The Land is the Source of the Law

The Land is the Source of the Law brings an inter-jurisdictional dimension to the field of indigenous jurisprudence: comparing Indigenous legal regimes in New Zealand, the USA and Australia, it offers a 'dialogical encounter with an Indigenous jurisprudence' in which individuals are characterised by their rights and responsibilities to the land.

Though a relatively 'new' field, Indigenous jurisprudence is the product of the oldest continuous legal system in the world. Utilising a range of texts, including films, novels, poetry, and 'law stories', C.F. Black blends legality and narrative in order to redefine jurisprudentia in Indigenous terms. This re-definition gives shape to the jurisprudential framework of the book: a shape that is not just abstract, but physical and metaphysical; a shape that is circular and concentric. The outer circle is the cosmology, so that the human never forgets that they are inside a universe that has a law. This law is found in the second circle which, whilst resembling the ancient Greek law of physics is a law based on relationship. This is a relationship that orders the placing of the individual in the innermost circle, and which structures their rights and responsibilities into the land. The jurisprudential texts which inform the theoretical framework of this book bring to our attention the urgent message that the Djang (primordial energy) is out of balance, and that the rebalancing of that Djang is up to the individual through their lawful behaviour; a behaviour which patterns them back into land. *The Land is the Source of the Law* concludes not only with a diagnosis of the cause of climate change, but a prescription which offers an alternative legal approach to global health.

C.F. Black is a postdoctoral fellow at the Socio-Legal Research Centre, Griffith University, and a Visiting Fellow at McGill Law School.

Discourses of Law

Series editors: Peter Goodrich, Michel Rosenfeld and Arthur Jacobson
Benjamin N. Cardozo School of Law

This successful and exciting series seeks to publish the most innovative scholarship at the intersection of law, philosophy and social theory. The books published in the series are distinctive by virtue of exploring the boundaries of legal thought. The work that this series seeks to promote is marked most strongly by the drive to open up new perspectives on the relation between law and other disciplines. The series has also been unique in its commitment to international and comparative perspectives upon an increasingly global legal order. Of particular interest in a contemporary context, the series has concentrated upon the introduction and translation of continental traditions of theory and law.

The original impetus for the series came from the paradoxical merger and confrontation of East and West. Globalization and the international-ization of the rule of law has had many dramatic and often unforeseen and ironic consequences. An understanding of differing legal cultures, particu-larly different patterns of legal thought, can contribute, often strongly and starkly, to an appreciation if not always a resolution of international legal disputes. The rule of law is tied to social and philosophical underpinnings that the series has sought to excoriate and illuminate.

Titles in the series:

Nietzsche and Legal Theory: Half-Written Laws
Edited by Peter Goodrich and Mariana Valverde

Law, Orientalism, and Postcolonialism: The Jurisdiction of the Lotus Eaters.
Piyel Haldar

Endowed: Regulating the Male Sexed Body
Michael Thomson

The Identity of the Constitutional Subject: Selfhood, Citizenship, Culture, and Community
Michel Rosenfeld

The Land is the Source of the Law: A Dialogic Encounter with Indigenous Jurisprudence
C.F. Black

Forthcoming:

Novel Judgments: Legal Theory as Fiction
William Macneil

Crime Scenes: Forensics and Aesthetics
Rebecca Scott Bray

Sex, Culpability and the Defence of Provocation
Danielle Tyson

The Rule of Reason in European Constitutionalism and Citizenship
Yuri Borgmann-Prebil

*Visualising Law in the Age of the Digital Baroque: Arabesques
and Entanglements*
Richard K. Sherwin

*Shakesperian Genealogies of Power: A Whispering of Nothing in Hamlet,
Richard II, Julius Caesar, Macbeth, The Merchant of Venice and
The Winter's Tale*
Anselm Haverkamp

The publisher gratefully acknowledges the support of the Jacob Burns Institute for Advanced Legal Studies of the Benjamin N. Cardozo School of Law to the series *Discourses of Law*.

The Land is the Source of the Law

A Dialogic Encounter with
Indigenous Jurisprudence

C.F. Black

Routledge
Taylor & Francis Group

LONDON AND NEW YORK

First published 2011
by Routledge
2 Park Square, Milton Park, Abingdon, Oxon OX14 4RN

Simultaneously published in the USA and Canada
by Routledge
270 Madison Avenue, New York, NY 10016

Routledge is an imprint of the Taylor & Francis Group, an informa business

Typeset in Minion by
RefineCatch Limited, Bungay, Suffolk
Printed and bound in Great Britain by
CPI Antony Rowe, Chippenham, Wiltshire

British Library Cataloguing in Publication Data
A catalogue record for this book is available from the British Library

Library of Congress Cataloging-in-Publication Data
Black, C. F.
  The land is the source of the law : a dialogic encounter with indigenous jurisprudence /
  C.F. Black.
    p. cm.
  Includes bibliographical references and index.
  1. Ethnological jurisprudence—Cross-cultural studies.   2. Ethnological jurisprudence—
  New Zealand.   3. Ethnological jurisprudence—United States.   4. Ethnological
  jurisprudence—Australia.   5. Indigenous peoples—Legal status, laws, etc.—Cross-cultural
  studies.   6. Indigenous peoples—Legal status, laws, etc.—New Zealand.   7. Indigenous
  peoples—Legal status, laws, etc.—United States.   8. Indigenous peoples—Legal status, laws,
  etc.—Australia.   I. Title.
  K190.B58 2011
  340.5′2—dc22   2010008408

ISBN-13: 978-0-415-49756-5 (hbk)
ISBN-13: 978-0-415-49757-2 (pbk)
ISBN-13: 978-0-203-84438-0 (ebk)

To my mother, Beryl,
my sister, Beverley,
and my cousin-sister, Mary,
with deep gratitude

Contents

Foreword

Observers of nature, especially herbalists, biologists and those who take water seriously, would readily accept the proposition that land is life. For the inhabitants of planet earth, the link between land and life is indissoluble. In his argument for the liberation of the 'wretched of the Earth', Franz Fanon argued that, for the colonized, land is life. This political argument is consistent with the biological insight that land is life. In this way, biology and politics converge. The convergence means that to disseize someone of their land is tantamount to the violation of their inalienable right to life. Thus ethics and morality come into the picture in order to ensure the recognition, respect and protection of the inalienable human right to life. The spheres of ethics and morality do not by themselves constitute positive law. Law, then, is necessary to enforce the recognition, respect and protection of the inalienable human right to life.

To the biological and political perspectives that land is life, C.F. Black now adds another dimension in the vigorous proposition that the land is the source of law. For some, a revered deity is the source of ethics and morality with which positive law must comply. For others, morality and positive law are separate independent spheres. These two contrary perspectives appear to be at odds with the proposition that the land is the source of law. According to one trend in legal philosophy, land is just a thing, available for naming, claiming and owning – individually or collectively. On this reasoning, the land is the object that becomes the subject of law whenever disputes arise concerning its naming, claiming and owning. Thus the land is not the source but the object of law. So it is that Dr Black's proposition is a contestation, an argument against the legal philosophical perspective that the land is merely a thing that fortuitously becomes the subject of law.

C.F. Black's proposition springs from an experience, an epistemology deeply rooted in the ancient wisdom of her people relevant to her Australia of today. Contemporary Australia is an invention of colonization, a veritable disseizure of a people's land, and therefore an abrogation of their inalienable right to life. By virtue of the questionable 'right of conquest', this invention named 'Australia' acted to silence the voice of the Indigenous peoples, the rightful owners of the country since time immemorial. It is no small matter that in recent times the parliament of Australia took the noble decision to apologize to the Indigenous peoples of the country. Dr Black's proposition is fundamentally a challenge to the legal philosophical perspective that the land is merely a thing. It is also the assertion and affirmation of the right of the Indigenous peoples of Australia to speak in their own terms on all matters, including the meaning of law. She draws from the well of her people's epistemology and wisdom to support the proposition that the land is the source of the law. Consonant with this, she uses homegrown terminology, especially the *talngai* and the *gawarima*. The former means light in the metaphysical sense, providing clarity to the penumbras of everyday experience. The latter is the description of a circular movement in which a story is carried over from one point to the next. The *talngai* and *gawarima* meet at the insight that motion is the principle of be-ing. Light moves one to illuminate the dark corners of experience, but this cannot happen if the light is static in the condition of permanent rest. Through the *gawarima*, the light of the *talngai* is continually enlightening the dark corners of experience. The meeting point between the *talngai* and the *gawarima* means the relationship is an experience and concept that is ontologically coeval with the insight that motion is the principle of be-ing. On this understanding, Dr Black invites three Senior Law Men, bearers of the ancient wisdom, to explain the cosmology, the relationship, and the responsibilities and rights that underlie the proposition that the land is the source of the law. Memory is the cement that puts the past and the present together, and the three Senior Law Men fulfil this function. The reader is invited to enter into this philosophy of law, to feel it in order to begin to understand it. For this to happen in a meaningful way, it is necessary to comprehend the meaning of 'Indigenous' espoused by Dr Black. It means, for her, 'a ritual sacred formula to produce good health in a knowledge system based on being within – *in*, a system of two; *di*, based on being within a productive or creative complementary system of relationships'.

Any Indigenous jurisprudence that was the victim of the Western invasion and conquest in the unjust wars of colonization is in vital need of a dialogical encounter with the West in order to assert and reaffirm the right of the Indigenous peoples to speak for themselves in their own terms. The jurisprudence of these Indigenous peoples, wherever they may be, is brought together, forming one community based on the shared experience of conquest in the unjust wars of colonization. One may ponder on the significance of the *Colonial Laws Validity Act* of the British Crown in order to appreciate this point. The common experience of colonial conquest is the well from which the Indigenous conquered peoples drink without having to renounce or repudiate their specific philosophical-cultural backgrounds. It comes as no surprise, therefore, that Dr Black is deeply immersed in the Australian experience while drinking from the common well of the experience of other Indigenous peoples. She draws a lot more from the American Indian, or Amerindian, experience compared with Africa. Yet she succeeds in making the Indigenous conquered peoples of Africa recognize their image in the mirror that she places in front of them. For example, we are introduced to the *Djang*, the primordial energy in constant need of balance and rebalancing. This concept is more than akin to the 'life force', dynamology or vitalogy found in the African philosophy of be-ing. It provides the basis for a polylogue among the Indigenous peoples of Australasia, Africa and the Amerindians. Memory and belief in the living dead ('ancestors') are sustained by the perpetual exchange of life forces in the holistic order of things. And so it is that the *Djang* cosmology is the affirmation that life is a complex network of dynamic relationships: a vitalogy.

The polylogue among the Indigenous peoples conquered in the unjust wars of colonization is not restricted to these peoples. As a challenge to the Western legal philosophical perspective, the polylogue is an invitation to the West – and, indeed, to all the peoples of the world. It is to be hoped that this invitation will be honoured, first, in the name of justice for and to all humankind, and, second, for the mutual enrichment of all the cultures of planet earth. Along this path there is a chance that *The Land is the Source of the Law* will make a lasting contribution to the protection and preservation of the only known liveable planet on which we all live.

Mogobe Ramose
November 2009

PART ONE

The Journey Begins

CHAPTER 1

My camp

'I want you to remember only this one thing,' said the Badger. 'The stories people tell have a way of taking care of them. If stories come to you, care for them. And learn to give them anywhere they are needed . . . Sometimes a person needs a story more than food to stay alive.'

(Borrows 2007: 13)

The Yugumbeh language of my mother's people[1] is a rich one. It stems from a land that was a virtual paradise, abundant in fish, birds and mammals. This abundance, however, did not lead to the erection of edifices to glorify some distant god or idol; rather, the Kombumerri people developed a rich intellectual and metaphysical world, aware of the galaxies as much as they were of the lifecycle of the smallest insect. Each entity was valued in its own right. My awareness of this heritage began with the repatriation of the remains of my grandmother's ancestors, a common story among Indigenous peoples of the world. But this story of return is a story of a beginning rather than end: it was the beginning of my learning of the Law, which had been denied to me due to an unacknowledged invasion – an invasion sanitized by such words as *discovery, settler society* and *colonization* rather than an acknowledgement that many thousands of men, women and children had died to keep Australia ecologically balanced. I feel a deep sorrow that these fallen warriors/soldiers are still not recognized formally, even by our own people, but rather airbrushed into the background as a Sorry Day, largely as a consequence of the settler society turning Australia into a First World nation. While the remembrance of this brutality and lack of recognition of those who gave their lives to keep their lands sustainable for future generations is not the purpose of this book, it is hoped that such remembrance will result from the impact of the book on the reader.

Returning to my story, the more I ventured into the remembrance of the world of my ancestors – and especially the revitalization of our Yugumbeh language – the more the stories came to me. And so, as the Badger advised, it was the stories – the vehicle for intellectual and metaphysical knowledge encased in feelings – that would reveal to me the Indigenous jurisprudence: why the Land is the source of the Law.

And so I turn to my clan's Yugumbeh language to assist me to elucidate the knowledge I carry in my genetic memory from those ancestors. I have chosen two words – two of my favourites, in fact – that will shape the jurisprudence in this book: *talngai* and *gawarima*. *Talngai* means light, which is used to enlighten in a metaphysical sense – what goes around the camp as knowledge. *Gawarima* describes a circular movement in which the information/story goes around a camp. In turn, it becomes a knowledge that is of a ritual nature and is therefore meant to heal through *feeling* the knowledge. This *feeling* of knowledge will be articulated through the *talngai-gawarima* jurisprudence actualized in this book.

The Talngai

I am legally patterned?

By telling a cosmological story from my ancestors' country, I am demonstrating how I am patterned into the web of Law stories that have weaved my ancestors into reality. This is just one of the Law stories that weave me into the web of reality of my grandmother's Kombumerri clan and my grandfather's Munaljarlai clan. It comes from my maternal grandfather's country of the Munaljarlai peoples of South-East Queensland, Australia. I have spent many years thinking about this story and revisiting while travelling around Aboriginal Australia. This account is my own rendering of the story, as each member of the clan will have his or her own account, for each telling passes on different elements that are important to the audience at the time of the telling. This telling emphasizes the breach of law of my own clan towards the hunting dogs belonging to a neighbouring clan, which, in turn, caused an abrupt geological change.

I was told once about these dogs, great hunting dogs they were. Not just ordinary dogs, hang around the camp types. No, these dogs were different – magic dog!

They say they even saw one of those dogs down on the Coast. A big black dog with red eyes. But I don't know for sure. Only old grandfather Bilum Bilum would know that. He was a clever man, knew all those old stories, Law stories – those Law stories that weave us all together.

But those dogs they had magic because they could hunt anything they wanted. They made that hunter happy. They would catch an animal, bird or fish and bring it back to the hunter.

That hunter he was a big strong handsome fella. He came from down south . . . made his way up the coast and up to the mountains and there he stood looking out over what was the beautiful hilly country of the ol' people.

That's before they got silly and got wiped out. And this is how it happened. This is how all that land got flattened out. Yeah, it lost all its lovely hills and pretty trees and so just became hard, baked land. It happened all of a sudden. I've been told this happen in other places. Maybe everyone got silly at the same time, so they all got wiped out.

That big handsome hunter was standing there looking out and watching for honey bees – he loved that sugar bag. That's another story how he found that sugar bag but I am not going to tell you that story. I am going to tell you this one about those dogs.

Those dogs saw a big *guraman*, that's a kangaroo, they chased after the *guraman* and before you knew it they had disappeared from sight, so the hunter didn't take much notice, he was just looking for those bees.

But what about those dogs, yeah, those dogs? They chased that *guraman* so fast that it had to pull up some of its magic and it hopped even faster and saw up ahead a lagoon, that was the Ilbogan lagoon in Bilum Bilum's country. When that kangaroo saw that lagoon, he jumped straight into it and turned himself into a *warrajum*. That's a water spirit, real special one. Makes that water, sweet water, special water.

But those dogs, what about those dogs, yeah those dogs. Well, they got mad at themselves for losing that kangaroo and so they didn't see those lazy young fellas coming along. They were supposed to be hunting but you know young fellas, any chance to sit down and tell stories about girls instead of hunting. And sure enough they thought . . . hey, let's catch those dogs then we don't have to do all that hard work huntin'. So they set a trap and caught those dogs and took them back to their camp and ate them up. Real good they were. Stupid fellas eating magic dogs!

Well that hunter, he knew his dogs had been eaten, he knew something bad had happen to them. He felt it on his skin, cause it started moving real bad right near his elbow. So he went looking for those dogs and found them. He found all those bones those lazy fellas had left in the campfire. He took those bones and made a special place for them up in the mountains. You can see that special place for miles all around. I like looking up to that place where those two rocks poke up looking like dogs watching me down on the coast. Makes me feel special.

But what about those fellas that killed those dogs? Oh that was bad and that hunter made sure they were dead. Then he did something that killed all the people. He changed that land with his magic – he made it all change, just in one day. With his magic he flattened that place out real flat and made that land real hard and black. That's now Munaljahlai country. That story reminds my Grandad's mob to be careful and follow the Law, otherwise the land might suddenly change overnight. A wipeout can happen any time. It happened before and can happen again. That's why we tell this story. To remind people, stay straight with the Law.

I am part of my family's history

My mother taught me to 'notice' nature. In so doing she taught me the Law of the Land.

My mother, Beryl Yuke, was born of a Kombumerri woman, Edith Graham, and a Munaljarlai man, Stanley Yuke. She grew up in a household that cared for her maternal grandmother. Sadly, Grandmother Jenny Graham was one of only a few Kombumerri women to survive on the traditional homelands of the Kombumerri. This land was invaded and eventually covered in concrete: it became the tourist city of the Gold Coast.

However, even though my mother's family witnessed the human-induced climate change of her traditional lands, and therefore had to adapt to the imposed culture, she was still able to pass on to me the habit of noticing nature. What I mean by this is that it was a subtle way, if not a subliminal intent, to pass on the importance of the Land as the Law, in a world bent on turning a paradise of natural environmental wealth into a poverty-stricken concrete mass of shining lights, high-rise apartments and artificial parks and waterways. My mother and her siblings had little chance of impacting on, or even comprehending, what was going on and what it would lead to. But then very few people are in a position to have such foresight, and still to this day are not in a position to see the impact of such madness. Perhaps, therefore, it might appear more sensible to consider that the planet is in a constant state of change and that the madness will also change over time and other priorities will supplant those of the present day. The knowledge to assist in that change comes from remembering stories from long ago, and that would appear to be my responsibility to my clans – to remember the stories.

The coming of a story

It is fascinating the way stories come to you, even though the Badger would appear to be telling us it is normal. There is a story I was told by a descendant of the farmer who cultivated the clan land of Bilum Bilum. In 1893, this farmer, rather than shooting Bilum Bilum or King Jackie Jackie and his clan, as was the practice of the day to acquire land, instead employed and handed down this story through the family over the centuries. King Jackie Jackie, as he was known to them, tried to warn the family of an impending flood. The farmer could see no evidence of this coming flood and therefore ignored Bilum Bilum's warning. Disappointed, Bilum Bilum then took his clan to higher ground and waited for the flood. The flood indeed arrived, and became one of the worst floods on record in South-East Queensland.

This story of Bilum Bilum and the flood came to me while I was writing up my doctorate. Not long after hearing this story, I changed my disciplines and moved from humanities to law. Ever since, I have felt that Bilum Bilum and other ancestors have helped chart my course through academia and the eventual writing of this book, as well as the use of our Yugumbeh[2] language to name the jurisprudence that will be developed in this book.

Journey through academia

My journey through academia revealed to me an array of stories from Indigenous peoples across the world. I found these stories fascinating and essential in aiding my children to build their character over time. Little did I realize that the stories which came to me were actually shaping my mind into that of a jurisprude. Therefore, on meeting William MacNeil (2007) and Shaun McVeigh (2006) of the Griffith Law School, I began to see Western law in a different way. Rather than finding the stories of Western law and their jurisprudence daunting, I found them *wanting* – especially as I began to mix with critical legal theorists (McVeigh 2006) and listened to their insights into the *wantings* of their law. I began to realize that this law could not help Indigenous peoples; rather it was a hindrance to them. As I enjoyed daily discussions with my friend Shaun McVeigh about the finer points of Western jurisprudence, sat through my doctoral supervisory sessions with William MacNeil, and engaged in other light-hearted discussions of popular culture, I began to shape my own understanding of Australian Aboriginal jurisprudence based on my personal experience and the texts found in this book.

Having said that, I could not even have begun such a narrative of Law without the dialogic engagement I experienced with my fellow Kombumerri, Mary Graham, and the formation of my understanding of the Australian Aboriginal world-view by Lilla Watson, on whose clan land I was born. Undergirding all this, however, was the essential engagement with the land of my ancestors, for it was that act of *walking the land* of my ancestors that actualized and authenticated the knowledge I had acquired through those dialogic encounters.

These journeys have also been literal, and have taken me into other Indigenous worlds where I have met guiding lights such as Hinsha Waste Agli Win, Mr Moana Jackson, Stephen Augustine, Joan Ropiha, Ephraim Barney, Ron Day, Adrian and Henrietta Marrie, Ahasiw Maskegon-Iskwew, Mogobe Ramose, Christine Zuni Cruz, Lyndon Murphy and Dale Kerwin. Then there are my colleagues, who helped to guide me into a deeper understanding of the dominant culture: Thelma Jackson, Bradley Sherman, Ben Goldsmith, Tony Bennett, Michael Meadows, Tom Round, Russell Bomford, AJ Brown, Michelle Barker, Larry Crissman and Julia Howell. I'm deeply appreciative of the life-saving editing of Sue Jarvis and Teresa Chataway. And I sincerely thank Richard Johnstone, director of the Socio-Legal Research Centre, Griffith Law School for the centre's financial support.

Finally, my gratitude must be expressed to my mother and sister, Beverley, to whom the book is dedicated. I thank my children, Ashley, Maleah and Kapun, and my grandchildren for just being there. Just as much, I thank my friends Glenda Donovan, Colleen Wall, Rita Mazzocchi, Kine Camara, Jonathan Richards, Robin Trotter, Donna Weston, Carol Ballard, Marianne Mitchell and cousins Marjorie, Leona, Shirley and Robin. Thanks to my clans, Kombumerri and Munaljarlai, and the 'living dead' on all sides of my family, and to the Lands of Gold Coast, Beaudesert, Kimberley, East Arnhem Land, Central Australia, Torres Strait Islands, Aotearoa, the great Turtle Island and South Africa.

Entering the gawarima

This book is shaped in a particular pattern – the pattern found on its cover. It is meant to evoke a sense of engagement, with the reader travelling through a series of camps and sitting down at each camp to listen to the

Law story conveyed there. There are nine camps in all, each with its own multi-level story, which in turn is encircled into a series of relationships with the other camps. Readers are asked to use their imaginations and perceive a circular pattern as they make their way around the camps. Allowing the imagination to flow with the reading enables a new layer of meaning to enter into what basically amounts to black letters on a flat page. The knowledge in this book stems from a multi-dimensional fluxing world-view. It is hoped that the reader will allow the joy of the flux of the Law of the Land to influence the way in which they receive the jurisprudence found in the following pages.

The main conversation in this book speaks in a triadic way: an Indigenous speaking to an Indigenous readership with the 'other' as observer. It is an appeal to Indigenous people to consider what makes their Law profoundly sensible and essential for the adaptation to climatic, economic and social unrest as energy and food shortages become evident, and to seek solutions within their own epistemologies and jurisprudence. I further contend that they should turn to their ancient narratives rather than taking a D'Artagnan-like musketeer approach of intellectually duelling with the Rule of Law, for I would argue that this approach has actually 'grown up' a whole generation of people who have neglected their own Law stories and succumbed to the 'Rule' stories of legal dualism. As Isleta Appellate Court judge Christine Zuni Cruz (2003) found as she travelled around the tribal courts:

> From the outset the elders exposed the attorneys' western knowledge of the law and procedure as laden with values and concepts in conflict with the Indigenous worldview of the people of Isleta. It is clear that two knowledge systems are vying for superiority in the development of tribal court systems.
>
> (2003: 2)

There is a dearth of books and articles on Indigenous jurisprudence and a glut of texts on Indigenous peoples and Western jurisprudence. The existing definitions surrounding Indigenous jurisprudence therefore have been influenced by the way in which Indigenous peoples have been assimilated under the Rule of Law. This assimilation process has taught our youth to regard Indigenous Law as something of a 'collective' version of Western law, whereas by travelling through the series of camps set out in the book, the reader will come to understand that the true source of the Law is the Land.

CHAPTER 2

The camp of the *talngai-gawarima*

Justice Blackburn acknowledged that the evidence from the Yolngu plain-
tiffs: 'shows a subtle and elaborate system highly adapted to the country
in which the people led their lives, which provided a stable order of
society and was remarkably free from the vagaries of personal whim or
influence. If ever a system could be called a "government of laws and not
men", it is that shown in the evidence before me.'

Milirrpum v Nabalco Pty Ltd (1971) FLR 141 at 267

This book is meant to open up an innovative theoretical framework that
draws on Australia's ancient Indigenous jurisprudence from Australia. It is
a jurisprudence that is aligned with jurisprudential influences from other
Indigenous legal world-views across the globe – for example, the Māori
representing the Pacific and the Lakota representing the Americas. The
book will bring an inter-jurisdictional dimension to this field, crossing
borders and comparing the Indigenous legal regimes of poetry as well as
'law stories'. Furthermore, this book will dissolve disciplinary boundaries
by utilizing a range of media: films, novels and storytelling. This interdis-
ciplinarity is consistent with the best in the Indigenous jurisprudential
tradition, with its blending of legality and narrative. The bibliography,
therefore, comprises predominantly Indigenous authors, as I wanted the
book to be the voice of the Indigenous and the way in which they see their
Law, rather than the mediated voices of the non-Indigenous, on one hand,

and the Indigenous voices that connote our legal tradition through a Western legal lens, on the other. The book is offered as an alternative legal reading for Indigenous peoples to explore and consider their own culture's legal theory. It contains a subjectivity that ensures the predominance of *feeling*: a continuous feeling for the web of interconnected relationships that patterns humans into their environment. The book is a dialogic encounter, so as to ensure a continued creativity in the intellectual engagement of law. Through the dialogic, the story of law is able to continue to flux through time. It gives the reader a freedom to engage, without having to take sides, to agree or disagree; rather, it reflects on the legal knowing told in each camp. I am, therefore, not setting myself up as an expert, but rather as a participant in a legal world that I find fascinating and life giving. It is a legal world drawing me into a relationship that guides me towards understanding my responsibilities to the Land. Conveying law through narrative ensures this independence of thought and avoids the need for textual critique. It assumes the reader does not come to this book for a 'how to' or 'a novel theory'; instead, it asks the reader to engage with the text and its legal rendering.

I articulate this 'actualizing' nature through a unique mode of jurisprudence: *talngai-gawarima*, a definition of jurisprudence that allows Indigenous peoples to be their voice of authority when expressing the jurisprudence of their ancient laws. This legal ordering is an act of naming – a naming of the Law that is rooted in the Land, a renaming of laws that to date have been mainly named 'customary laws'.

Zulu intellectual, Mogobe Ramose (who is Chair of Philosophy at the University of South Africa), states in his critique of the term 'customary law':

> [C]ustomary law is not a neutral, value-free scientific classification in the sphere of jurisprudence. On the contrary, customary law is, properly construed, a historical and value-laden experience and concept. As a historical experience, customary law is the manifestation of power relations often privileging the position and ideas of the powerful over the weak. Seen from this perspective, African customary law is the name conferred by the conqueror in the unjust wars of colonisation upon the living law of the Indigenous conquered peoples of Africa in general and South Africa in particular.
>
> (Ramose 2006a: 363)

Ramose argues that this value-laden conceptualization includes the term 'Indigenous'. In this context, an Indigenous person denotes the oppressed rather than a rootedness in a particular locality. For an understanding of my use of the words 'jurisprudence' and 'Indigenous', I have drawn on ancient sources. As Ramose (2006b) asserts, 'oppressed' people must take control of their intellectual landscape – and therefore their future – by choosing the meaning of the words they use. Accordingly, I use a definition that best expresses my understanding of the words 'jurisprudence' and 'Indigenous'. It is a paradigm that articulates a more ancient Proto-Indo-European[1] understanding of the word 'jurisprudence': *juris*[2] – a sacred formula to make ritually pure (and so engender good health); prudence[3] – the wisdom to see what is virtuous.

This paradigm rests on the flux of the two, the coming into relationship of the Law. The In-di-gen-ous[4] is the human personification of the Law of Relationship – that which produces two. In this case, we are concerned with two moieties: women's and men's law and business.

in – being within
di – two (two laws: the flux)
gen – produce
ous – full of.

Hence the overall meaning I attribute to the words 'Indigenous jurisprudence' can be translated as follows:

A ritual/sacred formula to produce good health in a knowledge system based on being within – *in*, a system of two – *di*, based on being within a productive/creative complimentary system of relationships.

I undertake this act of legal reclamation and also answer the call by Senior Law Woman Lilla Watson. In the early 1980s, Lilla taught me and other Indigenous people to challenge the 'terms of reference' being used in policy and university education in our home state of Queensland, Australia – especially in relation to child welfare and women's issues. Watson was an advocate of both Franz Fanon and Paulo Freire. In turn, Freire's work influenced my own, especially in relation to addressing the reality of another culture. I have built on that early education by prefacing the word *jurisprudentia* with the words *talngai* and *gawarima* from my Yugumbeh language.[5] The Yugumbeh word *gawarima* describes a circular movement in which the information/story goes around the camp (now the meeting house). Added to this word is *talngai*, which means light. This light is used to enlighten in a metaphysical sense – what goes around the camp as knowledge. In turn, it becomes a knowledge that is of a ritual nature and is therefore meant to heal through *feeling* the knowledge. This *feeling* of knowledge is articulated through the *talngai-gawarima* jurisprudence in this book as a series of concentric circles.

Shape of the Jurisprudence

To shape the *talngai-gawarima* jurisprudence, I have used the triadic organizing principle of concentric circles. This triadic model is replicated throughout the book. Just as the ability for a pattern to replicate is the sign of innovation and flexibility, which in turn allows growth, so the replicating of the pattern will bring about a growth of the book that shapes it into a scholarly work that will appeal to the Indigenous mind and offer a non-linear approach to knowledge. The use of concentric circles as an organizing principle is not original. For example, the work of Santa Clara Pueblo scholar, Greg Cajete (1994: 71), advocates its suitability as an organic organizing device in academic works, especially for the articulation of an Indigenous intellectual landscape.

Moreover, this ordering aims to reflect the importance of theoretical discourses emerging from Indigenous classical thought and narratives. An example employed throughout this book is that offered by Kanienkeha (Mohawk) Taiaiake Alfred (1999: xxiii), who bases his theory on the Rotinohshonni condolence ritual (1999: xx), expressed in three parts. The first, 'Peace', concerns initiating a dialogue. The second, 'Power', is expressly political, focusing on Native American political culture and leadership values. And the third, 'Righteousness', restates the main themes, bringing them into the contemporary context and applying them to the most important challenges facing Indigenous peoples today (1999: xxiii).

However, I provide an alternative interpretation of the circles. I construct the visual representation as follows: the outer circle is the cosmology, so that humans never forget that they are inside a universe – and that a universe has a law. This law is located in the second circle, which resembles, among other things, the ancient Greek law of *physis*.

Louis Wolcher (2004: 264) wrote succinctly about the transformation of Heraclitus's word *physis* to that of the Romanized *natura*, which, in turn, brought down the law from that of the galactic to that of the earth-bound and exploitable Mother Nature. It is interesting to note that, in the case of Heraclitus, he dismissed his fellow great thinkers who propagated the civil society rather than the adherence to the dynamic and flux-ridden *physis* of the universe. As Wolcher has argued, Heraclitus turned his back on those who basically could not accept that 'god played dice' with humanity – for example, Einstein and his realization that the fundamental laws of quantum mechanics are not fixed, but fluxing (2004: 265).

Furthermore, this fluxing law is based on relationship, which is termed in this book the 'Law of Relationship'. This relationship orders the placing of the individual in the innermost circle and defines their rights and responsibilities. In the following sections, I explain the concepts found in each circle in more detail.

Cosmology

To come into the Indigenous world and its fluxing *physis*, the outsider must first enter the cosmology of the particular group with which they wish to engage, otherwise the knowing of the people is only superficial. This is because a people's cosmological Creation story and events define their principles, ideals, values and philosophies, which, in turn, inform the legal regime.

Furthermore, I contend that a cosmology can be regarded as being not unlike a theory. For is not theory a story of how things occurred, what is valued, and so on? Hence a Creation story becomes a particular group's theory of how things came to be and, more specifically, how people should lawfully conduct themselves in a particular place. The difference here is that in the Creation story, the emphasis is not on answering abstract questions of existence; rather, it is on understanding how humans were patterned into a certain tract of land.

The Law of Relationship

This second of the concentric circles examines the legal system. My readings of the Senior Law Men and other Indigenous scholars indicate that the concept of the Law of Relationship is the most appropriate term to emphasize the centrality of the legal relationship in the edifice of the legal ethos – that is, the Land is the Law. The Law of Relationship is about a balance of difference (Alfred 1999: xiv).[6] The shape is a dyadic structure of two major moieties. These moieties do not form an oppositional binary, but complement one another to achieve the balance, which actualizes the rhythm of relationship. The shape and pattern of this Law of Relationship creates a body of law which, in Australia's case, 'vibrates in song' and is 'woven across' *Corpus Australis*. This is expressed in the concept of song-lines, or Dreaming Tracks, which criss-cross the body of the continent. I view these tracks as trade routes of intellectual property – an intellectual property that affords the owner the songs that sing up and actualize the Law of the Land. This concept will be dealt with in more detail in the various camps.

The Law of Relationship is a pervasive concept in other Indigenous laws. For example, Gunn Allen (1992: 18–19) has pointed out that: 'There is an old tradition among numerous tribes of a two-sided, complementary social structure. This dyadic structure ... emphasizes complementary rather than opposition.' Like most gynocratic tribes, this is the way the Pueblos are organized: into a moiety system that reflects their understanding of ritual empowerment as dialogical. Throughout the book, this diversity of expression is explored – be it the Mohawk balance of opposites, the Māori creation opposites or the Pueblo dual governing theocracy. The manifestation of the Law of Relationship, therefore, has as much diversity as the ecology of the earth itself. The Law of Relationship, in its human centrality, is about 'never being alone', while, metaphysically, it is the balance of the Land's energies.

Responsibilities and rights

This last of the triadic circles – and the most crucial – concerns the responsibilities and rights of humans.[7] It will be shown that, within this jurisprudence, when responsibilities to the Land are taken up, this results in automatic rights. Those rights combined with the human right become the voice of authority – that is, the validity of law. That voice is born out of experience and an actualization of the law. Central to this knowing is the development of a voice of authority based on the classical narrative and thought transmitted by Senior Law People in conjunction with the patterns of the law that rest in the land. Rights, therefore, are not a given: they are earned responsibilities.

The Pattern (Methodology) of the Book

Having described the fundamental characteristics of the circles, the following is an overview of the pattern or methodology of the book. This pattern is not unlike that of the common traditional image of people travelling from one camp to the next. It consists of a series of lines that appear to move from one set of concentric circles to the next, so that they converge into a larger circle as I move from the beginning of the book to the end, in which the overall concepts are joined up. Each camp, therefore, is a camp of concentric circles in which *talngai-gawarima* jurisprudence is discussed through a reading of the narratives of the Senior Law Men or of the contemporary literature relevant to the case studies, which tests that theory.

Meeting the Senior Law Men

The jurisprudential narratives informing the theoretical framework of this book are found in the metaphorical camps that contain the recorded oratories of three well-known and respected Senior Law Men of Aboriginal Australia. These narratives provide a legal ordering based on the classical thought of their clans' legal ordering. I shall refer to these elders as Senior Law Men through the honorific acronym of SLM to acknowledge their long and arduous education and training in the jurisprudence of Indigenous Law. It is an education that includes the knowledge of the language, laws, ecology, philosophy, ceremony and songlines of not only their own clans, but also surrounding clans.

Each Senior Law Man has allowed the documentation of his thought in an attempt to enlighten the Australian general public regarding the seriousness of the country's environmental situation due to the current global ecological imbalance, which, in turn, will make it difficult and costly for the present majority population of Australians to continue their contemporary lifestyle.

Each narrative provides the jurisprudence that underpins each level of the triadic circle, yet gives an emphasis to different circles. That is, SLM Neidjie exemplifies the cosmology; SLM Mowaljarlai exemplifies the Law of Relationship; and SLM Marika exemplifies the rights and responsibilities of the individual.

To elaborate on this pattern, I begin with the outer circle and the work of SLM Neidjie as documented in *Story About Feeling* (Neidjie 1989). I was introduced to SLM Neidjie's work in the late 1980s by Aboriginal elders Mary Graham[8] and Lilla Watson.[9] At that time, they were using his work as the major text for an innovative course on Indigenous Knowledges at the University of Queensland at Brisbane, Australia. However, it was not until I travelled to the northern part of Australia, which is the homeland of the Senior Law Men, that I could fully appreciate the finer aspects of SLM Neidjie's prose relating to law. *Story About Feeling* encapsulates the act of mediation between humans and the primordial energy known to SLM Neidjie's people as the *Djang*. I use this term throughout the book, as I consider that its very tone connotes an ancient power, a *physis*. This camp reinstates the *Djang* as *physis* and stresses its need for balance if humanity is to survive on this planet. It is also a foundation circle, in that it argues that an understanding of a people's cosmology is a prerequisite for any legal engagement with those people. To bring about that understanding, however, a movement from the abstract to that of the subjective through the act of *having feelings* – not emotions, but rather a sensitivity to one's surroundings – is explored. Those feelings are extended to other realms, including the Land itself. The significance of those feelings is obvious, in that they bring the human into relationship with the world around them, but, more importantly, into jurisprudential ordering. It will be demonstrated in this camp that, without the necessary 'affect' of having feelings, a legal discourse is not possible – let alone an understanding of the jurisprudence of Indigenous laws. In this camp, the relationship between the triadic communities discussed by Ramose (2006a, 2006b) is explicated. Here also, the concept of the 'watcher' is introduced, which leads to the next camp and the watcher as the 'witness' of another law.

The following camp introduces the reader to the gift. This gift is a law that witnesses. This camp shapes and patterns the Law of Relationship and the importance of having two laws witness each other. That gift is offered by exemplar Senior Law Man David Mowaljarlai of the Ngarinyin People of north-western Australia's Kimberley region. The pictorial account – *Yorro Yorro* – is a travel diary of SLM Mowaljarlai's journey with photographer Jutta Malnic, and articulates the *talngai-gawarima* jurisprudential reasoning underpinning the concept of 'walking the land' and 'actualizing' the law and its associated knowledge.

This journey is a jurisprudential account of the Ngarinyin cosmology in which SLM Mowaljarlai reveals to Malnic the finer points of the law laid down by the Wandinja Creator Beings. Through this account, SLM Mowaljarlai explains the Law of Relationship and its Ngarinyin pattern of law known as the *Wunnun* sharing system. Furthermore, he introduces the reader to the jurisprudential concept of the continent of Australia as a body – *Corpus Australis* or, to use the Ngarinyin word, *Bandaiyan* (Mowaljarlai and Malnic 1993: 205) – a body into which the law of the *Wunnun* sharing system is woven. This camp is, therefore, interlaced with conceptual nuances unfamiliar to Western notions of law. This account, more than the others, requires careful reading, as many paradigm shifts are required. These include the concept of procreation and freedom of choice in relation to laws. But perhaps the most challenging aspect is the concept that the continuity of a species is dependent on human intervention through the 'painting of the image'.

The last camp of dialogic engagement with the Senior Law Men deals with the innermost circle of the triad. This circle pertains to the rights and responsibilities of the individual, especially to questions of legal authority. SLM Marika is the exemplar Senior Law Man. His autobiography, *Wandjuk Marika Life Story*, was written in tandem with Jennifer Isaacs (1980), a well-known Australian photographer of Aboriginal art and craft. The significance of the content of the book is that SLM Marika undertook this autobiographical exercise in an attempt to recover the *power of definition* of his people's law and history – in other words, their intellectual property. His people, most commonly known as the Yolngu, are one of the most anthropologically studied people in Australia.

However, as will be argued, this scholarly attention did not bring these people good health. I draw on the work of Richard Trudgen (2000) and his account of why the Yolngu, even after having been given every possible advantage in Australian life, still have a high death rate. I will discuss his book, aptly named *Why Warriors Lie Down and Die*, and the experience of warriors such as SLM Marika; the reason for their demise will be explored. With regard to the vexing issue of Aboriginal health statistics (Australian Medical Association 2006), the health of Indigenous people in Australia is a blight not only on Australia's international standing as a First World country, but also on other First World countries with Indigenous minorities. The link between 'taking back the power of definition' and, as Ramose asserts (see earlier), the power of 'naming' is an important tool in reclaiming a people's intellectual landscape. I contend that the voice of authority must be vested in the knowledge that emerges from the Land, and that the mental health of Indigenous peoples will only be restored as a result of balance between the Land and humans.

These camps of dialogic encounter with the thoughts of the Senior Law Men and the thoughts of the reader are by no means the final authoritative voices of the cultures and laws they exemplify, however, for it is only by walking and singing the land that it is possible to truly know a law and in turn the people who emanate from that land.

PART TWO

Camps of the Senior Law Men

Entering the Camps

I will now take the reader to the camps of each of the Senior Law Men and reveal what I have learnt from carrying out a jurisprudential reading of the works they bequeathed to the world. These accounts are the perspective of each Law Man, and the legal rendering is my understanding. For a more contextualized and in-depth or authentic account, one must travel to the Senior Law Men's lands and spend years with the clans truly to be able to understand the meaning of their law as it is actualized on their lands. That all takes time and effort, and I hope the glimpse I offer of what I have learnt will encourage readers to spend time with these people and learn from their ancient and ecologically sound law.

CHAPTER 3

Feeling the *Djang*: The camp of Senior Law Man Neidjie

As mentioned earlier, in the previous camp, I was introduced to the works of Senior Law Man (SLM) Neidjie by my educators, Lilla Watson and Mary Graham. However, it was the work of their colleague Bob Willis (1990), in particular his honours thesis on SLM Neidjie and the term 'lawful behaviour', that made me consider SLM Neidjie's work beyond an aesthetic piece of Aboriginal prose on the Australian Aboriginal world-view. I found, as I read and continued to reread SLM Neidjie's prose, that I began to feel as if I were carrying around prose of great depth. Moreover, as I began to ponder the developments in quantum physics of the 1990s, I found myself referencing SLM Neidjie's writings to make sense of what I was reading. It was as if the abstraction of quantum theory was leaving out half the story. The poetics of SLM Neidjie gave me a feeling for the knowledge in the abstraction of the quantum theory. As Hannah Bell (1998) learnt from the Ngarinyin people (discussed in the next camp):

> For the Ngarinyin, the world is received and transmitted through direct communication with nature, understood in ritual through performing and visual arts, and consolidated into law of being and doing through the medium of dream in readily accessible altered states of consciousness. In order to experience the world through these media you must suspend your more familiar intellectual thinking in favour of sensory receptivity, awareness, and

responsiveness. Above all, you must observe nature mindfully, listen to the elements carefully and receive knowledge subjectively.

(1998: 135)

This subjectivity, as discussed in this camp, is the cultivation of feeling – specifically, feeling as a way of shaping and experiencing knowledge from the landscape and the universe itself.

Entering the camp of Senior Law Man Neidjie

This camp introduces us to the *Djang*, its protagonist SLM Neidjie and his Buntji people. The jurisprudence that emanates from this camp is both innovative and timely in a world experiencing global warming. It is a camp that I hope opens up to the reader an ancient jurisprudence, one which has largely been ignored due to its colloquial nature. As in Australian Aboriginal art – which I regard as its predecessor – the legal knowledge found in such works has gone unrecognized, as it does not fit into the formulaic jurisprudential scholarly papers, let alone reference the Western or Eastern jurisprudential greats; rather, it references its own source of wisdom – the primordial energy, the *Djang*. A universal energy or *physis*, this energy is not without personality and influence, however.

The subject matter for engaging with this energy is the philosophical prose of Senior Law Man Bill Neijdie of the World Heritage-listed Kakadu National Park of Australia's Northern Territory. However, I must state at this point that this camp contains *my* understandings and not those of his people, the Buntji. It is up to each individual of the Buntji people to experience his or her own understanding. My intention is to bring this work to the public at a time of great need for a jurisprudence that premises the environment/*Djang* as the law, rather than some human-centred set of norms that have to this point aided and abetted anthropogenic global warming (United Nations Intergovernmental Panel on Climate Change (UN IPPC) 2008).

To explore the establishment of law in any Indigenous culture, one must first enter the cosmology via the cosmological narrative. Central to that narrative are the constitution of authority and the jurisprudence that legitimates such authority. It is by understanding the cosmology that an outsider can come to terms with the manner in which the laws of that society and the individual's behaviour are understood. Senior Law Man[1] Bill Neidjie[2] of the Buntji clan of Northern Australia offers a collection of classical thoughts in his book, *Story About Feeling*. This cosmological account is accompanied by its strategies for knowing.

This understanding is based not on an abstract adjudication of the empirical norms; rather, as SLM Bill Neidjie explains, it is built on the individual's *feelings* about and *experiences* of the world. In other words, it is the individual who eventually must take responsibility for becoming the *voice of authority* to his own experience of the Law. So it is the individual who is constantly testing out his experiences through his relationship to his surroundings – whether seen and unseen. To feel the Law, which is posited in the Land, requires a communication with the unseen. This *feeling* of the spirit world and the reliance on that feeling as the basis for knowledge keeps the individual mindful of his own actions and so leads him to *internalize* the law, rendering it intimate, in contrast to the West's reliance on external prompts and norms. Thus, on entering an Indigenous cosmology, the outsider learns to have feelings for the cosmology and that process to take responsibility for her feelings (and her behaviour). SLM Neidjie (1989) offers a guide to connect with feelings in a lawful way through his book, *Story About Feeling*, a poetic cycle that I call 'oratory'. By commenting on these oratories, I offer a jurisprudential reading of this text.

This reading, however, is framed within the Australian Indigenous legal *logos*: Land – rather than humans and their customs – is the source of the Law. Through my commentaries on SLM Neidjie's work, this *logos* will become apparent.

Story About Feeling can be said to contain a series of poems, but I call these poems 'oratories' in order to emphasize their spoken and public quality. Unlike Western poetry, which is often individualized, SLM Neidjie's poems are collective – designed to enable us to 'feel', as a group, that the Land is celebrated as the Law. Moreover, they contain 'secret' knowledge that SLM Neidjie feels needs to be heard. This then renders them, as Laguna Pueblo scholar, Paula Gunn Allen (1992: 73), argues, ceremonial rather than popular literature.

Perhaps the best description comes from Pueblo Indian philosopher, Dr Greg Cajete.[3] When speaking of the Indigenous educational methods of the Americas, he refers to the poetic chants called 'flower and song':

> The Aztec developed schools called the 'Calmecac' in which the Tlamatinimine, the philosopher poets of Aztec society, taught by using poetic chants called 'flower and song'. Through formal and informal methods, the Tlamatinimine encouraged their students to find their face (develop and express their innate character and potential); to find their heart (search out and express their inner passion); and to explore foundations of life and work (find the

vocation that allowed the students the fullest expression of self and truth).

(Cajete 1994: 35)

This, I would argue, is the intent of SLM Neidjie's oratories. These moments of 'flower and song' were recorded by Keith Taylor in spasmodic encounters over several years. These oratories were then set down in *Story About Feeling*, a small book now known as Aboriginal philosophical poetry.

To begin these commentaries on SLM Neidjie's oratories, I will first present his words. *Story About Feeling* is told in dialect – what would officially be called Aboriginal English, or 'blackfella's speech'. So the tone is self-consciously colloquial:

> This story e can listen careful
> And how you want to feel on your feeling.
> This story e coming through your body
> E go right down foot and head
> Fingernail and blood . . . through the heart
> And e can feel it because e'll come right through.
>
> (Neidjie 1995: 1)

SLM Neidjie, as an Aboriginal Australian would put it, is 'having a yarn' – a conversation. But the conversation here is not with another person; rather, it is with the Land of Australia, its geography but also its cosmology – and the Law underpinning it. So the seemingly 'naive' language is informed by an extremely complex, indeed sophisticated, set of ideas – ideas that the uninformed or dialect-deaf reader will miss. I follow this evolution with a jurisprudential reading, using the triadic theoretic model of concentric circles of cosmology, the Law of Relationship and rights and responsibilities (diplomacy). I devised this triadic model to make it easier for the uninitiated in Indigenous classical thought to understand the writings of Senior Law People.

Cosmology

> Instead of putting their surplus energy into getting more food out of the landscape, Aborigines expended it on religious and artistic development in a huge release of intellectual effort. For them there was the religious and artistic imperative. In that sense, Aborigines, supported by their technology and skills, were able to float above the harsh

vagaries, the great stresses thrust upon them by an ever-changing
continent.

(Jones 1990)

Cosmologies are safe places: they are the circle that encompasses all one
perceives to be reality. It is from these safe places that people get a sense of
who they are and how they fit into the grand plan. SLM Neidjie's intention
in this compilation of oratories appears to be to situate the individual in a
cosmology in which maintaining balance is paramount. What is being
balanced is the *Djang* – the primordial energy – which, in turn, is the basis
for Law. That force or energy comprises legality, rather than the governance
of men. By shifting the emphasis from that of the governance of humans to
that of balancing energy, SLM Neidjie explains why the sensory and affect-
ive activity of *feeling* is fundamental to understanding the law. The development or maintenance of that sensory/affective activity is through the
constant enactment of the Law of Relationship with the unseen/spirit world,
which, in turn, develops in the individual a familiarity with not only the
unseen, but also the inanimate and the world around them. That development interconnects the person with that world – intellectually, psychically
and physically. This is not to suggest conquest: humanity here does not
colonize cosmology. Rather, the world around humans moves from being
a space subordinate to the human desires to one of a superior informant,
of the human's need for survival – a survival based on the interpenetration
of the knowledge found in the seen and unseen.

Story About Feeling

In *Story About Feeling*, the preface introduces the reader to the 'story'
of *feeling*:

> This story e can listen careful
> And how you want to feel on your feeling.
> This story e coming through your body
> E go right down foot and head
> Fingernail and blood . . . through the heart
> And e can feel it because e'll come right through.
> (Neidjie 1995: 1)

The intention of this paragraph is to situate the person inside their body
as the site of law: 'This story e coming through your body.' Hence this
lawful behaviour emanates from the person in his or her most corporal

form ('foot', 'head', 'finger', 'nail', 'blood') and not from something outside the self – an external adherent to a legal regime. This grounding brings
the person into relationship with 'feeling' and the internal law of other life
forms, both seen and unseen, as depicted in the following extract:

> Tree, grass, star . . .
> Because star and tree working with you.
> We got blood pressure
> But same thing . . . spirit on your body,
> But e working with you.
> Even nice wind e blow . . . having a sleep . . .
> Because that spirit e with you.

So the body of the person is connected with the body of the land ('tree',
'grass') and even the cosmos ('star'), for both have 'got blood pressure',
inextricably linking 'spirit' and 'body'. 'That spirit e with you,' writes SLM
Neidjie – a notion he takes up and develops, casting 'spirit' as mobile,
moving in a liminal space, a space of further communication with the
unseen. What is that space other than the space of 'dream'?

> You might dream moon,
> Or you might dream water, storm.
> You might dream tree, wind . . .
>
> Oh anything e can dream . . . that dream e's true.
> You having a sleep
> But your spirit over there where you dream.
>
> Daylight e come back.

'Dream', of course, has a very precise meaning for indigeneity, different
from that of the West – pre- or post-modern or psychoanalytic. For the
Dream here refers to 'the Dreamtime', a time out of time, more appropriately called 'the Dreaming', a state of timeless being in which the spirit
resides.

Translations

In the following, I set out my translation, which constitutes my own
understanding, rendered in standard Australian English. Then I will turn
to my commentaries on the *meaning* of the original 'broken English' text,
in which I quote small parts of the original text. The following translation

should be thought of as a synopsis of the longer commentary. It has retained the original paragraphing. I will use the first paragraph as an example of the method I am using:

> This story is for all Australians. Prior to this it was restricted
>   knowledge, which we did not share with White Europeans.
> We didn't like them.

I will now translate the rest of the text.

> White Europeans must understand that those who live in Australia
>   must understand the culture, and the restricted knowledge about
>   the Dreaming.

> The Dreaming is complex. It is our cosmology.

> Indjuwanydjuwa [the Ancestral Being] laid down the two-way moiety
>   system of governance. He made everything including the rain and
>   people, but he also made a governance system, which we refer to as
>   'Business'.

> Well they [Europeans] have their Biblical creation story.
> We also have a creation story about Indjuwanydjuwa, which we pass
>   on to our youth.

> Young people have a natural curiosity about their 'origins'.
> They feel they need to know and have answers to the mysteries of life.
> Everyone feels the same.

> The *Djang* is the *logos*. It is very complex.
> The Dreaming is mysterious.

> The source of the energy of life is powerful
>   and if you tamper with it you may destroy yourself
>   or may cause untold damage.
> [Note: the tampering with the microscopic atom brought into being
>   the atomic bomb.]

> If you tamper with it, can cause havoc
>   in the same way as a cyclone, it has no boundaries.
> The effect of the disturbance could cause

destruction in Croker Island, Elcho Island or Brisbane.
The *Djang* can cause cataclysmic damage.

We are all sitting on top of the *Djang.*
This primordial energy runs through the earth.
We do not fully understand this energy.

From our observations, the source is energy
that traverses the planet and one cannot be
sure if there is a disturbance in one country,
a fault lines effect will not cause a cyclone,
flood, etc. in another country

That is why mining disturbs us.
We are not sure of the full implications.
You can try and it might be alright.

However, it is us who worry about the consequences
because once it has happened it is us who will know
it is too late.

The *Djang* is the dream of the power of the King Brown.
[King Brown is a creative energy.]

Balanda (Yolngu for White person)! If the Aboriginal person
gets annoyed its because he wants you to stop the mining.
But the Balanda have to have the *Djang* explained to them first
This is a difficult concept to explain
So Aborigines are hesitant.

They may be hesitant because they may be aware
of some fault line effect that has caused a catastrophe
in another place, therefore they are fearful to express this awareness.

An example of a cataclysmic event might
be a plague called *mia mia* (sounds like smallpox)

Another example is a rock (raw uranium).
If you touch it you will die. The old people learnt
from experience about uranium. You have been warned!
Prior to this that knowledge was restricted.

We call the primordial energy the *Djang*,
What do you call it?

The *Djang* is a difficult concept to accept.

If you do not pay heed to this warning
You will be breaking the law – a
   primordial law which applies to all of us.

It's just the same as in your own country,
   if outsiders come and break the law
   it affects all of you.
You begin to worry a lot and that makes you feel weak.

He won't accuse you of lawbreaking. That's not his role.
He won't do that. (He is a watcher, not a policeman.)

Commentary

This 'Dreaming' is the starting point of the oratory: 'Big name . . . *Djang* Dreaming e listen.' That Dreaming, however, is not just 'for us', but also for the 'White European'. This is a bold departure in Indigenous literature, art, theology and jurisprudence because, traditionally, the Dreaming and the knowledge it affords is 'secret before', restricted to 'no matter Aborigine'. But SLM Neidjie's oratory is that 'This story not for myself . . . all over Australia story.' Why all Australia – especially an Australia often tone deaf to Indigenous stories? Precisely because it is 'the Balanda' – the 'White European' who is introducing imbalance in the land, provoking a crisis – a crisis of which SLM Neidjie, as an Aboriginal spokesman, is 'fright' – seeing it as terrible and terrifying.

    What alarms SLM Neidjie is the reckless exploitation of the land, as represented by 'mining'. 'Oh some mining might be alright,' writes SLM Neidjie, parodying corporate rationalization (ranger mining); however, he adds in an increasingly ironic tone, 'you try e might be alright.' Mining here is a metaphor; it extracts something, it creates something, disturbing atmosphere and its harmonies: 'You might spoil any body, so matter where/Same as cyclone, if you spill it.' How is mining related to weather? How does extraction lead to the creation, and chaos, of a 'cyclone' – or, even more lethally, a 'disease' ('Some sores . . . what we call *mia mia*/But this one, *mia mia*, biggest . . . just like boil')? So this disturbance is now rendered as a bodily pathological symptom (a 'boil') writ large on the body of the land. SLM Neidjie provides a diagnosis of this pathology and the dying land, locating this chaotic cosmos in the release of *Djang*. It is *Djang*'s implosive release that is the source of the problem, for *Djang* is the very organizing principle. *Djang*, in a word, is Law. But when it is tapped into inappropriately – as with mining – it becomes a disorganizing principle, confounding and confusing, blighting the land. Only by feeling the Law of the *Djang* will the Balanda be able to instinctively do what is right. So SLM Neidjie is not a prophet of doom in the wilderness, but rather a leader and Law Man who gives the people a law by which to live, one that draws them into the cosmology of the *Djang* – hence the Dreaming of Australia. By understanding Australia through the Land – as the Law – Australians will feel the imbalance themselves and realize something must be done. To learn to feel SLM Neidjie's oratory offers practical and democratic exercises in what amounts to an engagement with other life forms – for example, an eagle – but also inanimate objects, such as a rock.

The Land is not SLM Neidjie's sole focus. His lens widens to take in cosmology. So SLM Neidjie opens his oratory with an apostrophe to the Ancestor Indjuwanydjuwa. This Being, just like many others in other Indigenous Creation stories, brings the cosmology to life and so establishes the Law: 'I want rain, I want people.' This accords with, and is in the tradition of, the many stories talking of Creator Beings, which, as here, 'think or dream' humans and the earth into existence. (This is as though to join in the debates surrounding the law of physics, of which some theorists see matter at its most fundamental level – for example, the sub-nuclear as being more like a thought than solid form.) In the case of Buntji, SLM Neidjie says they dream of a snake-like energy, which the oratory renders as dream of the 'King Brown (Irwardbad)'. A 'King Brown' is a highly poisonous snake in its earthly manifestation, but in its representation, it is an enormously dangerous energy. It is an emblem of the *Djang* and a force that reverberates through all Creation and the universe: '*Djang* is biggest one.'

Balancing this force, according to the Buntji, is the 'Law of Oober', which appears in SLM Neidjie's oratory as 'two way e made', an Indjuwanydjuwa-created 'double helix' that, like the laws of physics, regulates, negotiates and binds energy (*Djang*) and its agent-emblem (King Brown). That law, a law of the cosmos as much as the Land, is the basis for SLM Neidjie's argument – as advocate of both physics and metaphysics.

The balance of the *Djang*, therefore, is the basis for the Law of Relationship: the metaphysical and physical relationship between people and the cosmos. This relational jurisprudence is, however, not only metaphysical (or physical), but geographical – between the people and the Land. For disturbances in the Land, according to SLM Neidjie, are the result of imbalances in the *Djang*: 'You might spoil anybody, no matter where. Same as cyclone, if you spill. First one might be east? No matter Croker, Elcho or Brisbane . . . same. That *Djang* will now do it.' So the reason for having 'feelings' is to keep yourself constantly aware of the activities that might cause an imbalance in the *Djang*, both locally and at a distance. For example, consider the importance attached to sacred sites – nodal points for the *Djang*. Indigenous Australians are acutely sensitive to any disruption of these sites' sacrality, precisely because such a violation throws the *Djang* out of balance. That *Djang*, of course, is not just an Indigenous force; it is one that connects us all – 'Aborigines', 'European' – 'story same'. So the *Djang* might be said to entail political principles, as much as a metaphysical or physical one. By connecting us all, it opens up the possibility for a democracy of feeling, of the land, of the cosmos. The cosmology, therefore, is a vibrating democratic sphere, where all Creation – including the planet itself – has feelings, and attention must be paid to those feelings through the monitoring of the balance of the *Djang*.

In the next section, we show how SLM Neidjie provides what is basically a helper from the unseen. In other words, it explores the consolidation of the interpenetration of the liminal space between the world of the seen and unseen. Moreover, it provides a confirmation of its existence and its 'relatedness' to the seen world.

Law of Relationship

The following translations are based on prose on page 107 of *Story about Feeling* entitled 'Spirit':

> The spirit of the Jabiru is Badbanarrarr,
> If you listen to this story
> You will feel the spirit beside you.
> This applies to everybody who listens
> To the story.
>
> I'm going to influence you
> And you will begin to feel the spirit.
> The spirit feels like wind.
>
> Someone may assume I am talking
> About the landscape, but
> I am talking about spiritual depth.
>
> There is a spirit world and
> It is parallel to this world.

You must become aware of the spirit world.
The spirit is in everything including the rock.

You may dream of a spirit or might find
something special in your pocket.
You may feel the spirit as something
Touching your hair, standing behind you
Or beside you.
While I am telling this story
You will begin to feel the spirit.
Yikes, I feel spooked!

When this happens, your hair might stand on end,
as you then can feel the spirit.
But don't be frightened.
He wants to communicate with you, so listen.
He likes you.

You can't see it so you begin to feel
Feel the feeling.

The spirit influences you.
He puts forth suggestions.

These suggestions the spirit puts forth
May lead to a pleasant surprise like
bush honey.

Commentary

Once again, SLM Neidjie is opening up his experiences to all Australians: 'This story for me, for anybody, for you too.' There is a lightness in this piece of prose that engenders a sensitivity: 'I can feel it, blowing wind.' This is the necessary sensitivity needed to communicate with a spirit: 'If you listen to this story here, E'll with you e'll be with me.' The referenced spirit is not a free-floating ghost, but rather a metaphor for the soul of another life form – animal, bird or mineral. In other words, to engage with 'difference', one must move to the most fundamental level of being – the level of spirit or soul. It is at this point of engagement that human characteristics vanish as the 'dominant interpreter' and *feelings* become the only adequate form of communication. Moreover, the oratory appears also to heighten one's awareness that one is being watched: 'and you'll get it because spirit e'll be longside.' That action can never be carried out in solitude, as the very air is full of the unseen and its potentiality to interpenetrate reality. Contained within that communication is an exchange of valuable knowledge. Ethno-musician Allan Marett (2005: 3) gives a solid account of the knowledge of his informants, Senior Song Men of the Wadeye people who enlightened him to the importance of the way the interpenetration of liminal space offers an opportunity of exchange of sacred knowledge for ceremony from both the dead and animal spirits.

In this particular piece of text, SLM Neidjie is trying to convey to his listeners that the spirit is already with a person and that he merely has to alter his state of consciousness by paying attention to his feelings rather than perhaps several hours of meditation. I would argue that this 'familiarity' with other states of consciousness is the hallmark of the Australian Aborigine. The protocol for communicating with other life forms is guided by the Law of Relationship. This law appears to dispense with rigid or embellished formalities and long periods of self-imposed isolation. Conversely, the opposite would appear to be the protocol for the Aborigine with a full exposure of intent. In some cultures, to reach this level of communication is seen as a specialist undertaking and one that requires a concentrated effort in isolation. The Aborigine would appear to be doomed to be drenched in the human drama. There is no escape into solitude, for, at every corner, a rock, a tree, a spirit is watching the actions of the Aborigine. Hence life becomes 'full-law' participation – fully engaged with all that surrounds us, both seen and unseen.

Therefore, when there is little resistance between the seen and unseen, it is much easier for the inanimate object to come through the liminal space and manifest: 'I don't known but you might find something. I find it couple of time in my pocket.'

The example given is that in relation to a *Badbanarrawarr*, the Jabiru: 'That spirit of that *Badbanarrawarr*, Jabiru, E'll be longside to you.' First, one may have a dream about a particular object such as a bird's nest: 'This one we say, "Only nest." But as SLM Neidjie goes on to explain, it is: 'But not really' – rather, it is a spirit: 'But something went in. Went under ground where the spirit for us.' What he is saying is that the nest, or even a rock, is the vehicle for the spirit that comes up out of the ground – the dwelling place of the *Djang* primordial force. Note that it is a coming up out of the land rather than an ordination from some divinity on high. The difference is the desire for relatedness rather than indebtedness. This relatedness is there for us to access at all times: 'That spirit e watching us. For you and me that spirit. Never lose. Always with us. With you 'n' me.'

SLM Neidjie then goes on to point out that 'Dreaming places' are also an extension of the 'relatedness to land' – they are there for everyone as repositories of Dreaming stories. But this is as a responsibility, not as a right. 'Must keep it. You must keep im story/ Because e'll come through your feeling. Even anybody.' Access to them is through having feelings. 'E can see . . . have a look!' This open invitation is a profound statement in itself. On the one hand, it explains the popular Aboriginal saying of 'I'm going to sit down country', which means 'I am going to sit down and listen to the country'. On the other hand, it is a major paradigm shift in the intellectual property notion of regulation. This would seem a breach of Aboriginal intellectual property, but instead it is a clever safeguard against humans' obsession with their own rights to have and control information. By ensuring access is only through having feelings for a Dreaming site, this ensures a built-in way of ensuring the visitor will not damage or steal from the site. It is a safeguard against 'abstraction' – where knowledge is gained through memory and analysis; if anything, 'objectification of the knowledge' is a prerequisite to authority over that knowledge.

The validation of what one may hear, however, is dependent on one's own experience of the wider community in terms of that knowledge. As mentioned earlier, a comparison with the teachings of the Wadeye Senior Law Men described by Marett (2005) reveals that when a new song from the dead is received, it is still up to the community to accept or reject that song as legitimate. This is the Law in other Indigenous communities, too, in relation to knowledge received from the 'unseen'. In fact, this process is no different from that involving scientific knowledge. The general public cannot simply carry out the same experiments which the scientist tells us are valid; it is only through the general public's experience of that knowledge that it becomes valid. This, therefore, maintains interrelated levels of the Law of Relationship between the site, the spirit of the site, the communicator and finally the clan (Marett 2005: 3). The completion of the circle of relationship becomes the Aboriginal environmental ethos – 'caring for country'. The clan must, therefore, care for the countryside if its members are to maintain access to the stories. If they deface the country, that ends their access to their intellectual property. Access through feeling, however, does not mean some kind of epiphany of the Dreaming and all that it contains, but rather offers 'bottom-level' knowledge; to access deeper knowledge requires initiations into higher knowledge of the site and the information contained. The higher knowledge is like understanding physics: the more you know, the more you realize that the universe is made up of an unknowable amount of information. The amount you want to know is based on how much time you have in your life to spend on such pursuits. As Indigenous societies are egalitarian, the clever man or woman is not seen as any different from the rest of the clan, so the pursuit of this kind of knowledge is purely personal. This lack of status also ensures a relatedness with the rest of the clan, rather than an exclusion from society in general, which, unfortunately, tends to be the outcome of a single intellectual pursuit in Western knowledge societies.

Therefore, for SLM Neidjie to abstract his knowledge into a book signals how urgent the situation now is. For this is a time when the secrets need to be shared. This sharing, however, is based on the 'graduation' of the Balanda regarding the realization of sacrality of sacred sites and the need for legal protection. Now the legislation is in place and there is a 'commonsense' understanding of the historical importance of sacred sites, SLM Neidjie has taken the next step and is sharing the 'secrets' of the 'lawful behaviour', which leads to the hearing of the stories of the Dreaming sites.

The moment of legal significance in this oratory is in the revelatory relationship between the human and the spirit, which is the basis of the actualization of law. This actualization is tempered by the development of the person's own inner voice of authority. Communicating with the inner space and relying on one's own voice of authority as the vouchsafe for the experience builds up in the human a sensory awareness of the effect of feelings and also the need for balance and taking responsibility for actualizing the Law in the Land. This, as I pointed out earlier, is the democratic process in action.

Rights and Responsibilities: Diplomacy

This section deals with the individual's rights to ancient knowledge that has been maintained by former generations and guarded by the dead, who become the sentinels of the sacred sites. It also looks at the responsibilities to act with consideration and due care when entering a sacred space. These spaces, we are told, are occupied by guardian spirits who must be acknowledged and respected for the responsibility they carry. The guardians are the Ancestors of the local clan, which brings about a familiarity in relations between the dead and living. The protocols, therefore, are about an ongoing relationship between people and the land, be they dead or alive (Marett 2005: 4). This is vastly different from the concept of political correctness or ritualistic behaviour, such as with the Native Americans who offer tobacco when entering a sacred space.

The second part deals with the knowledge found in the caves – for example, the paintings. The oratory asks the reader to think of the paintings as though reading a written text containing knowledge for future generations.

Paintings

The following is based on the prose entitled 'Painting' from page 69 of *Story about Feeling*:

> Well, we'll be dead
> and they can see our painting
> because behind us all the children . . . right back.
> They can keep on look this painting and bone.
> They can see us if they behind us.
> This country for us.
>
> When we are dead the future generations
> will see the paintings.
> They can look at the paintings and
> know the country is there for them.
> This is the generic protocol for all situations.
>
> As we can see 'this country is for us'.
> If you go to the cave you have to call out.
> Let the spirit know you are coming,
> especially if you are bringing a stranger.
>
> Otherwise if you do not take due care
> you will get sick, very sick.
>
> You have to call out to the spirits
> who are your ancestors as they'll be
> waiting for you and expecting you to
> give them notice so that they don't
> harm the stranger.
>
> This is the protocol of the Dreaming.

Based on page 107 of *Story about Feeling*:

> Then you think, I'll go somewhere else,
> maybe to look at a painting.
> You go and look at the painting
> and you begin to read it just like a newspaper.
> All the little marks are just another form of alphabet.
> You have your form of literature and we have ours.

That spirit is telling you to read those paintings
and feel what is good in them for you.
Then that spirit is telling you to go
and take photos of what you see.

Once you digest all this knowledge and
the finer details found in the marks,
you will digest it in your sleep and move to
a higher level of understanding
– been dreaming a good dream.

Commentary

This protocol of consideration or act of diplomacy comes out of the dream – 'Because that's the dream' – the cosmological Dreaming. It is the cosmological Law of Relationship – the law between the actions of the living and the responsibilities of the dead to guard the land or site.

Sacred spaces, just like halls of learning and religious establishments, require certain diplomacy in terms of approach. In the West, this approach is based on the knowledge that a divinity of power dwells within the walls of the establishment, with the Aboriginal, it is based on family relations: 'Yes you father, your grandad, your aunty,/They'll be waiting for you./You must signal, yell out . . . they'll listen. They know you.' It is the family relationship that once again shifts the reverential behaviour from that of an above-and-below relationship to an egalitarian relationship with the living and dead, still seemingly related but occupying different dimensions in time and space. It is as if the dead are still fully employed in the affairs of humans. They are not removed to some dead zone, forgotten in time but, as Marett discovered, 'full participants in the lives of the living and their ceremonial relationship to land' (Marett 2005: 4).

The same applies to all sacred spaces: 'Each place, no-matter here, all over.' An approach is made by calling out to let the spirit know you are coming and maybe bringing strangers. The spirit has a responsibility to care for the sacred space of future generation 'because behind us all the children'. The spirit needs to know if strangers are being brought to the site: 'New man might be stranger . . . you got to yell out.' The spirits need to know the stranger is being 'managed' by their Aboriginal host and will not cause trouble: 'Because wrong spot, wrong place.' In Central Australia, it is part of land council protocols that a new recruit must realize they are putting their host in physical danger if they go off and do as they please; this is due to the host's reciprocal relationship with the guardian spirit (Central Land Council 1998).

This familiarity, once again, would seem to generate a *feeling* – 'They know you. They will know' – rather than an abstracted ritualistic act of reverential behaviour. The reverential connotes a distance in relationship, if not a deference or homage being paid to that which is being revered. The Aborigine does not revere the dead or the spirit of a sacred site, but rather has feelings for the concerns of the spirit and its duty to protect a site: 'You might get sick or very bad sick. Because wrong spot, wrong place.'

The concern relating to sacred sites is much about the *Djang* power as it is the content of the cave paintings found in these areas. These paintings, SLM Neidjie points out, need a closer examination and understanding of their meaning: 'Big mob you read it all that story, e telling you all that meaning.' The Law Man asks us to first understand that the paintings and the markings are like the marks that make up the alphabet, which, in turn, become the script of the newspaper: 'That's the same as this you look newspaper.'

However, to understand the meaning once again requires the effect of feelings: 'That meaning that you look . . . you feel im now.' So the idea is not to enter the cave and try to decipher the markings, but rather try to 'feel' the meaning. In other words, the markings are not an alphabet or hieroglyphic, but a mnemonic for intuiting a feeling, which, in turn, brings meaning: 'You might say . . . Hey! That painting good one! I take im more picture.' However, the feeling is not something about which you have an epiphany while looking at it; rather, it is something that seeps into your unconscious: 'All that mark they make it, when you go sleep/You dream,' which then permeates your dreams and 'Hey, I bin dream good dream!' And so you have a good feeling about the painting, the cave and the cosmology from which it sprang. This, in turn, becomes a self-authorizing way of acknowledging another tradition, another life force and even another dimension of existence – that of the dead.

Conclusion

From the time of the invasion by the settlers to the present day, the Australian Aborigine does not, on the whole, appear to have seen the advantages of or the reason for the emphasis on the material world as displacing the metaphysical world. The universalism of humankind appears to have a 'glitch' when it comes to Aborigines – it is Land not humans at the centre of the universe. Why is this so? How does this affect Law? The answer lies in the affect of Indigenous Law and conceptual understanding of the Dreaming. All this is built on having 'feelings' for Land. These feelings were felt through a democratic/egalitarian process in which it was up to the individual to become the 'voice of authority' and so own and regulate their feelings in line with the greater *Djang*. These people somehow understood some of the fundamental laws of physics and the importance of developing an intellectual property regulatory monitoring process requiring the individual to take responsibility for their own actions.

So there was not only clear understanding that to move beyond the laws of the Dreaming was illogical and a breach of the Law of Relationship; it was unthinkable due to the 'feeling' they had towards Land.

The explanation for the 'glitch' of the Australian Aborigine is still given today: it is that the laws that control or advance technology are not in alignment with the Dreaming. That is, they are detrimental to the spirit of the Land. As Chairman Galarrwuy Yunupingu (1997) of the Northern Land Council states:

> Land is very close to the Aboriginal heart and we can actually feel sorry for land, like you would feel sorry for someone who has been hurt. We give land ceremonial names as a sign of respect and this is very important, like respecting your elders. We acknowledge the land by giving it a title that is not used every day; a special name so we always remember what it means to us. Our relationship with the land is much closer spiritually, physically, mentally than any other relationship I know of.
>
> (1997: 6–7)

Land was never perceived as a resource but always addressed as a 'thou'. As Marett (2005) learnt from the Senior Song Men of Wadeye, as he entered their cosmology the position and relationship to Land moved from that of the external objective sense of 'place' or 'home' to an animate relatedness of 'love' of Land (2005: 319). And so the cosmology that, for SLM Neidjie, is the basis of the Buntji people is one of a democratic space inhabited by a multiverse of beings, of which humans are just one manifestation.

Finally, this translation offers a timely jurisprudence for consideration alongside that which has shaped our world into its climatic stage of our history. It is an ancient jurisprudence offering a philosophy of law that premises the *Djang*, or primordial energy, as that which shapes the legal behaviour of the individual – a law that cannot but help make the individual responsible for their behaviour towards the planet on which we live. For it is not more regulation and imposition of laws that we need, but rather a realization by individuals that they have the ultimate responsibility to take due care.

Acknowledgement

This chapter was published in 2009 in a modified form as 'A Timely Jurisprudence for a Changing World' in the *International Journal for the Semiotics of Law*, 22(2): 197–208.

CHAPTER 4

The spider or the web? The camp of Senior Law Man Mowaljarlai

I asked Senior Law Man Mowaljarlai:
'Which was more important, the spider or the web?'
He replied: 'The web, of course.'

Entering the camp of Senior Law Man Mowaljarlai

On meeting Senior Law Man Mowaljarlai, I felt I had walked into a mythical world – a place where the normal becomes abnormal and where the surreal seems real. This man's very bearing was markedly different. Moreover, his knowledge was vastly different in its philosophical tone, depth and approach. He said he wanted to give the Western world a gift based on the Law of Relationship – the gift of lawful behaviour. This was a concept developed by Hannah Bell, who worked closely with SLM Mowaljarlai and his people to establish the Bush University, an audacious project that challenged the academic world of Australia to acknowledge that there are other ways of knowing this continent and other legal forms of governance. The aim of this gift was to develop a two-way process of governing Australia in a more ecologically sound manner. Bell (1998) wrote a book entitled *Men's Business, Women's Business*, to alert Australians to the importance of understanding the underlying Law of Relationship of two forces as the blueprint of natural law and, thus, the blueprint for all aspects of life. This double helix of relationship comes out of nature and, therefore, is the law nature has devised to sustain life. Those who live by this law in turn live a lawful life, one that brings respect for difference, but strives for harmony. The purpose of this book, by means of the journeys around the camps, is to reveal this law to the 'other', who, in turn, may take time to investigate its legal feasibility and innovation by visiting the landscape and the people from which the law comes into effect. The following account, as mentioned already, is my understanding and not that of the clans that inhabit the land of the mysterious and beautiful Kimberley, a resource-rich land that holds treasures far beyond the mineral resources that pollute the air and the minds of men:

> When the Wandjina walked back to their homes they waded knee deep through the roots in floodwater. They put the pattern down again after the wipe out they started Life all over again. What they manifested then is what we are looking at today. That's what we go and show people, what we know. That's why we call ourselves Wandjina people. Everything started all over again after the ice age. It was creation again! What happened after the ice age is this mob now – Wandjina again.
>
> (Mowaljarlai and Malnic 1993: 181)

This camp offers a radical philosophical approach to thinking in the twenty-first century. As that thinking is ancient, coming from one of the oldest traditions of thought in the world, it is not surprising to discover that the wisdom on which it is based arises not far from some of the oldest geological formations in the world (Wilde et al. 2001: 175).[1] So what makes it radical rather than conservative? Its radical nature comes from the very fact that it is built on a substantial body of classical thought, one that resonates to some of the tenets of quantum physics rather than simply conforming to norms associated with custom and practices.

There is very little information written down by Indigenous Senior Law People; rather, there are voluminous accounts written by non-Indigenous authors *about* Indigenous people. And now we have a growing body of accounts written by young Indigenous people who have not been through the gamut of life experiences, let alone had access to the finer points of their own Law and the important associated *feelings*. What is called Aboriginal Law is nothing more than the sad and quite appalling behaviour of Western law towards Aboriginal people. As Anishinabek legal academic, John Borrows (2007: 30), laments: 'Despite its potential to do otherwise, the [Canadian] law has both inadvertently ignored and purposely undermined Indigenous institutions and ideas and thus weakened ancient connections to the environment.' Furthermore, as Chief Justice Yazzie (2005: 122) of the Navajo Nation relates, Navajo law is based on relationship, not force, so the US federal law is incompatible with the Navajo world-view. These complaints are similar across Indigenous nations. This book addresses those connections to the environment and relationship and examines the legal philosophy that orders them. In other words, it is an account of the great intellectual tradition that underlies Australian Aboriginal Law – a body of Law that, like all laws of the world, is particular to place and people, but also has a commonality across traditions, such as Western legal thought.

This account of an Australian Aboriginal legal philosophy is, therefore, just one account; furthermore, it is my personal interpretation, one born out of experience as well as readings. However, there are legal norms and principles that resonate with Indigenous legal systems and sources throughout the world, as mentioned earlier. Those legal systems are articulated through the narrative, be it oral or written. Fundamental to an Aboriginal Australian, however, is the source: the Land, or primordial energy. From the Land comes the Law (Graham 1999: 105) and that law is realized through the Law of Relationship. The human vehicles for these narratives of Land and Law are the Senior Law People. They are persons who have gained extensive knowledge since early childhood of the epistemology, ecology, languages, oral literature and esoteric knowledge of their nation's classical thought. If anything, they remind one of the classical scholar, adept at music, art, languages, poetry, literature and science. Such internationally famous artists as SLM Wandjuk Marika (1995) are a prime example and the ordeals and perils of such learning are found in his 'life story' (see Chapter 5).

I first met Senior Law Man David Mowaljarlai of the Ngarinyin People, from the great rocky landscape of the Kimberley area in the isolated northwest of Australia, when, as a producer for Radio National (ABC), Australia's national broadcaster, I interviewed him back in the early 1990s. Ever since that meeting and the amazing depth of insight he offered to my programme, I have followed his work, which is outlined and examined in this camp.

SLM Mowaljarlai was an enigmatic figure in the Aboriginal political world of the second half of the twentieth century. His enigma lies in the very (seemingly) 'apolitical' nature of his politics – a politics that resisted the activism (and easy solutions) of the period. Instead, his politics were of the mind as much as matter. SLM Mowaljarlai fought tenaciously for the recognition of Indigenous jurisprudence as a worthy field of study at the tertiary level. In fact, he gathered enough support to establish a 'Bush University'.[2]

SLM Mowaljarlai's pictorial travel diary, *Yorro Yorro* (Mowaljarlai and Malnic 1993) was written in tandem with photographer Jutta Malnic and records their journey to the iconic cosmological figures of the Wandjina, the Creator Beings whose ventures mark the institution of the Law. This seemingly simple pictorial account is misleading in terms of its genre. Despite its 'picturesque' quality, the text is dense in its conceptual content and requires a number of intellectual paradigm shifts in relation to the Law and its source. Then it becomes evident that *Yorro Yorro* is a classical oratory and an engagement between the 'uninitiated' and the Senior Law People of the Kimberley.

What is revealed is nothing less than the cosmological beginnings of *Corpus Australis*, told through classical history and thought – as yet not appreciated by non-Indigenous, let alone Indigenous, scholars. SLM Mowaljarlai offers *a gift* of law – as he states, 'we have a gift'. Hence this camp is concerned with this gift of law, a law that 'witnesses' another law: the Law of Relationship does not set out to supplant, but rather to come into a double-helix relationship through its dyadic structure with human-made law:

> All these northern tribes have a belief system based on a philosophy of relationship, that in all of existence there are always two-two moieties (groups), two energies, two genders, two dimensions of existence such as above and below, seen and unseen, action and idea, generative and receptive. The dynamic of relationship holds that neither one is viable without the other, that survival and increase are dependent upon their interactivity, like the dual strands of DNA whose chemical bonds govern the growth and life of an organism.
>
> (Bell 1998: 18)

To address this gift of jurisprudence, I follow the triadic template, which I feel reflects the Indigenous world-view: cosmology, Law of Relationship, rights and responsibilities. First, with regard to cosmology, I deal with the actions and activities of these great Creator Beings, the Wandjina, who are deemed responsible for the law known as the '*Wunnun* System of Sharing' – a law that transverses the whole continent and gives shape to the Law of Relationship. This 'institution' of law is discussed in its historical context and its unique concepts. The second part of the narrative from this camp addresses the pattern of the *Wunnun* sharing system, a system that is read not for its altruistic value, but rather as a 'logical' responsibility. This logic is Indigenous and demands two 'witnessing' opposite moieties,

Wodoi and Djingun. The last part of the narrative deals with the rights and responsibilities of the individual, particularly in relation to the continuity of what is called their totemic species. That relationship is embodied in the *gi* relationship. I argue that this responsibility is one of preservation of species, effected through images, thoughts and song.

It is not an easy task to appreciate this alternative history and body of law, and a close reading is therefore required. Let us begin with the debunking of a myth, one that propagates the perception of Aborigines as the most religious culture in the world, which does their culture a great disservice. I argue that Aboriginal law, as patterned into the landscape of *Corpus Australis*, renders this culture one of the most secular – or, more correctly, nomological – of societies. This nomological or lawful cosmology explains why Australian Aborigines, though deemed one of the most spiritual people on earth, are, at the same time, devoid of prayer in their rich ceremonial life. How is this so?

For far too long, issues relating to Aboriginal cosmology have been treated as theological, rather than as questions of law, in the sense of a law as *physis*.[3] The intention of this book is to shift this line of questioning away from this historical paternalism – that is, the 'simple faith of the simple people'– and move it towards a more rigorous and respectful space, one that fosters questions of law. This, in turn, will elucidate why the Senior Law Men, such as SLM Mowaljarlai, SLM Neidjie (1989) and SLM Marika (1995), have stepped beyond the limits of localization of orality[4] and turned to the global potential of the written to offer what one might describe as a 'background briefing' to their jurisprudence. Their intention, it will be argued, is to move the paradigm of Aboriginal Law from that of a 'Genesis' story of Aboriginal *lore* to a story of the genesis of Aboriginal *Law*. Hence, these written texts can be seen as an appeal to the literate mind, assisting the print-oriented cultural agent in their understanding of the shape and patterns of Indigenous law. Therefore, these writings have a specific (and limited) purpose, and are not intended as a pseudo-dogma or a codification of the law. That is, they are not meant to last for all time – in fact, these writings are as transitionary as the lives of their authors, wandering far afield and on walkabout, attempting to reach a new audience – that is, modernity itself.

Cosmology

I now turn to SLM Mowaljarlai and the cosmology of the Ngarinyin people and an exploration of how they understand the Law of Relationship and its classical canon.

Creation of the Kimberley

In his account of Creation, SLM Mowaljarlai was able to lay down a timeline in a linear fashion. This would appear 'out of character' for Indigenous thought, which is formed around circular concepts of time (Graham 1999: 105). However, SLM Mowaljarlai's intention was to 'share' his law and so bring it into 'relationship' with the dominant paradigm of Australian law; therefore, he had to turn to concepts like linear time that the outsider would understand. Here is his timeline, based on sources cited earlier.

Timeline
1. Before Our Time – Narkundjaja – before Creation
2. Lalai – the active part of Creation
3. In the Beginning
4. Way-way Back – Ancient Time
5. Flood and Ice Age – interruption, Wipeout
6. Stone Age – Munggugnangga
7. Long Time Ago – Djuman Nangga
8. In the Olden Days – 'When we all still live in the bush'
9. Yorro Yorro – from the Beginning to the present and onwards.

As long as we are standing up with everything in Creation; as it was in the Beginning and will be for as long as nature regenerates itself. Ongoing creation, perpetual renewal of nature in all its forms.

(Mowaljarlai and Malnic 1993: 204)

Such a timeline evidences that there were both intellectual structures in place to sustain a historical narrative and legal structures to govern the maintenance of that narrative – and the knowledge it narrates. Hence, the seemingly fanciful myths contain this knowledge of origins and sources of how the cosmos and its law work – and are sturdy enough to withstand the vicissitudes of time, especially those 'times of trouble' that cata-strophically punctuate the timeline: catastrophes like the Ice Age[5] or Imperialism – the New Ice Age. The timeline reflects the survival of this knowledge and the persistence of law, a law perpetuated by the Wandjina. But who, or what, are the Wandjina?

We learn from the travel diary of SLM Mowaljarlai and Jutta Malnic (1993) that the caves in the vast sandstone valleys of the extremely humid Kimberley region are filled with images of the Wandjina Creator Beings. These images are unique. Rather than the finely executed designs found in the x-ray art of the north of Australia, the Wandjina are rather large, cumbersome entities that remind one more of spacemen than the ethereal representations of beings for which Australian Aborigines are noted. Their full – even satisfied – forms are suggestive not so much of humans or godlike figures, but rather stratocumulus clouds.[6] For they float along, inert and cloudlike. To extend this cerulean analogy, the nose of Wandjina is actually a lightning rod – that is, the *place where the power comes down*.

Even more significantly, they are devoid of a mouth. As Senior Law Woman Daisy Utemorrah suggests: 'He has no need of a mouth, he sends his thoughts' (Mowaljarlai and Malnic 1993: 133); the implication here is that it is the power of thought that emanates from the Wandjina. This is reminiscent of Paula Gunn Allen's (1992: 11) account of the Keres Pueblos Spider Woman, who weaves the world into being through her thoughts.

So the Wandjina animate the landscape of the Kimberley and, more specifically, the territory of the four original clans of Ngarinyin, Wunggarang, Wunambal and the former Worora. In other words, their role as Creator Beings is fulfilled as they create their reality through thought and feeling. Within this reality is the Law. What, therefore, is the relationship of the Wandjina to the Law?

To answer this jurisprudential query, I will start with the 'Wipeout' in Ngarinyin cosmology – the catastrophe, which necessitates the second coming of the Wandjina and so indicates that the Law is not dependent on human governance or its continuance in society. This is significant because it is at the time of this second coming that the Law is laid down – that is, the *Wunnan* system that comprises the jurisprudence of the Law of Relationship. But just what is this Wipeout? SLM Mowaljarlai gives us a clue to it in his story, relayed to co-author Jutta Malnic, of the coming of the Kallawa Anggna Kude[7] – a star with trails, in other words, a comet. This comet crossed the sky and caused the subsequent flood, leading to the Wipeout:

> When Mowaljarlai translated the Kalumburu tapes of the five old men, he had found that some ancestor stories were going back to when the islands originated, and even further back, to what the Birrimitji, the In the Beginning people, had seen before the Ice Age. One song told about a flood, long before the last, that was brought on by Kallawa Anggna Kude, a star with trails.
> (Mowaljarlai and Malnic 1993: 194)

As mentioned in the opening quote, the 'Wipeout' brought about a new start.

What is the significance of this alternative cosmology and its account of the source of Law? The significance lies in the fact that law is not made by humans, but rather ordained and deposited into the land by the primordial energies. Therefore, the source of Law is beyond humankind and their individual concerns; rather, it sits in the realm of eons of time, time in which land is obligated but then re-fertilized by the precipitation from the cosmic energies of the big bang of the universe. Put simply, the law is the *physis*, and to appreciate Aboriginal Law the outsider must connote law with a universe of galaxies that come and go, that die and re-fertilize. As famous anthropologist Andreas Lommel – who visited the people 30 years earlier – realized, his errors in reading *Yorro Yorro* were largely due to his own cultural arrogance:

> My stay had been too short to engage with their spiritual concepts to the depths revealed now, in this work. Nor had I become aware of a complex knowledge of the constellations in the Milky Way. But this now is magnificent. The statement here that aboriginal people always knew of galaxies beyond earth's solar system, it is resounding.
>
> (Mowaljarlai and Malnic 1993: x)

Not only was Lommel surprised that the Ngarinyin Senior Law Men were aware of other galaxies, but he also notes their maturity and 'modest reservation about their extensive knowledge' and, as he quotes: 'We only know about the Milky Way, that's as far as we can go.' Lommel recognized that the maturity of these people meant they did not have to impress the whiteman. As I discovered from SLM Mowaljarlai, to understand an Indigenous jurisprudence that stems from the Australian continent, it is necessary for a paradigm shift to occur in which the understanding of law begins with an understanding of the *physis* rather than the Romanized *natura*, as explained by Wolcher (2004; and see later).

Law of Relationship

The shape of the law

What emerges from the cosmological discourse is the realization that, to understand the law, an appreciation of the shape and pattern of law is an essential prerequisite. Not only must one 'know' of the cosmological foundation, one must also experience it. In doing this, the law is actualized and realized. What, then, is this realization and actualization? In this section, the shape and pattern of law will be realized. This actualization is achieved through a 'walking of the land'. This very act of actualization is what Jutta Malnic has captured in her photographic account of her journey with SLM Mowaljarlai. Through her images, Malnic has given us a sense of the journey and the experiences that actualize the law. This elucidation occurs on the journey taken by Mowaljarlai and Malnic, as detailed in *Yorro Yorro* (1993). There, SLM Mowaljarlai engages in debate over classical thought with various travel companions. These include Senior Law People such as Jagamurro the *banman* (medicine man) and Senior Law Women Daisy Utemorrah, as well as other Law People they meet along the way, such as Hector Darngnall, Violet Jormary and Paddy Neowere. The continuous dialogue that takes place as they travel across the land is recorded by Malnic in both words and images.

What do we learn about law from this discussion and the accompanying images? By incorporating the two media, the reader is able to get a sense of the difficulties, the concern and urgency about the need for protection of the sacred sites. But even more, the reader is drawn into the classical narrative and its account of law, handed down from the times of Creation by the Wandjina Beings. To begin, another paradigm shift is called for – a shift that moves the image of the continent of Australia from a large tract of real estate, national parks and natural resources into that of a body – a large human body lying in the surrounding oceans:

> I'll tell you something, how we see this country. The whole of Australia is Bandaiyan. The front we call *wadi*, the belly-section, because the continent is lying down flat on its back. It is just sticking out from the surface of the ocean. Deep down underneath are the buttocks, *wambalama*, from where the leg joints run into the pelvis and right across to the other side.
>
> (Mowaljarlai and Malnic 1993: 191)

Hence the shape of the law described by SLM Mowaljarlai in the Ngarinyin jurisprudence is an organic image – that of a human body. Thus, the 'shape' of law is a body.

I now turn to the second question of law – the pattern. How, then, is this body tattooed with this pattern of law? SLM Mowaljarlai uses the motif of the fishing net to demonstrate to Malnic the manner in which all Aboriginal people are linked up in this intricately woven web:

> I want to show you something. I want to show you how all Aboriginal people in Australia are connected in the Wunnan

system. The squares are the areas where the communities are represented, and their symbols and the languages of the different tribes in this country from long-long time ago. The lines are the way the history stories travelled along these trade routes. They are all interconnected. It's the pattern of the Sharing system.

(Mowaljarlai and Malnic 1993: 190)

Some might take umbrage at SLM Mowaljarlai's attempt to classify the whole of Australia; however, just as Cajete (1994: 35–36) asserts in relation to the Indigenous laws of the Americas:

Regardless of tribal culture, Indians of the Americas share common metaphors of Indigenous knowledge and education. It is because of such shared metaphors that the development of contemporary Indigenous philosophy of Indian Education is possible.

This is also SLM Mowaljarlai's intent. He is using metaphors he feels will analogize the shape of the basic principles and values of the Law of the *Australia Corpus*. The *Wunnun* system, as quoted here, is analogized as a sharing system, criss-crossing the whole body of the continent, in turn an organic trading system that emulates the law of the sharing system – *Wunnun.*

A further realization of Land as the Law comes from the understanding that Law is not dependent on human action for its continuity, for the Law is already posited in the Land. If anything, man would appear to be a redundant species when it comes to maintaining the Law, as shown in the following dialogue between Malnic and SLM Mowaljarlai:

What about the areas where there are no Aboriginal people still surviving, or at least not living traditionally there any longer?

You're wrong there thinking like that. The land remained, you can't get away from that. It acts for the people and their imprint is still there. If the land sinks into the ocean, the symbols will still be there. Only if the whole continent is blown to pieces and nothing is left of it, then it will be finished.

(Mowaljarlai and Malnic 1993: 192)

So SLM Mowaljarlai is addressing a fundamental question of law – a question asserting that the human merely actualizes that which is posited in Land. He is asserting that the focus on the human as the site of ownership or law is misleading. Moreover, Law is not 'portable' from one country to another – for example, by colonization – but rather stays posited in the original site where the Creator Beings 'laid down'. The actualization of that Law is through the engagement in the *Wunnun* sharing system of law.

I will now address the Law of Relationship and its replicating nature. This aspect of law is what brings the body into a vibrating whole of song. This rhythm of law is popularly known as songlines, which are said to criss-cross the country. The song is about trading in intellectual property on the mundane level, but on the profound level, it is about a continuous checking of the consistencies in the law – a consistency that does not eliminate regional variation but actually celebrates difference. How is this so? How can difference or parallel laws exist in one region?

I will now give an account of how this difference is perceived through the Law of Relationship. It is a law that is dyadic in its structure, and that replicates itself throughout the whole of Creation. As mentioned at the beginning:

> The dynamic of relationship holds that neither one is viable without the other, that survival and increase are dependent upon their interactivity, like the dual strands of DNA whose chemical bonds govern the growth and life of an organism.
>
> (Bell 1998: 18)

This dynamic relationship, as mentioned earlier, is not unique to the Ngaringin or to the cosmology of the Wandjina. This 'fluxing' relationship, the concept of 'relational others' working together, was understood as far back in the West as the time of the Greek philosopher Heraclitus. Louis Wolcher (2004: 264) wrote succinctly about the transformation of Heraclitus's word *physis* to that of the Romanized *natura*, which in turn brought down the law from that of the galactic to that of the earth-bound and exploitable Mother Nature. It is interesting to note that, in the case of Heraclitus, he dismissed his fellow great thinkers who propagated the civil society rather than an adherence to the dynamic and flux-ridden *physis* of the universe, as Wolcher has argued, Heraclitus turned his back on those who basically could not accept that 'god played dice' with humanity – for example, Einstein and his realization that the fundamental laws of quantum mechanics are not fixed but fluxing (2004: 265).

SLM Mowaljarlai therefore tells us the story of law in which the Wandjina Creator Beings have embedded the law into the landscape; in so doing, they have given to *Corpus Australis* a body of law – a continental body of law embedded into the patterns evidenced throughout nature.

Rights and Responsibilities

I now continue with SLM Mowaljarlai's story of law and what it reveals about the manner in which humans are patterned into the *Wunnan* system, as well as the associated rights and responsibilities actualized within the system. Furthermore, I discuss the relationship between humans and their totems, beginning with the concepts of 'image' and 'thought':

> I am giving you this image of the earth shaking itself. This image was given to us in song. Images overcome Earth power any time.
>
> (Bell 1998: 190)

To appreciate the importance of the phrasing ('Images overcome Earth power any time') requires a paradigm shift on the part of the reader, an understanding that power resides not just in the material (the earth), but in the abstract (the image) – that is, 'thought', since creation of the Indigenous world comes from an act of 'thought'. The metaphor used to explain this thought relates to the manner in which the brain works. Using an analogy from quantum physics, Wolf (1985: 24) suggests we cannot see a thought, yet we can actualize a thought – that is, observe it as 'electrical activity' in certain parts of the brain. This activity is not stimulated by the brain itself, but rather occurs in response to activities in the body and, furthermore, activities at the cellular level – with the cellular level having a consciousness of its own making and organizing (1985: 24). Therefore, the use of the metaphor of a cloud to describe the Wandjina connotes the 'deep knowing' of the Ngarinyin. It is important to have at least an elementary understanding of physics if one is to understand the cosmology of the Wandjina of the northern Kimberley of Australia, as the Wandjina culture is steeped in conceptual nuances relating to physics.

Returning to the creation of the world of *Bandaiyan – Corpus Australis –* we learn that creation began in much the same manner as in many global traditions – that is, the fertilization of a 'primeval substance'. As SLM Mowaljarlai says, before Creation there was '*ngallalla yawun* – everything soft like jelly' (Mowaljarlai and Malnic 1993: 132). During the Lalandi time of Creation, Wallanganda 'let fresh water fall upon the earth'. This, in turn, activated the Creation process between Wallanganda and the Earth Snake, Wunggud (1993: 132):

> In Lalia, Wallanganda came down to Earth. He came on order of Ngadjar, the Above One, the Master of All Galaxies, the One Beyond Our Understanding – to bring life to this planet. He came from above, from Sunrise Country, from the place where the

power comes from. He had sent all that water business. Now he came to put life into it.

(1993: 133)

The fertilization of the 'primeval substance' is from the 'water business'. This is not water as we know it, but more a cosmic rain of energy, a type of universal energy force. Here, SLM Mowaljarlai is trying to convey, through allegory, that Land is embedded in and with (legal) thought. This act of embedding is a continual action or reaction between the universal forces of, on the one hand, Creator Wallanganda and, on the other, the Earth's snake-like energy – *Midjelna*: 'As above so below.' This relationship is, unfortunately, not a happy one, but it is a productive tension that brings forth all Creation by way of the intervention of a Creator Being. The effect of that Creation is 'thought' – a seemingly continuous array of thought-like rays of the sun. Some have misinterpreted this phenomenon as sun worship, but I would argue that the rays of the sun are an analogy for this energizing thought process.

The recipient of the 'thought' is the 'Earth Serpent' Snake. She actualizes her role in the Law through three actions:

> Three expressions describe this action which extends to all *wung-gud* holes: *lulu njuwanignari*, 'she slid down the waterhole and stayed there'; *dunggo moni*, 'she edged out a place where she wanted to stop'; and *ada njuma*, 'where she reigns'.

Once in place, the Snake then becomes the 'back' from which all things grow. Owing to its wave shape, the Snake captures 'thoughts' that fall from the galaxy in the 'sweet waters' (Mowaljarlai and Malnic 1993: 133). So, before anything can materialize, an image projection (thought) precedes its appearance or manifestation in reality (1993: 133).

SLM Mowaljarlai reveals it is 'she' – the Snake – who controls the rhythm of all cycles: wind and weather; tides and currents; climate and seasons; reproductive, menstrual, growth and lifecycles. Furthermore, he asserts, she has her own powers: powers to destroy, to heal (restore her own substance), to clear the way, smash up rocks for gorges and rivers; and powers over the physical conditions preceding the embodiment of all creatures and growing things (1993: 133).

This almighty power, however, works in a binary relationship with Wallanganda, who sends – on a continuous basis – 'batches of energy to earth', perhaps analogous to solar bursts from the sun. The energy is then 'stored in the *wunggud* pools as images' (1993: 133). The pools contain

templates (thoughts/images) of all Creation. It would seem, in this cosmology, that it is not a 'seed' from which life blossoms; rather, it emerges
from 'images/thoughts' of humans engaging in a ceremony in which they
'touch up' the images that the Wandjina left for man. At this point, a
quantum leap is required, as this is a unique understanding of Creation.

SLM Mowaljarlai writes:

> When man, now identity man, left his home shelter for the open
> country, his totemic identity and source of secured supply
> remained in safe deposit in the paintings. He would return there
> to stimulate the idea of the Seed-Gift, ask for increase in the line
> of his totem, and be himself refreshed.
>
> Life-force is boosted by touching, retouching, stimulating and
> acknowledging the man-totem identity in various ways. The result
> is an increase in supplies.
>
> Every totem has a spirit, a *gi*, and it is the spirit of the totem
> which a person represents. This spirit rejoices in the presence of
> the brother-person.
>
> (Mowaljarlai and Malnic 1993: 138)

The concept of the *gi* can also be found in other traditions, such as the
Navajo *k'e* (Yazzie 2005: 130) or the Japanese *ki* (Doi 1981). Both are about
relatedness and dependence, a positive dependence and sense of belonging.
There is also an interdependence that ensures that 'shaming' within the
cultural bounds has an affect on the members of the community. The
Navajo concept is particularly beautiful, in that on the first laughter of
the newborn child, the *k'e* is embraced by the community and a feast is
held for the child by the first person to hear the child laugh (Yazzie 2005:
130). And, just as in the Ngaringin case, the fact that the spirit rejoices in
the presence of the brother (sister) person evokes a *feeling* rather than an
esoteric or prayer-like response. This shift to 'relatedness' (brother/sister),
as mentioned earlier, brings about a different jurisprudential approach to
the rights of the human. Humans' rights become more a case of rights to
human feelings. Feelings bring about the correct intellectual engagement
and lawful behaviour. A similar concept is found in Ubuntu philosophy, as
articulated by previously mentioned Zulu philosopher, Mogobe Ramose
(2002). Ramose argues for the importance of 'relatedness' as the vehicle
for humanness, conveyed in the expression *umuntu ngumuntu ngabantu*
('a person is a person through other persons') (2002: 41). SLM Mowaljarlai
takes this concept a step further, elucidating a gateway not only to 'the
other', but to the Law in the Land.

Returning to the theme of identity of man and the statement 'Life force is boosted by touching, retouching', so relatedness has a very physical dimension and this is a major paradigm shift. For fertilization and growth, life force is the product not so much of seeds as of sites – sites to which one requires access. So Indigenous land claims are not merely economic, not even spiritual; they go to the core of our being, our life force. For it is the site that gives life, not the seed. The water lagoons are important to the Kimberley tribes because they represent more a site of the original Creation than because they are a source of economic development (fishing, etc.). By recreating, not reproducing, those actions, they bring energy and so life into the world (Morris 1991). Hence, they do not call on the favours of a Creator, but rather pattern themselves into the same creative process. So there is an immediacy of action through actualization, rather than, say, waiting for a response through the intermediary of prayer.

This also discloses why Aborigines do not privilege paternity as the central factor in Creation, as the West (obsessively) does. However, let me first say that it is not that paternity has no role in procreation; rather, it is that this law has another view of the procreative process. Paternity was seen as a 'side-effect' of the actions of the human–*Wunnan* relationship. Rather than the male being viewed as the giver of semen, he is seen as the carrier of a 'thought' that impregnates a woman. The same logic applies to other creative processes – for example, hunting, which entails the 'touching up' of a painting, in turn evoking an animal image as thought. As previously mentioned, SLW Daisy Utemorrah says the Wandjina brought the 'thought', not the 'word'.

So there is an overall power in the universe defined through the title *Ngadjar* – the unknowable universal force (Mowaljarlai and Malnic 1993: 133). The knowable is framed in the interactions between Wallanganda and Mindjilan – that is, the creative energies from above to the life-giving earth from below. It is the tension between these Wallanganda and Mindjilan that actualizes creation. Humans are patterned into this Law of *physis*, and participate directly in its creation through maintaining the correct mental balance, which in turn actualizes the Law of Relationship – or, as Wolcher (2004: 268) puts it, theory suggests 'destiny needs you more than controls you'.

The following quotation reveals SLM Mowaljarlai's understanding of how (hu)man-totem Wandjina patterned humanity into their rights and responsibilities:

In the Beginning, human beings were one with their totem – man was yam, sugarbag, owl, etc. . . . man was present in every kind of food.

A person is inseparable, from his totem. Man and totem hold, guard and are bound by each other's life energies. 'That is why we say, 'Man was yam or wallaby or sugarbag at first,' Mowaljarlai asserts. 'They were first one with their food totem.'

This man-totem form is very important; the creator did not make any kind of seed to continue a line of species. Instead, he packaged the Totemic Principle into man, giving him responsibility for the continuing renewal and well-being of another kind.

(Mowaljarlai and Malnic 1993: 137)

In this passage, the question of law relates directly to the human's rights and responsibilities. The human's right is to bring into being the assigned species – the brother/sister *gi*. And the human's responsibility is to keep actualizing that right to continue the species. This binary of rights and responsibility therefore leads to a desire for diversity rather than homogenization. It is a diversity based on an ecological pattern and desire for balance and one that is totemized as a natural element or creature. So identity is not an effect of skin colour or features, but of ecological alliance and personality. SLM Mowaljarlai's alter ego was a hibiscus plant, just as mine is a stone.

The right/responsibility binary embeds in humans in an assured balance and functions as an ecologically based population monitor (Mowaljarlai and Malnic 1993: 137). This legal right, therefore, is meant to pattern a management system of resources – a pattern that, if applied to the whole of Australia, would require humans to see themselves as responsible for a specific species of food. Of course, some may say the normal fighting for resources would take over. But would it? Perhaps we would not have the wholesale slaughter of some species – such as happened with the bison of Native America and which immediately sets up a resource imbalance in nature for the preference of a particular species. However, with a legal system that emerges from an understanding that humans have a direct impact on and responsibility towards their food resources, we may see more interest in balance, rather than simply the acquisition of resources.

This patterning with a *gi*, as mentioned earlier, brings about the sentiment that: 'This spirit rejoices in the presence of the brother-person.' On seeing the brother/sister, the feeling evoked – as we have learnt from SLM Neidjie (1989: 107) – brings about a relationship with the human, a relationship that assists the person to access necessary resources. This relationship with the *gi* is, therefore, a profitable relationship as well as a responsibility. Just as when the human touches up a site for the continuation of a species, so, too, does the human receive the psychological benefits that might represent what I call a 'euphoria of alignment'. Furthermore, it localizes the human and affirms a sense of belonging. That belonging is localized, but it is, at the same time, *universal*. This *gi* and its touching up connect the person back to their classical histories, to their times of Creation. Therefore, as Malnic discovered, the Ngarinyin are constantly realigning themselves with the original Creation – they are not just building on a founding myth, but rather recreating that narrative on a daily basis, and in so doing achieving a continued balance by never forgetting their connection to time and space. This circular motion and motive undergird the Indigenous reality. This places the person, as another Senior Law Man Bill Neidjie of the Buntji People (1989: 107) asserts, in alignment with the *Djang* or primordial force of the universe.

The *Djang* in the Ngarinyin cosmology, however, has a more 'human' personality and turns on notions of choice – as evidenced in the process of walking one's country as SLM Mowaljarlai did. The core premise disclosed by SLM Mowaljarlai's journey is that Aborigines are well aware of having a 'choice' in all areas of their lives. They are not mindless naive nomads on walkabout,[8] but rather are aware of the laws of the universe and the ability to either live with the pattern of law into which they were born or to choose to make their own law that facilities their desires to be the source of their Creation. This story of choice is actually a narrative, which is continually played out throughout the history of many societies. Western nations, for example, desire to industrialize – and this, as MacNeil (2007) argues, is what has brought forth the 'monstrous body' of Western law.

Western law was diverted from its original duty, which was a *revelatory* role of nature's divine intention, to that of an *instrumental* role of following up behind technological development. This development, as I argue elsewhere (Morris 2004b), leads to a biotechnological world that imagines itself the creator of both humans and new species in the future. Therefore, I argue that the following classical narrative is atypical, rather than ancient, if the correct reading is applied.

The Earth Serpent – Midjelna

[T]hen the Snake uncoiled and stretched out. She became Midjelna, 'the one that unwinds her rings and stretches out looking'. Her body was sprouting with a kingdom of living nature. From here she would take over from the Creator. She would persuade man to reproduce by sexual intercourse only, without the spirit portion that put him under the Law of the Universe as

Wandjina (hu)man. Midjelna offered independence, joint management and knowledge of her own realm and powers – she
offered the earth.

With this offer of independence, the all-encompassing harmony
and order were disrupted. [Hu]Man could now choose to consider
spiritual matters or ignore them. The communities soon became
aware of the necessity for social laws.

(Mowaljarlai and Malnic 1993: 142–43)

If I turn back to the triadic model to 'read' this narrative, the meaning
that emerges is this: on a cosmological level, it could be argued that we are
reading about the birth of the ego – that is, Midjelna's choice; at the
level of the Law of Relationship, it is a revealing of the law of the universe.
If, however, the human chooses to be the creator, then a social law
(human-made) is 'posited' or instigated. On the level of the rights and
responsibilities, the human is perceived as a fully independent being who is
able to be lawful. If, however, the human becomes a devotee of Midjelna –
that is, devoid of the spirit and the universal law – then the human can
become an autonomic individual, a discrete entity oblivious to context – of
other selves, spaces, geographies, environments. So what Midjelna offers is
'independence, joint management and knowledge' of her own realms and
powers – Midjelna offered the earth.

And so the assertion of Midjelna's power and the subsequent choice
leads to the same conclusion as that experienced by Heraclitus. The dry-
adic flux-laden *physis* is left behind and the civil society – in the form of
social laws – is constructed and enforced with brick and mortar. Nature
loses its dynamism, and so becomes Mother Nature in joint management
with humankind – the creator of humanity's own destiny.

However, the Ngarinyin chose to persist with the spirit-laden Law and
to maintain the balance through the acknowledgment of opposites and
their necessary dynamism. Opposites are equal in all ways – there is no
gender divide at this foundation level; rather, each moiety contains male
and female – men's and women's law. As for the Ngarinyin, this 'living
with Wanganella' in turn makes him responsible and intertwined with
other species. A reading of the image or *gi* power could lead to an
assumption of a god-like creative power, but only if you assume humans
are superior to other species. If anything, it reminds the human that
they are codependent on other species. So the responsibility of being a
creator is to maintain a balance – as against the reproducer of self,
which has led to the out-of-control replicatory behaviour of the icons
built in humans' image. This replicatory madness sees nature reduced to a

ready resource and wallpapered into the background of humankind's achievements.

Conclusion

To conclude, I claim that the outer circle of the triad I have been using – cosmology – explains that the Ngarinyin system of law comes out of the Wandjina and the laying down of the law after the 'Wipeout'. After such a 'Wipeout', life and law must be reintroduced by the Wandjina. This cosmology places SLM Mowaljarlai's journey into context. As the reader moves through the Wandjina lands of the north-west Kimberley, they learn how to read the Land. And so an act of translation occurs. This translation is of the Law of Relationship.

SLM Mowaljarlai was as adamant as SLM Neidjie that the Balanda had to hear the Law. For SLM Mowaljarlai, it was essential the two laws work together to actualize the 'sharing system' because, just like SLM Neidjie, he felt an urgency – 'there is no time; time is running out' (Mowaljarlai and Malnic 1993: jacket cover, back page insert). This is the significance of SLM Mowaljarlai's work: it actually works to produce a template for sharing the management of *Bandaiyan – Corpus Australis*. This is the gift of the *Wunnun* system.

Finally, the rights and responsibilities of the human are intertwined with their codependence on their *gi* – a codependence that they choose. In making that choice, they are then sustained by their *gi*, which, in turn, patterns them into the Land and brings about a balance – a balance of the *physis*, a balance of Law. It is through this balance that they then find the authenticity of their classical thought – an authenticity that does not look to others for verification, even if they appear dominant. Rather, it looks to their sense of belonging to the Land.

CHAPTER 5

Health and land: The camp of Senior Law Man Wandjuk Marika

The Yolngu people have achieved many firsts in the Aboriginal world and have been leaders in many sectors relating to Indigenous people, from ground-breaking Land Rights Acts to internationally famous rock bands such as Yothu Yindi. All this demonstrates that the Yolngu are as capable as any other Australians of making their mark on the world scene and are more than capable of standing up for their rights. But that did not give them what was most important to their future: respect for their Law stories and validation of their rich intellectual reality.

The health of a people is dependent on the stories that come to them (Borrows 2007: 13). In the time of SLM Marika's youth, stories abounded; they intertwined and patterned people into an array of meta-physical experiences and knowledge. But then bauxite was discovered on his people's lands and there were promises of great riches that would bring the seemingly disadvantaged Yolngu into the twentieth century as equal citizens before the Balanda's law. Instead, mining brought nothing save the vagaries of Western civilization. The story of the Yolngu is a common one, duplicated across the many resource-rich areas of Australia and, therefore, is an important learning tale for all of us. It was a significant story for me and my understanding that money alone will not bring good health and sound mind; neither does it protect people from the ravages of alcohol and rampant diabetes and other diseases.

But then I came across *Wandjuk Marika: Life Story* (Marika 1995) and found hope. It is an account that Senior Law Man Marika shared with his long-time friend, Jennifer Isaacs. This, of course, will be a different account to the one shared with, say, his sister Bunduk or his son Malawan. This life story, therefore, elucidates that dialogic encounter between Wandjuk and Jennifer and his experiences as he took his Ulysses-like journey from his Dreaming site out into the globe as a famous artist and returned to his home as the custodian of the powerful Dreaming site of Yalanbara.[1]

A story of law and health

The spirit belong to that land which is a most important
Creation,
Like Yalanbara,
I have moved there,
I had so many struggling, so many bad habits,
Then I move to live in my special area,
So I can get more power, more understanding,
Have more feeling, kind and strongly and see the way
Very clearly,
Because there is special feeling from the land.

(Marika 1995: 131)

Entering the camp of Senior Law Man Marika

This camp of SLM Marika gives the reader a glimpse of the important link between health and land. As I learnt from reading *Wandjuk Marika: Life Story*, there were times when SLM Marika lost his voice of authority and so found the need to return to the land of his ancestors to clear his mind and find his power – a power which, as we learn from the earlier quotation, was actualized from the Land.

This led to the formulation of my previously mentioned etymological account of the word 'jurisprudence' and its essential element of health as the legitimizing factor of a law's right to have jurisdiction over a domain. For I would contend that if a law cannot ensure the health of a people through the understanding of its jurisprudence, then it is merely a set of rules to regulate their movements and their goods.

Senior Law Man Marika's autobiography, *Wandjuk Marika: Life Story* (1995), as already mentioned, was written in tandem with his lifelong friend Jennifer Isaacs,[2] a veteran photographer of Aboriginal art and craft. SLM Marika undertook this endeavour in an attempt to take back the *power of definition* of his people's law and history – in other words, their intellectual landscape.

But before we read SLM Marika's account of law, I will first contextualize his account, as there is a misunderstanding – especially in Australia – that money will fix any problem. During my travels across the continent of Australia, I was repeatedly and vividly struck by the same deep apathy in many communities that I found in Arnhem Land.

Why Warriors Lie Down and Die

What does it mean to be outside the Law? What does it mean to turn a deaf ear to the voice of the Law posited in the Land? What is the result of silencing the voice of authority? These are the questions posed by Richard Trudgen in his book, aptly named *Why Warriors Lie Down and Die* (2000). The following story is the stimulus for the book:

> About the middle of 1997, a community nursing sister who had been in Arnhem Land for many years asked me: 'Richard, what is wrong? The people now have good water supplies, good sewerage systems and good housing. But they're still sick and dying. What else do we have to do? What's missing? Have we done something wrong?' Like many others, she had believed that if the people's living conditions improved, their health would improve. Now she had been in the community long enough to see that this was not so.
>
> (2000: 218)

Trudgen's book was thrust on me as necessary reading when I flew out of Arnhem Land, basically asking myself the same questions as the nurse in the quotation. I had flown to Arnhem Land on a research trip, expecting to find a 'success' story that I could write up in my report. As it happened, the man sitting next to me in the plane was a project officer from Arnhem Land and he handed me the book to help solve my dilemma. I learnt that the book had been written at the behest of Senior Law Man Dr Djiniyini Gondarra after observing the practices of Richard Trudgen in dealing with the Yolngu. Trudgen was trained by the famous Brazilian educationalist and champion of the oppressed, Paulo Freire (2000), who moves beyond the 'ignorance' that assumes that, among 'the wretched of the earth' (Fanon 1965), poor health conditions and poverty are due to economic disparity and that equal rights and personal autonomy will solve the problem. Such a view sees these complex issues purely in terms of a politico-economic solution. This kind of thinking is obsessed with the 'intersection' of the problem, and has failed to comprehend what these people have been saying. Trudgen – like Freire – began with the cosmology of the people. Moreover, again like Freire, he entered the psyche and logic of the oppressed to engage in a meaningful dialogue. This dialogue, however, must be contextualized. Freire contextualized his understanding of the people through the examination of education systems, while Trudgen contextualized his through health.

Trudgen's work pinpoints poor health outcomes, stemming from the invalidation of the intellectual landscape – the 'intellectual' being both the physical landscape and a landscape patterned with ideas of culture and of law. Not only is this patterned land invalidated, but so are the voices of authority that articulate that culture and law. As Trudgen (2000) points out, this invalidation is further compounded when the voices of authority are incapacitated from monitoring or making judicial decisions about the types of knowledge allowed to be valued in their society. What counts as knowledge and who decides? This act of judgment is vital to all societies. For it is through its own intellectual landscape that a culture decides what is good for future generations and what is detrimental to a stable society.

These symptoms led Trudgen to suggest that those who bring this 'other' socio-economic model need to see things in a new way. At first, this seems to lead back to the ghetto of the 'intersection'; however, Trudgen goes in a different direction, offering more substantial analysis by posing the question around the concept of control. As Zulu legal philosopher Ramose (2006b) points out, 'naming' and 'control' are binary factors. To be in control of a society, it is necessary to name it, drawing your governance models from your own classical thought rather than that of another. In the case of the Yolngu, Trudgen (2000) observed their powerlessness even though they were reaping the socio-economic benefits of the dominant by asserting their political rights through the land council system.[3] However, this system of 'self-determination, self-management and currently self-reliance and self-sufficiency' resulted in 'warriors' who were 'laying down and dying'. What Trudgen observed was that the people felt their loss of humanity when they had to apply another culture's notion of 'being in control'. This loss of humanity, in other words, represents a devaluing of their spirit and an assimilation of their very being.

This profound lack of understanding of such fundamental ideas is not just known to the Yolngu but has been part of the political discourse for many decades. Yet we still see Aborigines pushing for leadership training courses, a move that assumes a young person can be plucked from a community because of their academic skills and that they will return after having been fully educated in the Western mainstream to lead their people. This is an assumption propagated by voices favoured by the media, rather than by a groundswell of followers. How is it that these educated Indigenous leaders seem unaware of the blatantly obvious pitfalls of a Western-constructed idea of leadership?

> As Freire observed so called leadership training courses are based on the naïve assumption that one can promote the community by training its leaders – as if it were the parts that promote the whole and not the whole which, in being promoted, promotes the parts.
> (Trudgen 2000: 207)

An assimilation, as Trudgen observes, means 'death' – not just of the warriors, but of all the people of the Land. So 'control' of naming and knowledge is vital to a society. As Trudgen (2000: 209) deduced:

> [W]hen the people have heard all the relevant information in a language they understand, initiated a response or intervention that fits their cultural ways, and then physically brought into being what they have decided upon, the problem seems to fade and almost disappear.

And naturally, as one would expect, good health ensues. Trudgen's realization led him to develop a series of questions based on his knowledge of Paulo Freire's educational model; these are important questions that validate the principles and values of a people. This reasoning is not so original, but rather implicit in any culture's well-being. It entails questions that recall what counts as knowledge; who has the power of definition; how the knowledge is organized and referenced; who is empowered to teach; and, more importantly in a world of 'Google the Genius', who is allowed to ask and answer questions. All these questions are implicit in the dominant educational system and its structures; however, my reference to Google reminds us that educators are once again asking those questions, especially in light of the other cultural influences of cyberspace, that break down the norm and introduce new voices of authority – voices with which, as Trudgen (2000: 209) points out, the Yolngu are also grappling.

These requirements are the same for any society, yet Indigenous peoples are not perceived as having the ability to conceptualize knowledge, other than as something relating to food-gathering and hunting. It is not surprising, therefore, that there is a lack of realization, even by Indigenous peoples, that they have a tradition of classical thoughts that bring forth a viable cosmology, a system of law and rights and responsibilities for the individual, who, in turn, takes on the responsibility to care for his or her land and people.

Cosmology

Let us now turn to the cosmology of the landscape that gave birth to SLM Marika as the authoritative voice of that Land's Law and a keeper of the sacred site Yalanbara – the creation place of his people, the Rirratjingu of north-east Arnhem Land, in Australia's Northern Territory. SLM Marika was considered the keeper of the source of the people's 'Book of Genesis' (Marika 1995: 32). He is the authoritative voice on the creative activities of the Creator Being Djangukawu.

The cosmological narrative known as *Djangukawu* is not the sacred or *manikay* version. This is the public story, which situates SLM Marika in the world and allows others to form relationships to him. The Creation story gives an account of the arrival of the two Wawilak sisters who are at the same time children of Djangukawu, and his two sisters Madalatj and Bitjiwurrurru (Marika 2000: 32).[4]

> It start from Djangukawu.
> He divided up two people, two Rirratjingu,
> And another thing,
> We are one clan, one language, one song and one
> everything,
> but He put it on two sides.
> When the ceremony times comes, then we come together,
> we come together, have ceremony for one people,
> Rirratjingu,
> A religion, the special ceremony,
> singing, dancing, burials, initiation and funeral,
> all that circle is going through teaching young people.
> We own two separate places.
> It's one large area, sunset on the other side around the bay,
> sunrise on the open seas, Yalanbara.
>
> (Marika 2000: 27–28)

What does this account of the Dhuwa jurisprudence tell us? It tells us that the first people materialized at Yalanbara and there began their journey of Creation, forming the mountains, rivers and waterholes. Also, they created different clans by giving birth to the many children who were subsequently divided up into Dhuwa and Yirritja moieties. These moieties were delineated through kinship and marriage laws. The laws relating to initiation and relationships with other tribes were also formed by the Dhuwa–Yirritja binary relationship. On cessation of these acts, the Creator Beings then became spirits. Sacred sites, therefore, are reminders of the Beings and Laws made in the cosmological beginnings.

As in the next stanza, it is women who create humanity and posit them in place, as though fertilizing the Land with humans and languages:

> They [two sisters] used to carry the people in these mats. When-ever they were ready to create the people in a different area with different languages of different clans, they used to open up the mat and that means those two sisters were the creators.
>
> (Marika 2000: 37)

What this narrative presents is an assertion that Aborigines are pat-terned into Land through a binary song of Law – the two sisters – and then the binary song weaves clans into relationship: 'Then Djangukawu made a song – two kinds, sacred song and public song' (Marika 2000: 37). Legal questions thus first require a paradigm shift away from custodianship or ownership, which connotes a being on top of land and so claiming rights to exclusive use of resources in some manner.

There is an overarching dyadic structure of Dhuwa and Yirritja moieties, each with their unique cosmology covering people, water, sacred sites and the biosphere (like plant sources). From this cosmology come their Law and their reality. It is this tolerant – indeed truly civil(ized) – approach to other world-views and access to land that distinguishes Indigenous juris-prudence from that of the Australian common law. For a great divide opens up here. The dominant culture does not understand a legal regime in which the *Land is the Law* and Indigenous legal jurisprudence does not understand *land as property*. This impasse or gap in 'legal translation' has led to more than just court battles.

Dyadic Structure

This binary jurisprudence is very different from the legal concepts encapsulated in the Aboriginal Land Rights Act 1976, which was said to offer Yolngu a right to autonomy. Trudgen points out that Yolngu have:

[L]and rights, but these 'land rights' are not recognised at Yolngu law; rather, they were created in a shape and form that suited Balanda law ... Yolngu do want the protection and rights the present legislation affords them over their estates. But at the same time, they dream of the day when these rights will be recognised in the form of their traditional tenure and the rule of law established in the *Madayin*.

(Trudgen 2000: 250)

To understand this law, Trudgen came up with the following list in consultation with SLM Djiniyini Gondarra. It is clear that he was trying to acculturate the norms of the body of laws known as the *Madayin*[5] to the common law notions of law through the latter's legal gaze and obsession with rules as a way of actualizing a law:

The *Madayin* encompasses the following. It includes:

- All the property, resource, criminal, economic, political, moral and religious laws of the people;
- Their Narra (restricted chamber of law) and other lesser councils;
- The objects that encode the law;
- Song cycles that tell of legal agreements;
- The trading highways that criss-cross Arnhem Land;
- The embassy sites on close and distant clan estates that give travellers and traders protection at law;
- The protected production sites (hatcheries and nurseries) for different animals, fish and birds;
- The correct conservation and production of plants and food such as yams;
- The husbandry of fish, turtles, animals, birds and so on;
- The restricted places for dangerous country, e.g. cliff faces or tidal whirlpools;
- Protection of the clan's assets;
- Controls to regulate trade and production; and
- Set diplomatic rules and regulations throughout all the clans and nations.

This complex *Madayin* system is seen as holy, demanding great respect. It was given at creation to establish and maintain a state of *magay*.

(Trudgen 2000: 13)

Yet such a listing unintentionally acts to abrogate the dyadic structure of the *Madayin* jurisprudence. The attempts at communication thus end up undermining the jurisprudential structure and therefore the law of the other.

This dilemma leads me to ask the reader to ponder the art of SLM Marika. His works are world famous and can easily be found on a search engine. For it is through art that the Yolngu have been able to articulate their Law. In a conference paper delivered in 2005, Kirsten Anker posed an important question to the Australian judiciary:

> In Australian native title claims, the Federal Court has the power to allow evidence of the claimants' connection to country to be presented in ways 'other than in the normal course of giving evidence'. Native title evidence commonly involves hearings 'on country' and the presentation of testimony in the form of songs, dances, ceremonies and paintings. This measure is partly attributable to the court's willingness to be 'culturally sensitive' and provide access to justice for claimants, but it is also an inherent part of native title's characterisation as taking its content from Indigenous law and custom – proof of a non-conventional title will involve non-conventional proof.
>
> But how, within the paradigm of Western law, does a painting (etc.) add to the probability that a particular claim is true? Is there 'truth in painting'?

Such questions demonstrate an attempt at cultural sensitivity, just as such sensitivity was Trudgen's goal. However, as we can see, something is lost in this process. Let me now examine what I regard as an important element of Indigenous jurisprudence, which needs a qualified Senior Law Person to make judgement: the legal reading of Aboriginal art. Painting the law needs a judiciary of competent Law People, who need deep knowledge of the Law stories to make judgements.

Painting the Law

The importance of SLM Marika's artistic masterpieces lies not so much in their exposition as in their content, for it is the story of Law that is sung on to the bark or canvas that actualizes the Law. SLM Marika's paintings can be found in most of the major collections in Australia and are also reproduced in his book. These paintings are stories of Law – Law paintings.

Paintings are not simply works of art, but rather are text or scripts. They are documents that detail the cosmological origins of mankind, the system of law and rights and responsibilities of the individual. This medium of knowledge transfer is not, however, a 'capturing' of the concepts but rather sung on to the painting. Singing accompanies painting and within the song is the Law. The travelling of the Creator Beings as they created an area is sung on to the painting. This connotes a movement and ensures that knowledge is not captured on a one-dimensional surface, but rather performed on to the surface, so giving it other dimensions as it is actualized. These multi-dimensional activities are said to give Indigenous people other dimensions of being.

Isaacs (1980) points out that SLM Marika told her that his father Mawalan handed on to him the full repertoire of Rirratjingu designs custodianship and taught him how to execute this knowledge through the paintings. SLM Marika then trained his eldest son, Mawalan II, who says his father still instructs him, in spite of his being dead (Marika 2000: 110). The importance of Ramose's concept of the 'living dead' and the continuity of important knowledge becomes evident in this relationship between father and son. This relationship is something that must be grasped if the reality of the notion of 'authority' in Indigenous jurisprudence is to be understood.

Rights and Responsibilities

This section relates to the manner in which the *voice of authority* is shaped so that the individual can take up their rights and responsibilities to Land. Fundamental to that formation is the valuing of that knowledge at an appropriate intellectual level. As Anishinaabekwe Nation scholar Leanne Simpson (2003) argues in relation to traditional ecological knowledge (an area in which the Yolngu are said to have made a major contribution in Australia):

> To include Indigenous Peoples and Indigenous Knowledge in research studies, policy developments, legislation and in environmental decision making, means that different decisions will be made. To use Indigenous Knowledge in a respectful and appropriate way requires Indigenous People. Our Elders and Knowledge Holders are our experts, they are the people with PhDs and they need to be at the table with enough power to use the knowledge within them to make decisions. Western resource managers, policy makers and legislators need to understand that

the respectful inclusion of Indigenous Knowledge and Indigenous Peoples requires that committees will be run differently, policies will change, and that different decisions will be made.

The Yolngu of eastern Arnhem Land are at the forefront of the movement to recognize ecological knowledge in Australia. However, the 'source' of that knowledge is being ignored, as SLM Marika has pointed out. I want to explore that 'blind spot', but first I will begin with a quote from SLM Marika (2000: 114), in which he tells of the story of his father's passing of authority in the form of his *djuta*:

> And then my father said to me, [as he is dying in hospital]
> 'Look, Wandjuk, my son, I'm no longer with you.
> I have passed it all on to you.
> You have to think hard
> And learn about many ways.
> Take my stick (*djuta*),
> Take my word,
> Take my energy,
> Take my courage.

This is a beautiful and poetic evocation of the passing of knowledge by an elder on to the next generation. The passing on of knowledge is not merely of remembrance of lessons learnt, but a whole repertoire of symbols, feelings and characteristics.

SLM Marika then contextualizes his inheritance and the means by which it is patterned into the Land. He then goes on to answer and deal with the source of the *voice of authority* – how and why he has the voice of authority:

> How could I learn all that? Well, that's a good question. Because I'm the top man's son. Because my father is the most important Man. He has more experience, he has more knowledge from his father, my father's father – because – I have many generations before me including the main one, Djangukawu our creation. We are the sons who know how to make, where to go, where to find the place.
>
> (Marika 2000: 114)

This knowledge acquisition (which some readers may perceive as a hierarchy) is, however, as always, subordinate to the Land:

> In his political days Wandjuk tells of how he tried to explain to the Balanda 'I was a man who pushed myself very hard against government law to make the Balanda understanding what the culture and what the land, how we love the land, because our land is most important and special because our land is from the Creation, because our land is the mother. The land has many things, power, experience and knowledge. That's what I explain to the government – to show them the land decorations, so they can understand.'
>
> (Marika 2000: 114)

The role of a ceremonial leader is pivotal to a tribe, as this leader is also a scholar of the classical history of the origins of their legal tradition and the surrounding clans. SLM Marika's role as a ceremonial leader, as well as that of a warrior, has attracted comparisons with great Native American statesmen such as Black Elk (Sioux) and Chief Seattle (Sugumish), who were both ceremonial leaders and warriors to save Native land in North America. The important similarity of these Native American figures to the Australian Aborigines is their role as a 'ceremonial leader' who is the 'master of ceremonial life and keeper of ritual and sacred truths'. It is a duty, this book asserts, that is more important than any political role, as it is the ritual that 'actualizes' the Law, rather than the fight for human rights of foreign laws that attempt to enforce civility. So if we are to understand the Indigenous Law, we must first understand that Law comes out of a ritual life, not a political fight. This is a message that the Senior Law Women of Wirrimanu of the Great Sandy Desert are also trying to filter into the Australian intellectual landscape:

> When the sacred is revealed, the imagination is infused with creative power – Living Culture – but when life is devoid of ritual, the connection with one's soul is lost and life begins to lose its meaning. When the soul is neglected, humanity loses its spiritual sensibility and is alienated from the Tujkurrpa, and thus from the self. The secularisation of life is one of the most effective forms of repression.
>
> (De Ishtar 2005: 292)

The importance of ceremony is well understood by other prominent Yolngu, including the Yunupingu brothers,[6] who have worked hard to establish the Garma Festival in which Indigenous culture is demonstrated and the voice of authority is securely in the hands of the Yolngu and the

Land. The festival is held in an isolated area so that the Land can influence and heal the participants. This 'contextualizing' of knowledge in the Land was influenced by Mandawuy Yunupingu's experience as a school principal:

> In the bureaucratic minds of Department officials, schools were associated with being away from all things Aboriginal. Schools in homelands centres upset all their categories. And I know from painful experience that when you upset white people's categories you'd better watch out.
>
> (Yunupingu 1994)

Mandawuy Yunupingu was not only a teacher, but also a Yolngu philosopher. He is an excellent exemplar of the Yolngu ability to articulate his people's philosophy. The following story is an extract from his 1993 Boyer Lecture, broadcast on ABC Radio National, in which he discusses *Ganma*:[7]

> Also, talk of *Ganma* brings another image to my mind. A deep pool of brackish water, fresh water and salt water mixed. The pool is a balance between two different natural patterns, the pattern of the tidal flow, salt water moving in through the mangrove channels, and the pattern of the fresh water streams varying in their flow across the wet and dry seasons . . .
>
> In each of the sources of flowing water there is ebb and flow. The deep pool of brackish water is a complex dynamic balance. In the same ways, balance of Yolngu life is achieved through ebb and flow of competing interests, through our elaborate kinship system. And I feel that in the same ways balance between black and white in Australia can be achieved.
>
> *Ganma* is a metaphor. We are talking about natural processes but meaning at another level. *Ganma* is social theory. It is our traditional profound and detailed model of how what Europeans call 'society' works.
>
> Of course Europeans have society and nature as quite different and opposed things. But for us, society and nature are not separate. We have Yirritja and Dhuwa, and these categories contain elements which are both natural and social. Also, of course, they have elements which Europeans call supernatural or metaphysical.
>
> (Yunupingu 1993)

So, according to Yunupingu's account, the Yolngu student is able physically to engage with the historical (*Ganma*) and philosophical concepts of their society by viewing the land. In so doing, the student learns the Law from the Land by observing its patterns. The Land becomes the great books of knowledge, obviating the need for students to carry the books around with them. Rather, they have only to observe their surroundings. For this intellectual landscape, when observed in such a way, brings land and theory into a relationship rather than divisive states of 'otherness' – land perceived as an object of 'otherness' to be studied through the theory of science, property law, geography, and so on. It is perhaps only the artisan/philosopher who has some sense of the Indigenous aesthetic approach to learning. Yunupingu is, thus, articulating the 'witnessing' element of the Law. The lawful youth must witness the evidence of Law as it is patterned into Land. This act of witnessing is shaped by the Yolngu classical narrative and thought, as articulated by SLM Marika's journey to Senior Law Man status.

Conclusion

Through this journey – not only of SLM Marika's account of his life, but also the examples offered by Trudgen and Yunupingu – this camp's discussion has brought forth a jurisprudence relating to the rights and responsibilities of the individual and the manner in which a voice of authority is shaped and healed.

It is by taking back of the voice of authority through events such as the Garma Festival[8] and education programmes such as the one suggested by the Yolngu that we are seeing some semblance of balance being restored. That recognition has also been given to Yolngu land management laws that are now being taken seriously in the north. The need to understand the Land better means that Indigenous knowledge is also being validated. But this should not create a situation in which the other validates the Law; rather, there should be a mutual respect for each other's knowledge to fulfil obligations to the Land.

This notion of the individual's voice of authority is not unheard of in other traditions. Taiaiki Alfred (1995) also offers another concept aligned to that of the Yolngu: the basic treaties of the Rohonshonni condolences ritual encompass much of the wisdom of the Senior Law Men. In this case, it relates to the role of the individual and voicing his authority through the decision to either participate or not in the governance of a traditional clan. As Alfred explains (1995: 5): '[I]t is the role of the leader to persuade individuals to pool their self-power in the interest of the collective good.' I would further point out that leadership is now ordained by non-Indigenous 'financing' sources. This was a complaint made earlier by Trudgen (2000) in relation to the dependency model, which eventually makes the 'warriors lay down and die', rather than stand up proudly in the knowledge that their ancestry is exalted for its worthwhile contribution. Leadership, as Alfred complains, is made up of *compradors* – or, as Murphy (2000: 56) argues, those who have the 'currency' to maintain power in the dominant culture. Therefore, when Alfred (1995: 5) says self-determination truly starts with the 'self with its inherent freedoms, powers and responsibilities based on a cohesive spiritual universe and traditional culture', it becomes obvious that SLM Marika has been shaped into the same patterns.

And so ends the reader's journey into the camps of the Senior Law Men and the jurisprudence that is revealed through a jurisprudential reading of the media they wished to use to tell us of their Law and also the world of the scribes who, through dialogic encounters with these Senior Law Men, attempted to educate their own cultures.

PART THREE
Travelling the Land

The Story Camps

I now want to take the reader to the story camps. These are the camps in which I will help the reader come to understand the *talngai-gawarima* jurisprudence as it pertains to modernity. The stories in the camps are women's stories and perhaps it is no accident that the scribes of the Senior Law Men were predominantly women. And it is women's understanding of the world that informs this book, as the author is a woman. However, before we enter the camps, I feel I should contextualize why I chose the stories of *Plains of Promise, Thunderheart* and *Whale Rider*: the choice stems from travelling in and engaging with the lands in which the stories are situated. I will now give an account of those journeys to contextualize the stories before moving into the camps themselves.

CHAPTER 6

The journeys: From camps of old men to camps of young women

Journey into the Dust

This journey continues on from the first camp and contextualizes the reason for the choice of the novel *Plains of Promise*. As I stated in my first camp, I began my journey of law by participating in the burying of the dead, the burying of ancestors whose remains in some cases dated back 1200 years. The burying of ancestors is 'sorry business', but it is also a time of growth and increased understanding of why these people lived and how my life has in some part been dependent on their deeds, as well as how my knowledge has come through the mitochondria of the continuous matrilineal line since invasion. It is this genetic material that has allowed me to understand my Law, even though the invasionary practices then and since have tried to wipe out that memory and disallow its validity through such common law constructs as native title – a legal construct created by people who lack the legal qualifications of a Senior Law Person, let alone the in-depth understanding of the Indigenous jurisprudence. As these fake authorities sit in judgement of matters about which they have no experience other than as observers, one wonders why Aboriginal people bother with such legal operettas. While this is simply my opinion, it is also one of the sources that tries to deny me the right to know my own Law – a Law that, I believe, is far more valid in its power to validate how I should live in the continent of Australia.

Having said that, I was still able to learn the following, written 20 years ago in a conference paper presented in the United States, which took me on the journey described in the next camp:

> A human being is a vehicle for the telling of a story. However, the story cannot be told without the land if the audience is to have complete comprehension. To talk of the great emu and the eggs it lays means nothing unless you can see the piece of topography that depicts this event, a group of copper green boulders.
>
> (Morris 1991)

I should qualify this by saying that one still does not have complete comprehension, but rather a *more* comprehensive understanding, if one views the land.

It was with this understanding that I entered the plains of the far north-west of Queensland, a state that extends into the northern interior. These great plains bring down sudden floods of torrential rain that rapidly fill the dry, parched plains of Central Australia. It is a strange land in that, if you do not have the educated eyes of an Aborigine, all you see are continuous, monotonous replications of scrub and wide-open horizons empty of cloud and mountain. But if you do have the eyes of an Aborigine, each bush holds the potential for an encounter with the surreal – as, indeed, the surreal is evident in encounters with the locals.

This is a land that seems devoid of humans, then, from behind some scrub, a bushman appears – or, more appropriately, one comes across a mob of people travelling along their Dreaming Track. That mob is not naked and woolly haired, but rather dressed (often) like Westerners and their associated family. They are a friendly lot, ready to know what you are doing burning up the bitumen in an attempt to get to the next appointment and seeming ridiculous in a pursuit of which these people are the antithesis. I also learnt on these journeys not to look too closely at such apparitions, otherwise you might find them too close for comfort at your next destination. It is not that I am giving them some semi-magical trait; it is just the way things happen. It what I call the 'Big Ears' phenomenon – Land has a way of nosing into your business. It listens and enters your head and soon you are encountering your curious thoughts played out in reality in the next town.

One soon becomes mindful of one's thoughts, words and actions in such places, as there is an energy moving around that embodies the trickster. At the time of my ventures, I was not aware of contemporary Native American literature such as Thomas King's (1994) *Grassy Green Running*

River, which narrates a story of Native American academics caught up in a world of interfering Creator Beings trying to do their best but accompanied by coyotes that just can't seem to get it right. This story provided many laughs as it brought back memories of my own adventures in 'Big Ears' country as an academic carrying out research into Indigenous media and breaches of intellectual property law. To my amazement, it was the Aborigines more than the whites who were doing the breaching – but while they were fewer in number, the whites benefited far more financially than the Aborigines did.

What this journey brought into strong relief was that the issue of intellectual property needed more discourse on law and the repercussions resulting from a breach of law, rather than a concentration on the ways in which the common law could accommodate Aboriginal rights – a goal that, I believe, is still under review.

But let us return to this journey into the plains – of the promise of return to Land – which is the premise of the book *Plains of Promise*. It was this journey and many encounters, both real and surreal, that brought a greater understanding. As I travelled this land, I witnessed the signs of the great Dreaming Track of the Two Dog Dreaming, which crosses over that land on its way to the east from the west – or was it from the south going north? It does not really matter, as this was not my story; rather, the point was that I knew I was crossing over the track. This crossing over is an acknowledgement that a great highway of Dreaming Law stories still exists, even if it is not laid down in bitumen. I do not know the full story – rather, I gained a sense of assurance that the Law is still there, that the crisscrossing of Australia with Law is still embedded into the Land and that the actualization of that law comes about by stepping on those tracks, as will be revealed in the story of *Plains of Promise*.

Journey with Hinsha Waste Agli Win

She just seemed to turn up one day at my university. Her appearance was said to be due to a conference, but I was soon to learn that her appearance was a beckoning by her Country to travel and learn how it is for those who live on the back of the Turtle. It was as if Turtle Island (known in the West as the United States) had come out to meet me. The venture into the cosmology of Turtle Island was at the behest of one of the most eminent Lakota scholar-activists, Professor Beatrice Medicine, an anthropologist who wrote extensively on the problems being an anthropologist entailed, but at the same time advocated the need for a voice of authority about her own people, especially as an American Indian woman. As an insider, she was much more attuned to cultural nuances and, more importantly, to the significance of the sacred. Her Lakota name was Hinsha Waste Agli Win, which means 'Returns Victorious with a Red Horse Woman' – a powerful name for a woman who carried out one of the most significant roles an Indian woman can attain in her lifetime, that of the 'Sacred Pipe Carrier' of the Sundance. In that arduous role, the chosen woman must dance non-stop for over 48 hours. This feat of endurance filtered into her later work, especially her tireless movement up and down Indian lands, educating young Indians about the importance of the Native American epistemology. As a descendant of the Deloria dynasty, she was following in the tradition of a famous Lakota family, whose members made an indelible impact on the representation of the Native American image in politics, academia, media and art.

My journey with Hinsha Waste Agli Win was, then, an authoritative one, one that not only informed me intellectually but also afforded a shift into another parallel legal universe. This journey into another cosmological account of the American South-West began in New Mexico at the Pueblos. This is a most appropriate entry point, as the Pueblo people have main-tained the oldest continuous Indian culture and legal system in the Americas (Waters and Fredericks 1977: ix). The landscape, like most of that in the South-West, is full of mystery and marvel. The open roads, the high mountains and the 'grande' rivers of the Colorado and Rio Grande are sights to behold. There is no doubt that you have left behind a world regulated by a human-made law and entered a parallel universe in which the great rivers and mountains order and inform behaviour and in which mere mortals scurry across the land like ants, busying themselves as though unaware of a larger and more advanced world. In this case, however, the larger and more advanced world is not inhabited by techno-logically obsessed humans, but rather by great stony beings who control the past, present and future through their stoic endurance. In partnership with these great mesas and bluffs are the elemental beings that storm across the landscape as wind, fire or snow, either blessing the Pueblo crops with their presence or making their absence felt through prolonged drought.

This isolation from humankind's 'dominion' over the earth is reinforced in the sobering images of humanity's 'nothingness' when gazing at the Anasazi cliff dwellings in escarpments of three rocky mesas rising abruptly out of the desert plain.[1] The enormous rocky mesas appear to put the man-made buildings into proportion in terms of their impact. Hence humankind's creative abilities are revealed as minuscule in proportion to such great stoic rock beings, which came long before humans and which will live long after humans have polluted or blasted themselves out of existence.

As we passed from the ruins into the present-day Pueblos, the continuity was evident. Permission was required to enter any one of the 19 'continuous' cultural islands, on the proviso that no images were to be taken with camera equipment or even a pen for drawing. This was my first 'experience' of intellectual property rights in action and it was the late 1980s – well before the fight had begun internationally for Indigenous intellectual property rights. Furthermore, this was my first encounter with a community that basically knew how to say 'no', a people who honoured their tradition of 'secrecy' surrounding their ancient knowledge. They were a people who seemed to be able to assert that 'our images are not for sale'.

Later in my career, I went on to write about and specialize in the area of intellectual property in the hope that an Australian Aboriginal community would also assert its right to say 'no'. Unfortunately, this still has not happened – but perhaps the Pueblo ability to resist was born out of longer experience of the exploitation of their images, such as the famous photographic collection of Curtis (1907–30)[2] or, in even more contemporary times, Hollywood. Furthermore, this is enhanced by the strong culture of secrecy, which is instilled in their children from birth. But, more importantly, this ban on intrusive technology – especially during ceremony – appeared to maintain the 'sacrality of place' that I could feel during the viewing of ceremonies such as the Reindeer Dance in San Domingo. To view a ceremony from ancient times without the flashing of bulbs allows participation in something holy, something old yet fresh, meaning a freshness from the past untainted by today's profanity of performances and its necessary lighting, sound, spectacular costumes and hyped talents. Hence the viewer of the Pueblo public section of their ceremonial dances is drawn into the cosmology of animals, large turquoise stones, harvests, songs and drums. It is a numinous world of the 'other', where the familiar is put aside and the experience of another cosmology is able to seep into your very soul; a world in which the particular, the crafted, the small, the organic and the beat of the drum are revered; a cosmology that requires the planting of corn and other crops. They are agriculturalists in a harsh land; this harshness, however, is not meant to drive them away but rather to make them as stoic as the mountains and rocks. Through continuous ceremonies, this inter-generational relationship with the Land ensures they remember how dependent they are on that relationship. The Law of Relationship is enacted daily. This constant renewing of their relationship with the Land – the mountains, rivers and particularly the annual rains – ensures they have strong values which are not easily substituted by another law just because they engage with that other law.

This is a world that stands, and is able to sustain itself, in total contradiction to its immediate neighbour, the pretentious 'art precinct' of Santa Fe or – even more 'off planet' – the technological 'sci-fi' iconic town of Los Alamos[3] and its infamous Los Alamos Laboratories. What could be more jarringly juxtaposed than those three worlds? Yet the Pueblo people are able to maintain their individual cosmology in light of these colonial giants of technology and exploitative consumerism. This exposure to such juxtaposed worlds 'welded' into my mind that an ancient culture can sustain itself if it will draw a line under what it will allow to be exploited. For example, a 'memorandum of understanding' (MOU) has been drawn up with three Pueblo communities and the Los Alamos Laboratories, as both wished to maintain their mutual understanding of the need for secrecy.[4] These MOUs are significant in their tentative recognition and respect that different cosmologies can coexist – one steeped in ancient tradition, the other 'hell bent' on exploiting the future. In the context of this book, the ancient can coexist with modernity if a pattern of commonality can be recognized – that is, a Law of Relationship can be found. In the case of the Pueblo and the Los Alamos Laboratories, that relationship is centred on the need for secrecy – secrecy in relation to ritual knowledge for the former and military secrets for the latter.

This ability for two parties to engage in a relationship that values and exploits each other's cosmology and values is demonstrated in the connection that exists between the Pueblo and the Santa Fe art world. The rich tourist trade of Santa Fe, and New Mexico in general, relies on the 'ancientness' of the Pueblo to draw people to the state. Therefore, the relationship is built on a respect for continuity: for the state, the exploitation of the image of the Pueblo; and for the Pueblo, the 'extra' income to support their subsistence lifestyle and to provide their young with an education about the wider world and its exploitive advantages.

After meeting many of the different Pueblo peoples, we moved on to the 'Indian trail', which led us into the cosmology of the Plains Indians and their tumultuous past in the 1800s. Driving through the expansive and silent lands of Colorado and Wyoming, and over into the Dakotas, I knew I was entering a cosmology exploited by Hollywood – a cosmology that Hinsha Waste Agli Win would slowly but surely wash away with her stories and historical remembrances. First, however, I will comment on the cosmology, beyond which I would argue many members of the general public have not yet moved.

The site of great buttes was enough to tell me I was moving into a cosmology full of the values and morality based on television greats such as *Gunsmoke, Wagon Train, Bonanza* and *Rawhide*.[5] I found myself half-expecting to see an Indian standing on top of some far off butte, holding a rifle and ready to shoot at our 'Volvo wagon train'. This is an image of Indian country that has subliminally been etched into our minds as a place full of brave cowboys and hostile Indians, a cosmology devoid of Indian women other than straggly squaws, their heroism and endurance eternally silenced. It is a cosmology that was retold by Hinsha Waste Agli Win, who showed me the images of Indian women in the mountain ranges – accounts of women such as White Buffalo Calf Woman, who rode into battle to save her brother by reaching down and swinging him up on to the horse. It was a history one could not doubt on meeting someone like Hinsha Waste Agli Win and experiencing her seeming boundless energy, which could only come out of a genealogy of strong and powerful women. It is also a cosmology in which the icon of a White Buffalo Calf Woman could signify nothing less than a buffalo's strength and endurance. These are powerful symbols, the authoritative voice of which resounds just as loudly, if not more, as that found in any written text.

With the guidance of the Lakota Senior Women, this cosmology of the Wild, Wild West was slowly reshaped into one that brought into prominence the great Creator Beings of the expansive countryside leading to the sacred Black Hills and Badlands of South Dakota, and the homeland of Hinsha Waste Agli Win at Standing Rock Reservation. This is the resting place of Sitting Bull – his remains were not returned until the year in which I was born, 1953 – more than half a century after his assignation in 1890. This journey to her homelands at Standing Rock Reservation brought stories of the heartache of Wounded Knee and the many other battles in which the descendants of the US Calvary still gloat at the eradication of 'hostiles'.

Now these great histories – until this point only known to me through the Hollywood narrative – were now being retold to me by the descendants of those warriors. I would assert that it is important for Indigenous people to be aware of the pervasive influence on the general populus that these old images of Indians still have to this very day when they think of a 'native' people – especially if the people become articulate and challenge the system. In Australia, the image is one of the docile native; however, if the native becomes public, or 'restless', then the savage is brought back into full view, just as any disturbance in Africa immediately brings up images of Shaka and the Zulu.[6]

We then travelled up into the most significant sacred site for Plains Indians: *Sapa Papa*, the Black Hills. We had a short stay at the home of

Art Amoittee, one of the foremost Lakota artists and an advocate of the importance of the Sundance.[7] The unusual land formations are said to be arranged in the shape of a heart and when the people did the four-day ceremony that travelled around the mountain, it was said to be done in the shape of a buffalo, as if continually rewriting this symbol into the text of the Land. Art reminded us of the wholesale slaughter of millions of buffalo – a shameful historical metaphor for the barbarianism of the westward shift into Indian land. The fact that this barbaric behaviour could rise to the level of leaving rotting carcasses all over the plains never ceases to amaze me, neither does the fact that disease did not break out and wipe out the whole population.

The journey through these major sites, the stopping and visiting with the people and the Land, shaped my cosmological understanding of the Native American, a cosmology that will be explored in the Camp from Turtle Island when we undertake a jurisprudential reading of *Thunderheart*. Our journey ended in Saskatchewan, which is, in fact, an extension of Plains Indian country. There we met students and staff of the Saskatchewan Indian Federated College,[8] where some of the best collections of works on Plains Indians can be sourced.

This entry into this cosmology therefore reshaped my understanding of the Plains Indian from a macho cult of the warrior and the great battles of Little Big Horn, Red River and Warbonnet Creek to that of White Buffalo Calf Woman and the annual renewal of the Sundance, the gathering of the pow-wows to demonstrate the pride of Plains Indian identity. It is a demonstration of pride that has spread to other Indian groups as far away as the Mikmaq of Nova Scotia, Canada. The annual pow-wows now provide opportunities for the Indians of North America to display their pride in their culture.

This reshaping of the cosmology was reinforced when I returned a year later and travelled to the Grand Canyon and into the Apache lands of Arizona. The viewing of the Grand Canyon is an unforgettable experience in that the human self loses any sense of significance in the presence of such a powerful landscape. This power of never ending endurance and the unbelievable craftsmanship of the original Creator Beings of that area give credence to a logic that perceives humans as being patterned into such grandeur – which is nothing less than straight-out commonsense.

This is a land in which the likes of Geronimo and his men and women battled with the cavalry for as long as possible before being brought in through the help of another Apache. The story is only just beginning to be told, although it still downplays the role of the 'Native bringing in the Native' with the American in tow. More importantly, it is a story of treaties – broken treaties. Instead, an American settler cosmology devoid of the broken treaties – *terra nullised*[9] out of history through the vilification of the Indian – still shows the astute student of history that at one point the Americans honoured their law and signed treaties with people they recognized as owners of land. This is a recognition that Indians and Americans alike are now trying to get their governments to honour and their historians to remember.

And so my journeys through the American South-West and up into the Great Plains brought me into the ancient cosmology of Turtle Island. This is a cosmology in which the Indians have their classical thoughts and narratives of the history of Turtle Island and its people, a cosmology in which many different Creator Beings and cosmologies make up this vast land. But these cosmologies link up in their laws of relationship to Land and the future. The following chapters will reference these journeys and the narratives from those whom I have met on these journeys, especially the guiding force of Hinsha Waste Agli Win, who now influences both me and her own people from beyond the grave.

The Māori Cosmology

I now turn to the Māori world and its cosmology. My first encounter with the Māori cosmology occurred not long after my return from Turtle Island. The issue of intellectual property protection had become a serious undertaking in law and the Māori were determined to get Indigenous rights on to the United Nations 'radar'. I had just finished a book on the subject of Aboriginal traditional stories and was therefore in a good position to argue for the inclusion of the protection of traditional stories. The First International Conference on the Cultural and Intellectual Property of Indigenous Peoples was held in Whakatane in 1993. The historical outcome of this conference was the drafting of the Mataatau Declaration,[10] which was then lodged with the United Nations. This *hui* (meeting/conference), however, was also my introduction into the cosmology of the Māori – an introduction to what I might call the *protocols of existence*. The *hui* was held on a series of *marae*, or meeting places, belonging to the host tribes of the conference. These *marae* are places of formality and protocol, each containing its own distinct character. The *marae* is made up of a sacred courtyard and a collection of buildings, including a meeting house. Each area has its own protocol. The courtyard is perhaps the most dramatic, as this is the point of entry into this symbolic representation of the founding ancestor. A ritual is carried out as the visitors are welcomed but also challenged to state their business. There is much singing, oratory and drama played out in this open theatre – an essential theatre, as it is within this drama and song that one is transported from the mundane of the outside world and Pakeha-imported law to the world of Māori law; law stemming from ancient Aotearoa. This ancient law has never left or been subsumed by modernity, for it is the very shape of the meeting house, which is built in a representative manner to reflect the protective nature of the founding ancestor[11] – an ancestor who travelled from the mystical Hawaiki, a sacred place to which Māori return after death.

Therefore, entry into the *marae* is an entry into another cosmology, another dimension of law. Carved walls and woven flax inlays surround the interior of the meeting house, a space empty of furniture and footwear, a place where the spoken word holds power and pledges become law. This is a law that is not enforced, but rather reinforced through song, oratory and ritual into the very character of each participant; it is a law that calls each individual to be a voice of authority on that in which they have participated and to which they have agreed. The *marae* is a place where the Māori individual is patterned into a cosmology and *whakapapa* (genealogy).

Perhaps the grandest *marae* is that of the Māori Queen, Te Arikinui Dame Te Atairangikaahu, at Ngaruawahia, Hamilton on the great Waikato River, banked by lush undergrowth and towering trees. It is a place reminiscent of the great river of Aunduin in *Lord of the Rings* (Tolkein 1954) This magical river runs past what is perhaps the largest and most ornate of *marae*; more importantly, it is the *marae* that is most steeped in history. This large complex hugging the banks of the Waikato River gives a sense of being in the presence of the *tikanga*[12] of the Māori, a place holding powerful *mana* (authority), its sprawling grandeur reminiscent of its past and present challenge to Pakeha legal authority.

My encounter with this *marae* was at the starting point of all great adventures into other cosmologies: the dead. I was visiting the Waikato University in Hamilton at the time of the passing of the Queen's brother, Sir Robert Matuta.[13] This was a moving and surprisingly uplifting experience, even though the protocol and ritual related to the passing of the body (on bended knee) and paying of respects to the females of the community. The whole process of entry, participation, partaking of a meal and final departure took nine hours. The calmness and sombre mood, set in the tranquillity of grounds dotted with weeping willows and women dressed in black, brought back memories of the royal grounds of Kyoto, the ancient capital of Japan. A sense of zen suffused the proceedings and brought forth many orators and mourners from all over Aotearoa. A ritual law was present as a guardian, guiding one's every movement in these holy grounds.

The Māori Queen and her role raise unique questions of law, especially in relation to the invaders and their right to declare their Queen's sovereignty over Māori lands. These questions of law are raised by Dorsett and McVeigh (2002) in terms of the justification of settlement, to say nothing of the breach of the invader's own legal system.

What, therefore, was the meaning of producing a replication of the British monarchy? Why had this institution lasted so long in such a hostile legal environment? The answer lay in one particular historical figure's attempt to make the *tikanga* visible to the invader. Through the establishment of the King Movement – *Kingitanga* – the Māori took the invisible and refashioned it into a visible form: they reflected back their system of governance to the invaders and their sovereign. More importantly, with the arrival of Wiremu Tamihana Tarapipip Te Waharoa, the *rangatira* of the Ngati Huau of the Waikato district, they imposed on it their sovereign's moral foundation (Stokes 2002: 185). For it was Tamihana's entry into the *Kingitanga* Movement that caused it to take on a shape that not only reflected back to the invader their act of sovereign imperialism – by declaring that they had a king and therefore the right to invade – but, more importantly, their moral authority. The ordination of the Māori king was by laying a Bible on his head: what more could the invader require? Tamihana's own historical roots, when given an Indigenous reading, came out of nothing more than feudal warlords bent on assuming overarching power and the use of the Bible as an indication of divine authority.

Wiremu Tamihana Tarapipip Te Waharoa was of particular interest because he addressed the question of how two legal systems could work in tandem: 'A Māori society in control of its own destiny, under a system of Māori law, working in partnership with Pakeha law, and participating in the benefits of Pakeha settlement' (Stokes 2002: 186). As a true *rangatira* and scholar, he was the first to turn to the Pakeha's moral authority, which at that time was to be found in the Bible. The Pakeha with whom Tamihana was in daily conflict were predominantly Christian and supported by missionaries. So Tamihana was examining not only the law, but the moral grounding that validated these acts of invasion and blatant theft. In other words, he studied the Bible to ascertain the principles and values by which these Christian people justified their right to steal. The Old Testament espouses the 'promised land' doctrine, which justifies invasion. However, Tamihana noted that the New Testament also called for brotherly love along with other moral concepts also found in the Māori *tikanga*. As is my intention regarding the outcome of this book, Tamihana sought a common ground when it came to the *tikanga* of both laws, so that a process of mutual respect and communication could begin.

The establishment of the *Kingitanga* occurred at a *hui* at Ngaruawahia on 2 May 1859, at which *Potatua* was installed as King (Stokes 2002: 185). The design was not that of chieftains ceding their authority to an overall sovereign, but rather the formation of a confederacy with a benevolent ruler whose role was symbolic, on the one hand, but representative of the *tikanga* legal system that had governed the Māori for millennia, on the other. The strength of the *Kingitanga* Movement was in 'foreign policy': the king was the figurehead, leader of a confederation of resistance. He was visited by, and sent deputations to, tribes all over the North Island (Stokes 2002: 186). Gorst points out that Tamihana saw 'the purpose of this ambassador of the people as to create a paternal sovereign to execute just laws to which all should yield obedience; and to oppose the progress of the Pakeha by passive and peaceful resistance, giving no pretext for war' (Stokes 2002: 187). In other words, he desired to establish a system of law to prevent warfare and to preserve the land in Māori ownership.

This ambassadorial role required him to travel around and confer with the King's Council, which was held in high regard:

> In all questions which I have heard discussed in the council, they have argued with calmness and good temper, keeping steadily to the point at issue, and facing all the difficulties. Calm in discussion, the strongest opposition never provoked person rudeness. It would have been impossible to gather a body of Māoris with whom the Government could have more advantageously consulted upon the management of the native race. The Runanga Ngaruawahai often acted as a judicial body: it appeared to be the last resort in cases which no one else could settle. Tamihana had hoped to set up a judicial system based on the King's Runanga which would overcome these conflicts with the local *runanga*.
>
> (Stokes 2002: 18)

In other words, Tamihana saw the value of the system of his own law and also saw how it could work in tandem with another law, which should not have found this court system so foreign.

However, it is in the nature of invaders that they wish only to impose their understanding and symbols of law and so the Treaty of Waitangi was established and signed. The signing of the Treaty of Waitangi was by only a few in the Waikato River[14] area and this was only because they feared they would become slaves of the British, 'but very few natives, they said, in this district had signed the treaty, and these few only on the good faith of the missionaries, the reason was, they were not, nor would they be slaves'

(Stokes 2002: 18). The Treaty of Waitangi was therefore in opposition to the *Kingitanga* Movement, which it remain to this day. The former represents an assimilation into a dominant legal system and suffers the fate seemingly preordained for such documents – lost to both the bowels of the archives and the cockroaches until the hostiles demanded its resurrection . . . that is, if anyone could find it![15] The sad state of repair of the Treaty today is testimony to my description. The Pakeha did not appear to be in the least ashamed of, or shamed by, the sight of a piece of tattered paper hanging in their national museum as a proud testament to their legal process and right to rule. Neither do they take responsibility for the continued antagonism of the Māori Land Courts based on the rights set down in the Treaty. Both sides still contest its meaning and intent.

Meanwhile, the other institution – that of equal legal rule – has persisted quietly but firmly; just like the Land itself, the intention is to endure rather than to win.

The Queen has since died and her son has become the new king. He, like *Potatua*, must consult a council – a council that is said to be reasserting the ideals of Tamihana and so calling for the disavowing of the Treaty of Waitangi. However, the *Kingitanga* Movement has no more legitimacy than the Treaty, for it also was made up of only the northern tribes that wished to be involved. More importantly, the movement is not really a matter of law – for the *Kingitanga* is the representation of Māori *tikanga* and the way that representation works in tandem with the Pakeha law.

The late Queen Te Aroha resurrected the original sentiments of the role of the ruler. She, more than any before her, had brought the role to one of international recognition through her regal ways and keen sense of diplomacy. It was said that then New Zealand Prime Minister, Helen Clark, wept openly at her funeral and stayed the full four days. This sign of deep respect also signifies to the Māori that it is through their conduct and essences of *mana* that achievements and true recognition come – not by Western legal systems 'begrudgingly' giving over to Māori demands, but through the personal conduct of what it means to be Māori. The Queen and her *marae* are symbolic of Māoridom; therefore, the voice of authority does not come from a Western legal right but from the exemplar of a Senior Māori woman and her display of *mana*. And so my learning in the land of the Waikato River came from answering questions of law. What are the ways in which the Māori have adapted to the invaders clothed as settlers? How have they tried to educate or reflect back to the Pakeha their morally bankrupt behaviour?

But the river had more to teach me and, as the great Waikato River brings forth the *mana* of the *Kingitanga*, it also brought forth another person who lives on the river. Tainui Stephens is a film director who has produced defining productions such as *New Zealand Wars* (1998). Stephens has become an expert in the use of film technology – just like the Lakota – and has refashioned the representation of history through Māori and Pakeha historical accounts of the New Zealand warring period of the 1800s.[16] What Stephens produced was a 'Māori' *Lord of the Rings*, but, in this realm, the worlds are those of the Pakeha and Māori. Stephens filmed authoritative Māori historians giving oratories of their *iwi's*[17] accounts of the great wars. To his credit, and that of the Pakeha historian James Belich (1988), they did not try to paint a 'politically correct' image of the Māori as peaceful Hobbits invaded by the Saruman and his Orcs, but rather a people already skilled in warfare and ready to take on the invader. It is through this documentary that we learn that the Māori were the originators of 'trench warfare', a model used to advantage in the European wars in which the Māori bravely participated. In this documentary, however, the skill of the Māori military man is brought to the fore, as is the revelation that it was only through 'pure numbers' that the Māori were defeated. Also, *New Zealand Wars* is one of the rare sources that reveal how efficient the Māori were as shipping agents, transporting fresh vegetables to the booming goldfields in Australia and California. These kinds of technological skill are played down for some reason, even in Māori accounts of themselves. The Queen's captain of her *waka taua*[18] has recently taken the arduous journey from New Zealand to *Hawaii* in a *waka taua* to demonstrate the navigation skills of the Māori and perhaps put to rest the idea of Thor Heyerdahl's 1947 *Kontiki* expedition raft, as though ancient people could only technologically design rafts rather than the great seafaring outriggers described in Cook's diaries as being much larger than the *Discovery* or as found in Aboriginal narratives from South Australia by David Unaipon (2001: 192) with their mentions of seafaring canoes.

There are many great stories in Aotearoa and my patronage into that world by Moana Jackson ensured I also saw the trials and dramas of the Māori's wrestling with the Pakeha to honour the Treaty of Waitangi. This endless struggle is played out through continuous battles, the latest being the 'foreshore'. One wonders whether the New Zealand Wars have ever ended or instead have simply taken on new shapes and patterns. They are still the same old stories and therefore give legitimacy to the need to read them for their jurisprudential teachings.

This journey into the Māori cosmologies of Aotearoa introduced me to the classic historical accounts of the beginning of the many and varied Māori peoples. By entering the body of the various *iwi marae*, I was able to be taught the creation account of the arrival of the Māori in Aotearoa; that arrival includes those who came from other islands, while others appeared from different dimensions – most significantly *Hawikii* (Tuaiwa Hautai Kereopa whanau 1998). My major empirical encounter with the great Waikato River allows me to give an oral account of the empirical knowledge I gained of the Land and its narrative of the Law of Relationship between the two laws of Aotearoa – laws that attempt in various ways to communicate the establishment *Kingatinga* Movement being the Māori response, while the Treaty of Waitangi was the Pakeha response. The former was steeped in tradition and protocol and stoic persistence of the Māori right to home rule, while the latter was the never ending duel between opposing 'readings' of the meaning of the Treaty.

The classic history in which these legal responses are situated, however, could not truly have been understood had I not watched *New Zealand Wars* and interviewed the film's director. It is the role of these modern-day bards to help people remember so that their historical accounts of oral history can be spoken by voices of authority.

My final journey to Aotearoa was to visit the land and sea that spawned the cosmology of the tale of the Whale Rider, originally related by the storyteller Witi Ihimaera (1987) in her book *Whale Rider*. After I had watched the film and begun to enter the story, I realized I needed to visit the land and sea of this story and thank it for its generous telling. And so I ventured on a holiday to Aotearoa, the first holiday I had allowed myself in decades. It actually seemed decadent being a mere tourist. It was hard to be in someone's country without spending time with the locals; however, this trip was a journey of gratitude and so off I went.

To travel to this isolated place – Whangara, north of Gisborne on the east coast of New Zealand's North Island – is a *Lord of the Rings* episode in itself. The locals appear to zoom around Mount Doom as though these death-defying narrow roads that slither up the side of sharp mountains and down into craggy gullies are the norm. There are no straight roads, which was hard on this 'land laid flat traveller' who was used to hundreds of miles of bitumen Dreaming Tracks. Instead, this land was a never ending curve of hilly sheep farms and waterways. At each curve lived a *tene phana*, the keeper of the waterway, which the road crossed ready to take your life if you did not pay your respects. As if that was not bad enough, there was the fear of the mountain goats known to roam out on to the road at their pleasure – and then there was the fog, that creature of mist that descended at a moment's notice. Once again, as a Pacific Ocean hugger, I thought driving through fog on roads that appeared ridiculously narrow when mainly inhabited by iron monsters – those long and smelly cattle trucks and logging trucks – was beyond the pale.

To make things worse, everything was so green! I was used to the red sand of the desert or the white sand of the ocean shore, contrasting against a sparkling sky of delightful brilliance. But here was that Middle Earth of the *Lord of the Rings*, deep green and dark with fog. I eventually made it to the coast and wondered how I would ever return to that mountain range.

The coast was a welcome sight, if not odd in that the hawks filled the skies – well, I was in Hawks Bay, obviously! I then travelled up to Gisborne and on to the beach of *Whale Rider*. The beach was covered in pebbles and black sand, again an affront to my sensibilities of what a beach should be: shells and silky soft sand. I suddenly realized there must be whole culture of how one enjoys a day out on the pebbles. Does one take a towel and an umbrella or a sturdy chair and wear rubber thongs (or flip-flops in New Zealand parlance) on one's feet? What stories must come from such sites, how different they must be to our own, for the land is engaged in such a different manner. But then this was whale country – there were no kangaroos here, only the possum, invading from Australia. The possum totem is honoured in our country; here the possum is a pest and its fur is used to sell back the pest to Australian tourists – most appropriate payback, I thought!

Tucked away from the keen eye of the tourist was the little village featured in *Whale Rider*. I saw it from a distance, for I was not there to say 'hi' to the locals. I was there to visit the cosmological space of the great Paikea – and, indeed, that very day a pod of whales was making its way down the coast.[19] This was whale country and a pebbled beach suddenly made sense, for the beaching of whales and the offering up of their bodies for the nourishment of the locals of ancient times would have needed a firm base. I paid my respects and returned to the trail of terror, facing the monsters of trucking industries and asking the benevolence of the *tene phana* to keep the goats in the hills. I returned safely and felt the journey had changed me for I now knew for certain that the country was in safe hands: the *tene phana* ruled the rivers and the whales patrolled the shores; pity the human who thought otherwise.

And so I end this tale of my journeys and now take the reader to the camps in which I intellectually actualize the knowledge I have gained from walking the land in which the following narratives are set.

Women's Business Caught Up in Men's Business

I will now take the reader in a new direction, having experienced the camps of the stories of theory, and draw the reader into the world of the late twentieth century, moving in preparation for a new millennium. For the stories from the next three camps are stories that overlap from one century to another. They are stories meant to prepare young women and men for a world in which women are no longer downtrodden by the religious history of the First World countries, but rather return to the rightful place of women of traditional societies and the equal placing with men as voices of authority and Law. As Hannah Bell (1998) asserts, she had to come to terms as a feminist in an Aboriginal society with the fact that there was a deficiency in her treaties when it came to the role of women. In the main, modern feminism still assumes the Western world has the upper hand on how to live on this planet:

> This unique window on the world opened my eyes to a concept of the feminine whose authority and nature is, I believe, integral to the health and well-being of all human societies. Through my friendship with Mowaljarlai I have come to understand the forgotten essence of being a woman in my own culture – which continues to extinguish, or render as invisible as the mother of my childhood, the Essential Feminine.
>
> (Bell 1998: 9)

This difference will be developed more fully in the following camps. These are stories in which women who initially appear to be tragic figures are re-read as protagonists with much to teach the young women and men of the twenty-first century. In other words, when the political 'ism' is taken out of feminism, then a remembrance of the song of the feminine can surface and a new jurisprudential reading can be revealed.

CHAPTER *7*

The camp of 'caring for country':
The world of *Plains of Promise*

Australia's Gulf country is dusty and dry, flooding with the same intensity as the sun sears the land. This seemingly harsh land, as poets like to refer to it, is, in my experience, one of the most surreal places to live in. It is a land in which a seaside breeze can bring messages from far away to the north to the flooded plains of the Gulf country. It is a place where mythological Beings still walk the land and leave their essence to assist the people – if they bother to spend the time to sit down country and take advantage of what the earth has to offer. It is country in which a Western education can do nothing more than make one ignorant of its power and Law. This is the setting for Alexis Wright's novel *Plains of Promise*.

Alexis Wright grew up far away from her home territory, but was drawn back to the land of her Ancestors through the stories of her grandmother. Just as her grandmother's narrative is about an inter-generational pull, so too is the reality of Australian Aboriginal women. More often than not, their story is one of return to country, of retrieving the stolen link to country that resonates deep in their genetic memory but struggles to emerge due to inadequate psychological skills to bring it forth. However, it eventually comes through, accompanied by a deep and powerful peace of mind. There is almost inevitably a deep anger as well, but once that has been explored there is a contentment in knowing you belong. For belonging is not about politics, passports or skin colour; it is about relatedness through a genetic memory of what it means to live lawfully in a landscape.

Entering the Australian Landscape

> Life was so different now that the white man had taken the lot. It was like a war, an undeclared *war*. A war with no name. And the Aboriginal man was put into . . . prison camps, like prisoners in the two world wars. But nobody called it a war: it was simply the situation, that's all.
>
> (Wright 1997: 74–75)

Alexis Wright's *Plains of Promise* (1997) is a highly potent tale of the Dreaming,[1] dramatic in its characterization of the Law of the Land and its people. It is a tale of creation immersed in the high drama of the hero's journey – a hero who actualizes the law through acts of lust, violence, love and never ending battles of shifting relationships. *Plains of Promise* leaves readers feeling they have witnessed the coming into being of something tumultuous, but conversely enduring – as enduring as the land itself, its law unchangeable. As Wright (1997: 1) writes: '[N]othing foreign could change the essence of the land. No white man had that power.'

Plains of Promise offers a template, or measure, for the actualizing of Indigenous Law in modern Australia. It is a narrative that reveals the 'bottom story', the story of the underbelly of the Law of the Land:

> In Yolngu (Aboriginal) society, as in all cultural groups, new knowledge is rejected out of hand if it is not built on existing, culturally accepted knowledge. Within their cultural knowledge base, Yolngu have a huge amount of knowledge about the world around them. For any subject Yolngu ask themselves, *Nha dhudi dhaw yuwalktaje* (What is the true, bottom or foundational story for this particular subject?) This 'bottom story' is the objective truth about a subject. Any new knowledge must not conflict with good solid evidence and culturally accepted truths.
>
> (Trudgen 2000: 207)

The 'bottom story' of *Plains of Promise* is an archetype that reveals an 'unacknowledged war' in the world it represents. This war has been conveniently reconfigured as 'a situation' by the invaders and so disallows any recognition of the need for 'rules of engagement' in conducting the war (Dorsett and McVeigh 2002).

Structure

This narrative is about the revelation of an enduring law and culture. Therefore, persistence and actualization of the law are its themes and it uses a triadic organizing device: the concentric circles (Cajete 1994) of cosmology; the Law of Relationship; and rights/responsibilities. Before entering this circle, however, I will sketch the plot of this inter-generational saga. I will then proceed to bring the reader into the world in which the Land is the Law – that is, the source of Law is the Land and it is the human engagement in actualizing the Law from the Land that brings about lawful behaviour. These concepts will become more evident through the jurisprudential reading of the cosmological story or Dreaming narrative of the waterbirds (Trudgen 2000: 303–4). This story has skilfully been woven into the narrative by Wright as a device to make sense of what appears – at least on a first reading – to be the senseless inter-generational trauma: that of the state of Queensland's stolen generation (HREOC 2005) 'under the Act'.[2] This will be complemented by the works of several Senior Law Men[3] of Aboriginal Australia. Second, I will turn to the Law of Relationship, contrasting *Plains of Promise* with the harmonizing of disparate opposites. For *Plains of Promise* represents a law that appears to divide and double-cross its Law Men, as personified in the challenges facing the character of Elliot – the young Law Man – who must bring about a rebalancing of the Law in the wake of the impediments imposed by the Old Law Council, made up of an unlikely group of inmates of the missionized concentration camp. Furthermore, his waterbird totemic twin, Ivy Koopundi, although portrayed as a dysfunctional victim of circumstances, is actually the source of the rebalance and both are descendants of Clever Men or Senior Law Men. It is through the high drama of the lives, loves and losses of these two people who share the same totem – the waterbird – that balance can be restored.

Third, and finally, I will explore, under the rubric of rights and responsibilities, the role of the individual as the gauge or barometer for the rebalancing of the law. This is a role seemingly forced on the individual: to answer the call of the powerful Land for the return of its own. But as a threshold issue, I will summarize the narrative of *Plains of Promise* before turning to my reading. The reason for this seemingly long summary is born out of what I call an Indigenous civility. That is, I actually believe readers must also engage in their own reading of the text, as well as can be offered under copyright constrictions.

The Story

In 1997, Australian Aboriginal writer Alexis Wright's novel *Plains of Promise* opened the Australian literary scene to a new dimension in Australian historical sagas.[4] This innovative novel was divided into four chapters. I will present a précis of each chapter, so offering the story as much as my critique.

The Time Keeper's Shadow

This inter-generational saga is set in a fictional northern Queensland mission named St Dominic's. It begins with the announcement of the death of a deranged woman from another 'country' (district). The dead woman's child, Ivy Koopundi Andrews, is the main protagonist. St Dominic's is a mission controlled by the missionary Errol Jipp and his distraught wife during the height of the era of the Protection Act in the 1950s. However, after the woman's death is declared a suicide, a spate of copycat suicides begins. All the victims torch themselves in the same way as did the distraught women. The child, Ivy, immediately comes under suspicion as the source of the evil events. The missionaries and Aboriginal Christians see her as the work of the devil. Unknown to the Christians, however, is the Council of Old Law People. They view Ivy's presence as a sign that a breach of traditional law has occurred and therefore must be investigated. In the meantime, the depraved Christian minister takes the vulnerable young girl and makes Ivy his sexual slave. This precedent allows the men in the community to abuse their power over the women. However, once the child is found to be pregnant with the minister's baby, she is condemned and her child is taken immediately to a southern state to be adopted out to hide the minister's criminal behaviour. Ivy is then forced into a disastrous marriage.

Her husband is Elliot, the young Law Man who is known as the Traveller. He is so named because he has been chosen by the Old Law people to travel hundreds of miles through outback Queensland and down to Lake Eyre along the Brolga Dreaming Track to find Ivy's kinsmen in the hope that they will take her back and so end the suicides. During his travels, however, Elliot meets the love of his life, Gloria, who is Ivy's cousin. Gloria also eventually ends up on the mission. As she is a beautiful woman, the depraved minister allots her to be the wife of his Aboriginal comprador, Delaney, who has to rape her to make her his wife. However, she still continues her affair with Elliot and bears him two children. In the mean time, Elliot has been forced to marry Ivy.

Elliot is resentful that he has had to marry Ivy and becomes violent. He is unaware that the Old Law Council had intended him to take care of Ivy until the arrival of Pilot Ah King, whom Elliot met on his trips south. The Old Law Council had decided that, as Pilot was a regular visitor to the mission, it would be easier for him to take Ivy back to her country without the minister noticing. Elliot is unaware of this arrangement and inadvertently kills Pilot during a dispute. Elliot then becomes more frustrated by his life and lack of acknowledgement for his brave deeds in relation to the Law. He takes this out on Ivy, who retaliates by burning down their house and stabbing Elliot – albeit not fatally. Both are flown out to hospital, but only Elliot returns.

Glimpse of Distant Hills

The next chapter moves 20 years ahead to Ivy's life in a mental health and research institute, Sycamore Heights. The story focuses on events leading to her release into the community. She finds a home with an unstable woman and, once again, inadvertently finds herself causing someone's death. This leads her to live a feral life. Eventually she is found by Elliot, who has settled down and become a community leader. Elliot returns with Ivy to the mission, which by now has become self-governing. He takes Ivy to an outstation outside the mission, where he cares for her and allows her to live a life undisturbed by people.

Victory Lane

The third part of the story deals with the political element of the novel. Time has moved on and Ivy's daughter, Mary, has become an educated woman who is not told she is Aboriginal until her adoptive parents die. She then embarks on a search for her roots through a political world. Like her mother, and through sheer coincidence, she ends up at St Dominic's mission as she is involved with a man from the mission. She also has a child and an unhappy ending.

Plains of Papery Grass

The last part deals with Mary's arrival at St Dominic's mission with her little girl, Jessie. In other words, she arrives just like her grandmother – Ivy's suicidal mother – with a child in tow. Elliot, recognizing Mary as Ivy's daughter, takes care of her, but does not reveal their relationship. No one reveals this, as they are ashamed of their past. Even Delaney, the minister's comprador and the husband of Elliot's lover, Gloria, has become an invalid and dies before he can tell Mary who she is. His sudden death is seen as untimely, as he tries to reveal the truth. It is then revealed that the Old Law Council was upset at the return of Ivy but capitulated; however, the arrival of her daughter and granddaughter is viewed as unacceptable. Elliot takes Mary to meet her mother, but does not reveal her identity. Mary only knows Ivy as some madwoman she meets in the bush one day with Elliot. As Mary and Jessie fly out of St Dominic's mission, the plane crosses Lake Eyre, which has now filled up with water after a 30-year drought (the time cycle of the novel). The mother and child both find themselves drawn to the sight and say they will visit next time. The story ends with Mary remembering the Dreaming story Elliot told them about the waterbird. He had assured Mary it was a true story and a real place in the Dreaming.

Creation Story

> If a beautiful bird was to miss the moment when the rest of its kind lifted from the Great Lake as the water was about to disappear, it would be lost. It may have been ready for days, even months, alongside the others. But when each day the birds lifted to the skies, perhaps the wind was not behind them so they landed on the water again, waiting for the next day and the day after that, and so on ... If a young bird was left behind it might have died. That is what happens when these kind of birds don't make the great flight. They die very quickly. But if it does not die, then this is what could have happened.
>
> (Wright 1997: 303–304)

The story goes on to tell us of the landing of the crows and their predatory behaviour towards the stranded waterbird. On realizing that the waterbird has a power to bring water to the lake, the crows fight over the bird. They eventually force the bird to travel with them and cause evil. The story tells us that 'the waterbird is able to send back the secret which makes the water return through unsuspecting carriers', but after generations of living with the crows, the waterbird's descendants go mad and so the lake dries up.

The Bottom Story

And so the 'bottom story' of *Plains of Promise* is the Dreaming story of the waterbirds. The waterbird in this Dreaming story is the human barometer of the law, embodied in the character of Ivy Koopundi. She is a barometer skilfully clothed in the dysfunctional outer image. The 'outsider' looking in sees nothing but despair at the plight of the 'poor dying natives', while the insider perceives 'a force of nature – a waterbird' finding her way home at the beckoning of the call of the 'Law of the Land'. Juxtaposed to this, like a double-helix relationship of similar dysfunctionality, is another waterbird – a male – personifying the image of the 'lawful' Aborigine, the young Law Man, Elliot the Traveller. Neither, seemingly, has rights or responsibilities. And both are apparently locked into the pattern of the law: the timeless *Wunggud* pattern of which Senior Law Man Mowaljarlai of the Ngarinyin says:

> The Ngarinyin worldview is based on the belief that the primary unit of life and existence is relationship. Mowaljarlai would say, 'There are always two.' Holding up the index fingers of his right

and left hands. He never held up two fingers from one hand. In describing relationship with two hands, he acknowledged that each participant or aspect of the relationship comes from a different side, has different functions and strengths, and responds to different brain or mind messages.

(Bell 1998: 21)

That pattern, as SLM Mowaljarlai asserts, is found across the whole continent of Australia in varying forms:

I want to show you something. I want to show you how all Aboriginal people in Australia are connected in the Wunnan system. The squares are the areas where the communities are represented, and their symbols and the languages of the different tribes in this country from long-long time ago. The lines are the way the history stories travelled along these trade routes. They are all interconnected. It's the pattern of the Sharing system.

(Mowaljarlai and Malnic 1993: 190)

It is a pattern that allows for movement across the great continent, as long as the Traveller stays within his or her designated pattern, itself given at birth. But, unfortunately, both human barometers – Ivy and Elliot – try to take what they want and then suffer the consequences. For both are pulled by the seemingly jealous land, determined to make them take up their responsibility to help rebalance the imbalance that has affected not only the present, but also the past and future of Lake Eyre and its fertility and its distant neighbours in St Dominic's mission. This lack of individualism might prompt an activist to cry out for human rights. In the end, however, Wright's story rejects 'politics' like this as nothing more than egotism wishing to deny its place in history and its associated responsibility. The ego is found wanting and selfish when the larger inter-generational picture is revealed:

For the Ngarinyin there is no confusion about identity, status, authority, and gender function for all people and all of Creation. Although the old system has been significantly disrupted since families and tribes have been semi-domesticated, Westernized, and Christianized, the original system, self-sustaining for tens of thousands of years, continues to resonate its primary truth in the present day.

(Wright 1997: 21)

The Dreaming story thus provides a vehicle for making sense of the tumultuous events of *Plains of Promise*. It places this dysfunctional and isolated mission into a larger sphere, that of the cosmic, where time and space become irrelevant and balance and ceremony are all important. This story can be called the ceremonial story, which brings order to the haphazard events that occur to the various female protagonists. This project is similar to those of other famous Indigenous writers, such as Senegalese film maker Ousmane Sembene's *Moolaade* (Sharmill Films 2004) and famous Pueblo author Leslie Marmon Silko's (2006) novel *Ceremony*. As literary critic Paula Gunn Allen (1992: 123) explains:

> What Tayo and the people need is a story that will take the entire situation into account, that will bless life with a certain kind of integrity where spirit, creatures, and land can occupy a unified whole. That kind of story is, of course, a ceremony such as Betonie performs with Tayo as the active participant, the manifestor of the thought [of Thought Woman, the creator].

As Allen further elaborates, the intention is to dispense with industrial time; the protagonist of any ceremonial healing story must be taken out of the mechanized time and brought back into alignment with ceremonial and therefore cosmic time so that healing can occur for both society and Land (1992: 123). This is the same as the project of *Plains of Promise*: it is about a 'return to country', a return to cosmic time and the Dreaming.

Cosmology

In the case of Wright's Dreaming story, we find that the waterbird, or Ivy Koopundi, and her ancestors and descendants were patterned on, and likened to, the Great Lake – figured as essential to its survival:

> Then the young waterbird had a child. So that the disappearing lake could be made to reveal its waters each year when the birds returned. The secret was passed on to the child. This meant that they should always live near the lake.
>
> (Wright 1997: 303)

And so the two – both human and land – need one another.

I will develop this concept further by referencing the work of Allan Marett (2005) in his ethnomusical account, *Songs, Dreamings, and Ghosts*. Marett was taught by the Senior Song Men of Daly River, in Australia's

Northern Territory, about the intimate relationship between the living and the dead and their co-relationship to the Land through ceremony. The ethno-musical study was done over 15 years of engagement with the Wadeye Senior Song Men such as Alan Maralung (Barunga), Tommy Barrtjap and Bobby Lambudju Lane (2005: xix) of the Daly River district and the enactment and singing of the *wangga*. Marett came to understand that:

> Reciprocal obligations like those that hold between the living and the dead, and among the living in matters of ceremony, also condition the relationship that both the living and the dead have to country. In the Daly region, country is conceived of as living and sentient, and as the source from which the living spring and to which the dead eventually return. The purpose of the joint work performed by the living and the dead in the production and performance of *wangga* is to ensure the continuity of this existential journey to and from country.
>
> (2005: 4)

In short, this is a calling to home. It is a sense of belonging, patterned on and spun into a web of inter-generational creativity and dynamic change. It is so mutable that the only way to know it – that is, the law – is to contextualize it rather than decree it in some static dogma, or alternatively into a universalism based on a human-centred natural law. The central focus of the law is thus not humans and their rights, but the maintenance of a sustained place in the pattern of the web. Therefore, land and humans are inextricably spun into a pattern of legal relationships:

> Person and place, group and jointly owned land, are bonded conceptually and semantically. Individuals take the most import- ant aspects of their identity from the spirit-beings with whom they are associated.
>
> (Williams 1986: 27)

The removal of people from their homeland is therefore more than just a matter of a 'stolen generation'[5] brutalized by human intervention for their moral good. It is about a rupture, which has cosmic and environ- mental consequences. This environmental rupture is further supported by an ontological genocide that negates the recognition of the Indigenous need to maintain legal integrity over their lives. As *Plains of Promise* reveals, there is a traditional governance system that must be adhered to in the choice of situating of housing and even seating. An ongoing adherence to this system, in my view, is a continued 'passive resistance' that now must deal with the invasion of the 'circle', which, in turn, negates the complexity of seating arrangements when issues of law are being discussed. This lack of recognition has much to do with the complexity of the system, 'the complex nature of how to translate these time immemorial boundaries into the confines of their present circumstance' (Wright 1997: 41).

Furthermore, a more fundamental understanding is missing, which is being silenced: the intellectual thought that goes with Indigenous Law. This is demonstrated by the experiences of Richard Trudgen, a health worker with over 30 years' experience in the tribal areas of Northern Australia. Trudgen's experience, after working with some of the most affluent tribes[6] in Australia, led to his own intellectual exhaustion. He was dismayed by the lack of 'progress' of Indigenous peoples, especially when provided with everything Western culture deems necessary for an affluent life. Instead, Aboriginal people rejected the materialism of the West in favour of a continuing 'dysfunctional' life. So Trudgen's insistence on the white cargo cult of Western education, health and wealth as the solution to 'Aboriginal problem' fell on deaf ears.

Trudgen's realization is based on his training with Brazilian educator Paulo Freire (2000) and Freire's radical philosophy for teaching the oppressed, which recognizes that an imposed leadership only leads by 'manipulating' and a 'submerging and dominating of the consciousness of their comrades' – or worse, by causing them to 'became strangers in their communities' (Trudgen 2000: 206). Trudgen saw this played out in the Yolngu communities, with disastrous results (2000: 206). There is another way, however – one that builds on the intellectual tradition of hundreds of millennia: namely, Indigenous classical thought, Indigenous science and Indigenous Law.

Elders such as Senior Law Man Djiniyini Gondarra (in Trudgen 2000: ii) were calling for the recognition of their intellectual tradition, one into which 'outside' information could be incorporated – if explained in Indigenous language and through Indigenous logic. In short, this is what Indigenous society, no more or less than any other civilization, requires of new information. Wright's narrative also portrays that intent.

Law of Relationship

To develop the concept of the Law of Relationship, I will refer again to the works of Allan Marett (2005: xix) and the knowledge he acquired from the Wadeye Senior Law Men such as Alan Maralung (Barunga), Tommy Barrtjap and Bobby Lambudju Lane (2005: xix). It will especially help to position and inform the actions of Elliot the Traveller as he attempts to cross the Simpson Desert down to the Lake Eyre Basin – the home of the Waterbird Dreaming. This account of Elliot's adventures is full of encounters and whisperings of unseen things and Beings. Marett's work gives substance to this liminal world and demonstrates its validity in the reality of Indigenous song tradition and legal patterning of relationship and reciprocity.

The Wadeye Senior Law Men explained to Marett (2005: 62) that:

> By singing the songs of the ancestors, and by dancing following ancestral precedent, ceremonial performers draw together the worlds of the living and the dead, and in the liminal environment thus created – a space that is both of the living and of the dead – the deceased person who is the focus of the ceremony is able to cross over and join with the ancestral dead.

This account enhances our understanding of the need for Elliot to sing his way across the desert. For it is with the help of his totemic other – the waterbird – that he is able to stay on the seemingly straight and narrow Dreaming Path:

> Elliot journeyed discreetly, singing the songs taught by his father and uncle-fathers, each step through the song-map unlocking the land . . . Sometimes his movements were as graceful as his totem, the brolga . . . Elliot knew he had reached the home of a great spirit – the Serpent, the greatest ancestral creator being; he should remain on guard, for anything could happen in this greatest of places . . . This was the instructed destination: the song-map must end here. He could only go further if he was given permission by the traditional elders of this place.
>
> (Wright 1997: 43)

From the missionary perspective, however, Elliot was seen by the St Dominic's missionaries as a showman and trickster, able to manipulate the energies of life and confound the people. But this ability was a subtext for his ability to feel the Law. He had been trained by his Senior Law Men to 'feel' the Law and, in turn, it gave him an intimate knowledge of the Law of the Land. Elliot was in a relationship with the Land. He understood the Law of Relationship, but it did not make him moral or ethical. Rather, as Graham (1992) says, Indigenous Law is amoral. And, I would argue, the Law of Relationship resides in one's spatial interior, not in the exterior.

To bring about balance, however, Elliot's twin is ever present in some form or other – be it her person or the negative influences of her ancestry, which continue to plague St Dominic's mission. To bring about a balance in the end, Elliot must not only find the source but also care for Ivy. This he fails to do and ends up having a knife fight with her, which sends them on to the next stage of their destiny. Ivy is confined to a mental asylum while Elliot is confined to the mission and the role set out for him by the protector, Jebb: that of a native in need of care and protection from the ugly realities of Western civilization. Even after the arrival of self-determination, Elliot's life is still within the confines of what is acceptable to the system. He cannot marry the love of his life, as community responsibilities have taken over and his love has fallen into disrepute. However, this has not killed their ongoing passion; it has merely imprisoned it in a 'web of respectability', which persists for decades, unable to find release.

Ivy's release from the institution sees her inadvertent return to the mission, as though a call is still being made to this seemingly mentally ill woman. Her return once again throws Elliot into the role of carer, but this time he takes on his responsibility and keeps her safe from the ravages of mission life. The Old Law Council is not happy, but Elliot appears to have learnt that he has a responsibility to this 'twin waterbird'. Her life, just as much as his own, has been subject to the Law and the annoying interference of the 'outsiders' law'.

Therefore, rebalance is at the core of the story of *Plains of Promise*. It is not about heroes or heroines and their great struggles, but rather how the rebalancing of the Land and its cosmos is achieved.

The Law Council

This story conveys the message that it is not a matter of remembering or finding a hero, but rather reactivating and reweaving the law slumbering under colonialism. This need for the reweaving is reminiscent of the tenacity of the spider[7] and its constant reweaving of its damaged web as it risks its own life in the urban jungles. In the same way, the Indigenous Law Person is constantly reweaving the Law. In De Ishtar's (2005) account of her experiences with the Balgo Law Women of the Western Desert region of Australia, she learnt that the law and ceremony were not static reproductions of ancient beliefs, but were constantly being injected with new blood.[8] She notes that a renaissance in ceremonial vigour had taken place in the 1970s (seemingly in a clandestine manner), in the hope that the missionaries would not become aware of these new influences that came from the Kimberley, further north in Western Australia. It was important the missionaries be kept ignorant of these developments and so the beliefs were incorporated with Christian elements and then passed on to communities as far south as the Kintore of Central Australia.

This clandestine behaviour is played out in *Plains of Promise*, as before the Law Council is able to begin the investigation and consider the evidence that Elliot has brought back from Ivy's homeland, a matter of boundary disputes has to be settled. These disputes refer to the manner in which Indigenous people, when forced into these missions, would try to establish their housing arrangements based on traditional kinship systems. This they considered 'a highly intellectual way of maintaining integrity over their lives, regardless of the white man enforcing his way of doing things' (Wright 1997: 41). Just because the invader ignored the laws relating to kinship taboos, it did not mean the people would automatically follow suit. *Plains of Promise* does much to reveal how little intellectual relevance the invaders' law had in organizing a suitable governance system for the inmates.

Continuing this vein of thought, Wright offers a new and original question of law. It would seem the rupture occurred long before the arrival of the invader: the invaders' effect on the original event would be symbolized more by the 'crows'. By this I mean that, in *Plains of Promise*, crows symbolize those who brutalize the waterbird. Therefore, a crow can be both an invader and an Aboriginal comprador. The crows' wanton acts exaggerate the breach of the original law rather than being the source. Repositioning the role of the invader from one of centrality to the cause to one at the perimeters of influence disempowers the invader's law as the 'determinant' of the future of the people. Furthermore, Wright's taking the breach back to the Dreaming is arguing that it is a breach that must be solved by Indigenous people and their legal system, not by the invader's legal system. It would thus be more appropriate to position the invaders as merely an irritant or as kin to a climatic catastrophe, which requires a concerted effort by the Indigenous people to 'reconstruct' their various societies, rather than intellectually constructing themselves always within the Western cosmology/reality. Graham (1992) has suggested that Indigenous commentators do not put enough emphasis on the need for the 'reconstruction' of the society – that is, the recognition that something has happened and that adaptive strategies need to be put in place – strategies that align with Indigenous governance styles. Therefore, Graham says, an 'ethic of resilience' needs to be fostered among community and policymakers. As Wallace (n.d.) points out, we must go back to the origins of Law and determine the problems.

The imbalance, as Senior Law Man Neidjie of Kakadu National Park in

North Australia has pointed out, does not necessarily emanate from the actual place of a breach, but may come from a distant part of Australia. In other words, people must be mindful of their behaviour as it may be having some unknown effect in another place – for instance, the removal of sacred stones could cause a breakout of a disease in a distant city (Neidjie 1989: 82).

The question of Law therefore pertains to the origin of the copycat suicides in *Plains of Promise*, which, on the one hand, are unheard of and, on the other, have become endemic to St Dominic's mission. In the novel, Wright alludes to the fact that she is referring to the new phenomenon of suicide – '[T]his is where it all began,' she writes. For suicide has become endemic to Aboriginal society, especially in rural areas. It is as if Wright were using *Plains of Promise*, and especially the Old Law Council, as a vehicle to work out this vexing issue pervading Aboriginal society.

The Dreaming story of the waterbirds points to an imbalance in the Dreaming as an unfortunate act of fate. In other words, *Plains of Promise* investigates, deliberates and makes a ruling on the case of the suicides. The deliberation is set out in the Dreaming story. The evidence is obtained by Elliot and deciphered by the Old Law Council, which then offers an explanation. Interestingly, the imbalance has come out of the Dreaming. That is, there is a fundamental fracture that has occurred in the relationship between the Great Lake and its people. This imbalance has been heightened and intensified by the invaders' intervention, which involved the rounding up of people on to missions and the deviant behaviour of the stolen generation, only accountable to mission law, which allowed 'crow-like' lethargic compliance. This mission law of regimented behaviour, however, did not guard against the influence of the Law of the Land.

As we are told in *Plains of Promise*, the retribution for the breach came in the form of a 'fog'. The invaders were not implicated in the crime, as it would appear that they were not relevant to the law – their existence was made *terra nullius* by the Land itself.

However, for the original inhabitants, the breach was deadly real: it called its people to rebalance the imbalance or else pay a price. Old Pilot, the negotiator on behalf of Ivy's people, told Elliot of the grim reality:

> After he died, more followed. Couldn't help themselves. Like they wanted to die. Some don't even wait to get sick, they find some other way to kill themselves to get someone else to do it for them.
>
> Those people get someone else to kill them tricky way. Tricking someone to kill you – that's something queer. So they don't even

know they gone and did it. Then sometimes these people get so sorry for what they done, they do it to themselves as well.

(Wright 1997: 93)

Pilot warns Elliot that if he does not bring the girl back, both his community and Elliot's will continue to suffer the endemic suicidal behaviour:

> If she don't come back it will get worse for this mob here, and for your mob as well. Just wait a little while – you'll see the evil spirits turn up at first light. You'll see that low fog crawling like a snake across the ground, sneaking around until it finds someone to take away. Someone not on the lookout. We all watch to see who those spirits will get hold of.
>
> (Wright 1997: 94)

This type of reasoning puts the cause of the suicides squarely in the hands of Indigenous peoples and so empowers them with a possible solution, if not their own intellectual deciphering of the situation. And just as in the earlier mentioned *Ceremony*, the cause denotes an imbalance in the ritual nature of the people. In the case of *Ceremony*, it is named as witchery (Silko 2006). The release from the curse of the witchery is only achieved through taking responsibility and not blaming hapless, disconnected whites, but rather looking to another more powerful source:

> The witchery would be at work all night so that the people would see only the losses – the land and the lives lost – since the whites came; the witchery would work so that the people would be fooled into blaming only the whites and not the witchery. It would work to make the people forget the stories of the creation and continuation of the five worlds; the old priest would be afraid too, and cling to ritual without making new ceremonies as they always had before, the way they still made new Buffalo Dance songs each year.
>
> (Silko 2006: 230)

Plains of Promise offers the same knowing, a knowing of the source of the imbalance. The Old Law Council, therefore, does not waste time blaming the invader or the mission tyrant, but rather the members of the Law Council know there is a major breach – although they do not understand who or what has caused this breach. They realize that Ivy is central to the breach, but are not sure why. For them, she is only a child of a disturbed woman, one who is haunted by some strange beings at night – beings from another sphere of reality. Crows and fire are motifs associated with this seemingly disassociated child. When the copycat suicides begin, they soon realize that fire, with all it connotes, is connected symbolically with this woman. That is, there is a drying up, a parched reality in need of cleansing water. The revelation of Ivy's ancestry, coupled with unintentional deaths, emboldens the Law Council to action – action of which the council is unsure and which, unfortunately, leaves Elliot the Traveller open to possible death. To carry out this rebalance is no simple matter, however, due to the interference of the unjust law and also the stupidity of human desire. One generation is not enough time to carry out an investigation into the source of the imbalance, let alone find the rebalancing solution, because the Land cannot make people do what it wants. It can only 'call'. The case takes over five years to determine the cause and 30 years to rebalance.

I will now return once again to the Law Council and its judiciary role:

> Elliot's information would need time for very careful consider-
> ation before any action could be taken. Those like Dorrie who
> listened for the spiritual messages and others who were expert in
> interpretation would all have to be consulted. This would involve
> listening to the re-enactment of those messages in song many
> times before any final consensus could be reached.
>
> (Wright 1997: 116)

Just as we read earlier in Marett's account of the Wangga song cycle and the interpenetration of the world of the dead into that of the living, so Dorrie relies on information from the spirits. Equally, just as the Senior Song men must also decipher a song and its meaning and the perfection of that song by constant rehearsal, so it is with Dorrie, with her new-found information:

> Old Dorrie was someone who listened to the messages blown by
> the morning and night winds. Dorrie could also hear and pick out
> familiar voices of deceased relatives whom she had never even met
> when they were alive. These spirits could be relied upon to impart
> important information.
>
> (Wright 1997: 115)

These parallel universes of reality inform many Indigenous worlds and, over millennia, have proved useful in the maintenance of the culture and Law (Morris 2004). The ontology of invisible beings is an important aspect of intellectual property debates. As I have argued in other fora, Indigenous Law is a full Law and the Western equivalent is half a law (Morris 2000a: 209–11). Only a full Law can appreciate the legal jurisdiction of the Indigenous reality – a reality that has been around much longer than the half law and is much more conducive to the continuity of the land as a viable resource for future generations. Therefore, it is intellectual madness to turn to a law that negates half of what is evident in the Indigenous person's daily reality.

The motif that Wright has used to describe that imbalance is that of a waterbird's inability to fly away with the other birds – in other words, the continuity of the ceremonial journey of coming to a place and leaving, the ebb and flow of the relationship with land. The seemingly nomadic life is one patterned by the relationship with land. This relationship has been ruptured – or, as it is expressed in *Ceremony*, 'this world is fragile', so it is the responsibility of the people to go to great lengths to re-pattern the law, not just blame the *terra nullius* invader.[9]

The fiduciary duty of the waterbird to journey and return has been breached. The waterbird has neither left in a correct manner nor returned. *Plains of Promise* therefore deals with this new question of law – that is, what happens when there is an unintentional breach of law. How is it recovered and how is restitution made?

This question would seem insurmountable, but looking at the manner in which the Law Women of Balgo were able to bring about a renaissance in ceremony and ritual, it is not an impossible feat. Rather, it is a matter of persistence and endurance. It is the ebb and flow of life and country, as the Senior Song Men have informed us through Marett's work. I will now turn to the actions of the individual within this relationship.

Rights and Responsibilities

'That girl. She was related to that old man, you know.'
Elliot listened, startled out of his sleep as Pilot went on talking. 'He's properly dead now. No one around could fix him up so that was it. I tell you, there was no one like him. He could fix up anybody just like he did for that dog there I told you about. You'd think if he was so smart he could have fixed himself up. But he couldn't. He got some sickness was took deadly even for him. In the end he just wanted to lie down and die.'

(Wright 1997: 93)

Elliot and Ivy Koopundi are the pivotal characters of the novel – the twin waterbirds who bring back the balance; however, the price of their heroism would appear to be basically their sanity – or is it?

In this section, I start by discussing the role of Elliot, legal twin of Ivy, then move on to discuss Ivy and her female descendants.

Elliot, as I have already argued, is pivotal in his role as the person who can actualize the Law. But he fails to do this through his own petulant behaviour. He is too ridden with ego desires and a sense of revenge that he ends up killing Pilot, whom he believes will seek revenge for the murder of his prized dog. However, Pilot is the very person who was sent to relieve him of his burden – Ivy. The murder of the dog is interesting, as the dog appeared early in the novel as a representation of the curative powers of Ivy's ancestor. The story about the dog's cure was to be relayed by Elliot to his Law Council so that they would understand the power of the Clever Man who was Ivy's ancestor. But Elliot dismissed this story as 'too scary' and so does not impart this important piece of the 'evidence', which the Law Council needs to solve the case. It is then either his sense of guilt or his own fear of the dog that leads him to kill the animal, a habit he later repeats. Elliot would seem to be cursed due to his own disrespect and, therefore, in the end finds his own life full of hatred and bad luck. This he cannot really blame on the missionaries, as he is not quite honourable himself or willing to discipline himself into becoming a full Law Person; instead, he becomes a victim of colonization and takes on a leadership role in the colonized system – one that is a façade or a way of gaining power in someone else's law, rather than enacting his own Law. Thus, the rights and responsibilities deemed to be Elliot's duties become too much for him and he reneges on them and leads the assimilated life, a half-life with no real love; he adopts a show of respectability and becomes a community leader by default.

I now turn to Ivy. Ivy is the linchpin connecting the past and the future, the apparent cure for all the never ending stream of deaths. Ivy is portrayed as battered by the winds of life, rather than dancing to the rhythm of the pattern of the law. She is as delicate as her totemic 'other', the waterbird. But at the same time, she is an enduring force and, in the end, dances a wild dance, a dance that releases to all the violence visited on her. Rather than fighting back and so destroying herself, she endures the violence, like a force of nature, and then finds herself back on the Land, left in peace to wander it like a waterbird, undisturbed by the imposed reality and laws of the invaders and compradors. She now has time to engage fully with the Law and its associated reality, which includes a continual dialogue with her traditional Lands off to the distant south. Her return and dialogue bring

back the waters to the Great Lake, *sitting down country* being the actualizing of the Law of Relationship between the human and the Land, which,
in turn, brings the balancing of the law.

Therefore, the return of Ivy to the isolation of the outstation near
St Dominic's mission was not, as some may think, further punishment
and isolation, but rather the giving of a lawful place – a rebalancing. It is a
place of solitude in which the dead can influence her and her duties to sing
up the Land and bring back the water to the Great Lake. She is able now to
sing to her Country, even though she is off country. As Marett (2005)
learnt, a person does not necessarily have to be on Country to be able to
sing to her Ancestors and ancestral land.

Furthermore, Ivy meets her descendants, even if in a seemingly mad
moment. Elliot takes Mary and Jessie to meet Ivy, whom he introduces just
as 'family'. The reader is left thinking that the half-mad woman is unaware
of the 'family'; however, in the days following, little Jessie reveals:

> But Jessie said she'd seen an old woman just like the one in the hut
> near their house one day. It happened when they first came to the
> community, when Mary was across the road. The old woman
> came into their house and gave her a lolly, Jessie said.
>
> (Wright 1997: 297)

So Ivy once again assumes the dysfunctional role, but is fully aware of
the coming of her own child. We learn later in the novel that her daughter
Mary also senses that Ivy is content when she reminisces about Elliot's
son's words: 'Besides, she's happy here' as she flies out of St Dominic and
observes Ivy busy with something on the ground. So, by the end of the
novel, Ivy is not a victim of the law, but rather finds peace in a semi-
conscious existence – an existence that is more in tune with what is
important to her reality. It is as though she has moved to the world of the
dead – and, as Marett (2005) learnt, mortuary ceremonies were important:
'We wanted to make her free to walk around in her country all the time,
and we wanted the people left behind to feel good.' (2005: 61)

Ivy's descendants

Turning now to Ivy's descendants, her daughter, Mary, appears also to
travel the dysfunctional road of her mother and grandmother once they
encounter the white man's law and just like her grandmother she gives
birth to a child, Jessie, by a man from St Dominic's mission, which then
eventually draws her to the source of the imbalance. So Mary also is firmly
patterned into the imbalance. However, Mary suffers from a different

dysfunctionalism – an ignorance of the power of the Law of the Land. Mary was born into a generation expected to be fully assimilated and to repel their heritage and Law, which stems from their birth country, and instead take on a heritage and law from another land – somewhere with its own law of the land.

However, as Mary grows and discovers that she is adopted, she gravitates to her cultural roots and land. This slow gravitation has a price, however – the price of biculturalism, a 'constructed' biculturalism defined by the dominant culture's terms of reference. The outcomes of such a construction are explained by Paula Gunn Allen (1992), who points out that the contradictory definitions of women represent opposing forces in American culture: in one culture women are represented as strong and capable, while in the opposing dominant culture they are viewed very differently: 'Through this destructive dissonance we are unhappy prey to the self-disparagement common to, indeed demanded of, Indians living in the United States today.' (1992: 48–49). She then goes on to list the self-destructive behaviour that includes mandatory alcoholism and domestic violence, reminiscent of behaviour seen by Trudgen (1992) in Australian Aboriginal communities: 'Some of us travel and move around a lot; some of us land good jobs and then quit them; some of us engage in violent exchanges' (1992: 48–49).

These 'hopelessly opposed cultural definitions of Indian women', however, are systematic of the opposing laws. And, just as in any colonized environment, the women of the oppressed nations suffer the bipolar behaviour that in *Plains of Promise* moves from dysfunctional to assimilated. However, this assimilation leaves Mary and her daughter ignorant of the power of the Law of the Land, which is drawing them back to their mother's home country. The country 'needs' them just as much as they need it, in order to know how they are patterned into the scheme of things – both historically and legally.

At the end of the book, we find Mary and Jessie promising that return and the lake refilling with the knowledge that the right people are coming home to balance the pattern – a rebalancing and relationship that are totally foreign and unknowable to those outside the pattern.

Conclusion

So, in conclusion, *Plains of Promise* reveals a saga of many layers. It is a story of multi-layered relationships with land, kinship and law. It follows the triadic circles and takes us into the cosmology of the people, their systems of law and finally the rights and responsibilities of the individual.

However, while one can easily be sidetracked by the dysfunctional aspects of the missionary concentration camps and the associated legal system, they must not be allowed to override the jurisprudential reading of Aboriginal Law.

Plains of Promise, when read as a legal narrative, is nothing less than an exegesis of the Australian *War of the Worlds* and the violence that it renders through the silencing of the possibility of another account of law in Australia. Unwittingly, this legal and intellectual silencing is perpetuated by Indigenous people themselves, through the critical imposition of Western-trained Indigenous leaders and academics on and off communities (Alfred 1999). Furthermore, the guiding words of Chief Wallace suggest we seek out the origins of the law rather than approaching it from the Western top-down model (Wallace n.d.). By beginning with a Western education, the 'fundamental approach' to legal issues runs against the grain of the Indigenous intellectual legal tradition.

Hence Wright rolls out a tumultuous saga, but then ends it with another story – a *bottom story*, which takes the reader to another level. It is a level in which the cosmological reality of the Law of the Land is explained, a story that is meant to explain through metaphor the trauma of the law of the waterbirds, a law depicted as a fog, an insidious force: 'You'll see that low fog crawling like a snake across the ground, sneaking around until it finds someone to take away. Someone not on the lookout. We all watch to see who those spirits will get hold of' (Wright 1997: 94). The fog in the novel is the representative of the unknown killer, the unknown source of the suicides. As Wright says: '[T]his is where it all began.' The cure for the suicides is a rebalancing or a returning to country of people: special people – the people the Land needs for its balance. The lake deems Ivy's family to be special – due to the waterbird totem, which, in turn, is an allegory of its Clever Man heritage.

The question of law being put forward by Wright, therefore, is that Land is not inanimate, but rather fully conscious and able to impact on people's lives. The Land has a story and it is the *story of feelings*. This is a story that SLM Neidjie has shared with Australia in his book *Story About Feeling* (1989), in which Land and Law are seen as unchangeable and empowered.

As Paula Gunn Allen (1992: 123) asserts, it is the living of the ancient stories in the modern stories that heals the individual – and, I would add, re-patterns them back into the Land and allows them to actualize the Law. That actualization, in turn, becomes the ceremony.

CHAPTER 8

The camp from Turtle Island:
Thunderheart

Entering the camp from Turtle Island

I now leave the camp of the dusty landscape of *Plains of Promise* and travel with the eagle to North America, the home of Hinsha Waste Agli Win – also known as Professor Beatrice Medicine – and her trail of tears, representing the stories of her people, both past and present. It is a trail that is entwined in the mythical world of the American Western movie.

I have chosen the movie *Thunderheart* on which to carry out a juris- prudential reading. *Thunderheart* is set in the Badlands of South Dakota. The term 'Badlands' is an appropriate one for the setting of a movie about the bad things that happened in the 1970s, but at the same time it is a dichotomy, for the Badlands are actually a magnificent national park, featuring rugged terrain that is full of mystery and colour as the sun moves across the horizon reflected in the changing colours of the rocks. *Thunderheart* captures those images, thus empowering the voice of the land as an integral part of the film. Throughout the film, we return to these images as though to frame characters and plot in time immemorial. For the story of *Thunderheart* is about the ancient impinging on the present.

Thunderheart was in the last stages of production when I travelled to the Badlands, so the film has considerable significance. The Oneida actor Graham Greene, star of the film, was the latest pinup boy among the Indian academics I met at the Community College on my way to the

Wounded Knee Memorial with Dr Medicine. This film therefore resonates as part of my lived experience in the Badlands.

More importantly, however, the film is based on real events that happened on the surrounding reservations during the 1970s, the heyday of the American Indian Movement's (AIM) support for Native Americans who were being oppressed by government-appointed governing bodies. The 1970s were a decade of revolution all over the Western world, starting with the London student riots in March 1968. The revolutionary spirit and action spread to the United States and eventually led to the shooting of both the father of the Civil Rights Movement, Dr Martin Luther King, and the champion for civil rights and presidential candidate Robert Kennedy. These shameful deaths epitomized the grim realities of life for Indians on reservations during that era. South Dakota was nicknamed 'murder capital of America' at that time, due to an unprecedented number of murders, including that of AIM activist Anna Mae Pictou Aquash.

This journey was the precursor to another trip, when I travelled a decade later to the homelands of Anna Mae Pictou Aquash, who was a Mikmaq woman from Nova Scotia. At the turn of the millennium, I travelled to Canada's East Coast and became acquainted with the Mikmaq tribe through Heredity Chief Stephen Augustine.[1] This friendship led me to become fascinated with the nineteenth-century Mikmaq quill worker and artist Christianne Morris (see Morris n.d.). In turn, this gave me a context for Anna Mae. Rather than knowing Anna Mae merely as a member of AIM with only a political past – that is, as a young woman from a poverty-stricken and residential school past who made her way down to the hotbed of Native American political activism – I was presented with a very different picture.

I was drawn into the history of the Mikmaq through my fascination for Christianne Morris, whose name was almost the same as mine at the time – Morris is my former married name. The more closely I looked at this woman, the more similarities I saw between her life and mine, even though she had been born in 1814. Yet I feel this was merely the 'bait' to get me to delve more deeply into the peoples from whom Anna Mae was descended. I was assisted in this search by Ruth Whitehead, who worked at the Nova Scotia Museum. I brought together the information I collected on Christianne in a manuscript on her life, which helped me understand how the 'living dead' work with those in the present to tell a history (Morris n.d.).

My journey in documenting Christianne's life is reflected in some ways in the film *Thunderheart* – albeit without the heroics. Rather, piecing together the information Ruth and others gave me brought me into contact with Anna Mae's land and her people's untold history from the perspective of a 'squaw' – a female who also lived through poverty and disease, as well as the blatant racism of her time. However, Christianne's journey was different, and her legacy can be found in portraits of her, together with artefacts and various documents, including a letter to the lieutenant governor pointing out that the Indian Committee Loans owed her a cow and seeds. It was quite evident from her life achievements that Christianne was not going to let the Indian agents get away with depriving her of her rightful entitlements. This may appear irrelevant in light of the political demands of today, but in its time it was a major step for an American Indian female to demand her rights. If anything, it showed the kind of female tenacity that gave birth to Anna Mae. These courageous women weren't going to let poverty and disease wipe out their tribes.

So I learnt the difference between a memorial to the death of a person and working with the dead. Anna Mae's legacy is one of a death – sorry business – while Christianne's concerns the living dead and the ways in which a living person may be influenced by the dead. Both are of great value, but, unfortunately, it is the always sorry business that garners attention, not cultural continuity.

As I mentioned during the exploration of my journeys to the various story camps, it was the powerful impact of Hinsha Waste Agli Win – an impact that continued to resonate many decades later – that made me understand the power of the Indian women of the mythological West. Once again, this is my understanding of what I have seen and learnt; it is not an absolute truth; rather it is but one take on the great saga of the West and the deep philosophy of the Law of the Red Road.

The Trickster of Politics

Leonard: It's a power deal.
Kelner: They'll kill you!
Leonard: Sometimes they have to kill us. They have to kill us.
Kelner: Look, I don't have to do this.
Leonard: You don't have any choice.
Kilner: I'm trying to help you people! Why can't you accept that?
Leonard: It's in our DNA – you have to do what old man says.
Kilner: What makes you such a threat?
Leonard: Because we choose to be who we are. We know the difference between the reality of freedom and the illusion of freedom. There is a way to live with earth and a way not to live with earth. We choose. It's about power.

(*Thunderheart*, discussing the FBI raids)

This camp examines power and the ways in which that power can be accessed. It also looks at the way the source of the power is sidelined in favour of a battle over the power of the 'other' – the white man's power and law. We enter the world of Hinsha Waste Agli Win and her people, as well as the majestic Badlands, which contextualize and frame many of the scenes of cosmological Law and power. This camp addresses a particular time in American history, a time that appears to circle back on a continuous cycle of rebirths of the same events, the same sad outcomes. The concentric circular nature of American history is sourced within the boundaries of the Badlands and the sacred Black Hills of the ancient peoples of that land. It is as if these small, isolated Lakota/Oglala[2] Indian reservations – inhabited by the remnant of the Great Sioux Nation[3] – are born to play out their lives on the stage of world history. It is through their heroes, both male and female, that the legends of the past and present are created. It is as if the Plains Indians, more than any other Native American people, have 'acted out' the cyclical nature of history as a never ending recycling of events, ever seeking balance; these events are captured in stories from which we can learn; stories that we can remember.

However, as we have become part of a globalized world in which history is but another programme on the History Channel to be consumed as edutainment rather than providing meaningful lessons about dangers that lie on life's path, the cyclical nature of history has been lost. Stories such as *Thunderheart*'s have been rendered politically incorrect because a white man wrote the script, rather than contextualizing the white man into the greater power of the source of the Law. For this story is about that source – the source of power that sustains peoples through historical atrocities that reduce the perpetrators to mere thugs with guns, unable to honour treaties or allow American Indians – Native Americans – ownership of their own lands.

As Duthu (2000: 149) explains:

> The court institutionalizes tribal sovereignty within the matrix of American democratic structure through language that alternately affirms tribal political existence into perpetuity and consigns such political existence to the whims of a superior power. This suggests that the nature of tribal sovereignty subsists in a field of contingencies, where the ultimate determination of the nature or scope of tribal power and rights operates in relation to broader national institutional imperatives.

This camp explores the concentric circle of the history of Wounded

Knee in South Dakota, the historical killing fields of the Plains Indians, both past and present. I first sketch the intersection as it is dramatized in *Thunderheart*, because these acts are themselves metaphors for the cosmic Law. Second, I turn to the Law of Relationship as it is personified in the characters of Levoi and Johnny Looks Twice, the leader of the resistance group ARM. Finally, under the rubric of rights and responsibilities, I explore the role of the feminine as the voice of 'the source', the call of the land itself. That 'feminine' is embodied in Maggie Eagle Bear, herself based on real-life Mikmaq Indian[4] activist Anna Mae Pictou Aquash,[5] who was murdered by two convicted members of the American Indian Movement (AIM).[6] This murder is contextualized through a short history of the events in and around the uprising at Wounded Knee – remembered by the Oglala people as the Reign of Terror, with its subsequent high number of unprecedented murders, including that of Aquash (see *Thunderheart*). This murdering of the feminine is analyzed in terms of the Grimm Brothers' tale 'The Girl Without Hands', which introduces us to the mythological motif of the handless maiden and has its ghostly equivalent in reality in the dismembering of Aquash's own hands. This motif is connected to the role of Indigenous women in governance, on the basis that it provides an exemplary tale of the continued denial by Indigenous men of Indigenous models of leadership, women's equality and all that this implies cosmologically – that is, as Kanien'kehaka (Mohawk) philosopher Taiaiake Alfred (1999) argues, the acceptance of the *existence of opposites* in the political as well as the social. This equality is not based on the Western notion of equal rights, but on the Law of Relationship, and on the balance not only of genders, but of the real world in which they are situated.

Thunderheart: The film

The film *Thunderheart* is a dramatized version of real-life events that happened on the Pine Ridge reservation in 1975 between the FBI and the American Indian Movement (AIM) over exploration for uranium and the pollution of the reservation water supply. The reservation was notorious for being the 'murder capital of the nation', with the highest number of violent deaths per capita in the United States at the time.

The film was directed by Michael Apted and scripted by John Fusco. It stars Val Kilmer. However, it is the spectacular Badlands that frame the plot and bring it into the realm of the mythical. For the hero comes to learn that it is the power of these lands that is the real source of Law, not some imposed paper-driven law from another people. A woman teaches him this valuable lesson, in the process losing her own life. The murder of this feminine source of knowledge and wisdom will become a central part of our learning in this camp.

The film engages the two laws that have jurisdiction over the lives of the people living there: the ancient Indigenous Law of the Red Road[7] and the recently encoded[8] Federal Indian Law of the United States. In the film, these laws offer very different paths to rights, self-determination and home rule for the oppressed Oglala. This difference is not just external – between two laws and two systems – but internal. This internal disjuncture is referenced through the actions of the two leaders, Johnny Looks Twice and Frank Coutelle, who represent their respective laws. Johnny Looks Twice, the leader of the radical pan-Indian group ARM, sees himself and his followers as the warriors of the Red Road and liberators of the oppressed Oglala. Conversely, Coutelle, the senior FBI agent heading the murder investigations, sees himself and the federally appointed governing body, Guardians of the Oglala Nation (GOONs), as the liberators of an ancient people who need to move into the twenty-first century. I argue that both leaders abuse their positions to instantiate their voice of authority.

Levoi is a young, zealous FBI agent of Native American heritage who has been reassigned as a Federal Indian Agent. His appointment is an attempt by his superiors to appease the ongoing conflict within the reservation between the traditionalists of the Red Road and the GOONs. Levoi is in awe of Coutelle, the legendary maverick of the FBI, and he believes he is the true voice of authority in the whole conflict. However, this perception changes through a series of revelatory experiences vouchsafed to Levoi under the guidance of the Medicine Man, Grandpa Reaches. Under Grandpa Reaches' tutelage, Levoi learns to *feel* the path of the Red Road and its legal authority. Levoi is assisted here by reservation policeman Walter Crow Horse, who acts as a jurisprudential boundary rider (Lester 1993),[9] constantly contesting Coutelle's jurisdiction on tribal lands. Through an antagonistic brotherly relationship, he also assists Levoi to trust his revelatory experiences as the *voice of authority*, which, in turn, guides him to the source of the imbalance – the strip mining in the sacred Black Hills.

Lurking on the margins of the story, peripheral rather than central to its theme, is Maggie Eagle Bear. Portrayed as part of the leadership of ARM, she is the only feminine voice of authority encouraging Levoi to 'go to the source'. That 'source' is, of course, a metaphor for the imbalance polluting the holy lands – *H'e Sapa* – by the mining interests. Only by returning to this source and listening to its representative – woman – does Levoi solve the murder; more importantly, however, he actualizes his role as the Holy Man. So Maggie, despite her seemingly small part in the drama, is in fact one of the major characters.

Her cold-blooded murder, at the hands of either the GOONs or the FBI's Indian mole, suggests that these rivals are really two sides of the same coin, committed to what Alfred (1999: xii) calls the realist fetishization of power, of control – to the point that it takes on a 'spiritual meaning'. That spirit, however, is one that murders the feminine in the shape of Maggie – murders her, indeed, in order to appropriate her position and access to the sacrality of the Land under the governance of the White Buffalo Calf Woman. Fools Crow himself recognizes and regrets this appropriation, because the whole point of the Red Road is called into question when detached from the feminine. So Levoi's project is to recuperate the feminine, listening to Maggie's call to the source, and with it an understanding of the source of his people's problems. In doing so, he learns to feel the Law, and actualizes his responsibilities. Only by 'feeling' the blood of his ancestors, *which runs through his heart like a buffalo*,[10] does he comprehend what it means to walk the path of the Red Road.

White Buffalo Calf Woman

> Sometimes the solution is to educate them on the source of our law. You see, a lot of criticism comes from people when they look at the so-called Federal Indian law system and look at its origins from the top down, starting with what is the position today and then going down, tracing it back to see how did we get there. We don't look at it from that point of view; we look at it from its origin of our law and how it evolved to where it is today and I think that is the essential distinction between how they view us and how we view ourselves.
>
> (Wallace 2001)

Following the advice of Chief Wallace, I turn to the Plains Indians' cosmological narrative of the coming of the White Buffalo Calf Woman (Wallace n.d.: 41). White Buffalo Calf Woman is the source of the Law, as Paula Gunn Allen (1992: 344) elucidates:

> She brought the Sacred Pipe to the Lakota, and it is through the agency of this pipe that the ceremonies and rituals of the Lakota are empowered. Without the pipe, no ritual magic can occur.

The source of the land is manifested as a recognizable spiritual entity, which instructs the newcomers in the Law and the lawful behaviour. She is not unlike Masaw, the guardian and protector of the Fourth World of the Hopi. On arriving in the Fourth World, Masaw instructs the people on how to behave in the New World (Waters 1963: 21–22). They, like the Sioux, were forced to leave their traditional lands due to an invasion; however, the Hopi were facing the invasion of the elements and abrupt climate change while the Sioux were in a state of flux in the 1700s, having been forcibly moved westward from the Great Lakes to the plains of the sparse Badlands. This new environment was totally foreign and demanded a new contract, a new system of law and, above all, a new contract with the spiritual guardian of the new country. The ability of a nation to renegotiate a founding contract was not foreign to the Great Sioux Nation – in fact, it is fundamental to any society governed by the Law of Relations that has an understanding of the 'flux of nature'.

Therefore, when a nation finds itself in a new ecological situation, there is an expectation that a new contract with the spirit of the Land will appear and validate the people's arrival. This does not mean the overarching cosmology has changed, but rather that it has been adapted to include new aspects to suit the people's situation. So cosmologies are far from being static – in fact, they are dynamic. Nowhere is this dynamism more palpable than in the coming of a messianic character. For the messiah connotes the need for the society to change, and carries with it an important message of transformation. That transforming message here is that of the new contract – with its source being the feminine. For White Buffalo Calf Woman is a messianic figure, said to be reincarnation of Whope from the ancient creation myth *Ohukankan* (St Pierre and Long Soldier 1995: 44).[11] This woman, said to be the embodiment of the feminine ideal, came as a sacred spirit and dwelt with the Lakota people for four days. Her purpose was to develop a new jurisprudence comprising the principles, values and rituals suitable to this new landscape. This constitutes the cosmological, or natural, aspect of the Law: White Buffalo Calf Woman brings with her a new contract with the Land.

This is different from peoples who bring their God with them from another land. This is about honouring the guardian spirit of a particular landscape, from which people wish to take the resources and benefit from them. It is about honouring the new land, not trying to superimpose something from another landscape, from another continent.

Cosmology becomes History

Through the character of Grandpa Reaches, *Thunderheart* is connected to the Wounded Knee Massacre of the 1890s. Because Grandpa Reaches – like his model, Fools Crow[12] – is a survivor of the Wounded Knee Massacre, he is also someone who sees all the problems still arising from the original

Wounded Knee, with its sorry tale for Indians because the violence it has bred comes not just from whites; as the ghost dance shows, it also emerges from within the Indians themselves, and it is an Indian who must bring back the balance – and not just any Indian, but a sanctioned hero, a descendant of the original holy man – Thunderheart.

This fiction has its basis in fact and so the *Wicasa Wakan*,[13] Fools Crow, saw the need for a new kind of leadership, thus influencing the writer John Fusco to develop the character of Levoi. From a young age, Fusco said he had an interest in Native American philosophy. This led him to the Pine Ridge reservation where, after five years of continuous encounters with the Pine Ridge Lakota, he had not only learnt the language, but also had earned the right to be taught and influenced by the *Wicasa Wakan*, Fools Crow.

I want to focus now on Fools Crow's influence and the match he supplies to writer Fusco as the character Grandpa Reaches. Grandpa Reaches is central to the film because his interactions with Levoi bring about a new leadership in the form of a rehistoricized cosmology. In short, Levoi becomes an avatar of White Buffalo Calf Woman through the historical agency of Grandpa Reaches. Interestingly, these interactions are themselves based on the writer Fusco's interactions with the real Fools Crow. Fusco tries to avoid the 'Indian trade' protocol in which he is frightened Fools Crow will take his expensive turquoise choker. Finally, Fools Crow catches him out and gives him a bone whistle. It is not until later that he realizes the intention of Fools Crow: the 'traded' bone whistle is sacred, a metaphor for the Law as much as the efficacy of trade. In receiving the bone, Fusco is given the power to tell this story. That is the true nature of reciprocity posited and actualized in 'Indian trade'. In *Thunderheart*, Grandpa Reaches 'Indian trades' Levoi his coveted Ray Ban sunglasses for a stone. That trade has legal and spiritual significance, auguring Levoi's acceptance of his role, predestined by Law; it brings him out from behind his expensive sunglasses – a metaphor for Western values. This embrace of the Law is predetermined earlier in the film: the handing of the sacred pipe for Levoi to smoke is a sign of the acceptance of the legal authority of the Red Road. The 'smoking of the pipe' symbolizes the legal act of 'truth speaking' as against that of 'swearing an oath on a Bible'.

The interactions – of taking and giving – are moments of legal significance because they are points at which Levoi engages with and understands the nature of the reciprocity element of the Law of the Red Road. But they also connote moments of fear. At the very moment Levoi accepts the pipe, the FBI agents blast their way in and Levoi turns his gun on Grandpa Reaches. The FBI's smashing of the 500-year-old rattle symbolizes the smashing of the ancient past of the Sioux. Seeing this action, Levoi is then brought to his senses and understands the real implications of the smashing of one law by another. At that moment, Coutelle's voice of authority as a liberator is also smashed in Levoi's mind. He must choose which law he will follow – one that tolerates the smashing of anything that gets in its way or one that makes him feel his ancestral blood. Even more than that, however, he hears the call of the feminine: the reason for Levoi's quest is not just personal – rediscovering his roots – it is political, psychological, jurisprudential and cosmological, laying down a new law that will rebalance the community, 'enabling the coexistence of opposites, extending relationship, responsibilities and respect to outsiders' (Alfred 1999: 137) – all within the parameters of Red Road jurisprudence. In short, Levoi will be cosmology becoming history – and history becoming cosmology.

The Law of Relationship

Let the world change you and you can change the world.

(*The Motor Cycle Diaries*)

The next part of the camp focuses on the intra-Indian fighting depicted in *Thunderheart*. This is a fundamental problem found in many Indigenous nations across the world. Both Alfred (1999: 137) and Lakota intellectual Vine Deloria[14] have pointed out that the competition between the traditionalist and the 'agency' or 'band' leaders is endemic. That is to say, government-installed leaders such as the GOONs of *Thunderheart* are a mode of governance based on the legal principle of *right*, as against the hereditary or traditional leadership and governance structure based on the principle of *responsibilities* – in this case, the Red Road.

This rather complex set of intra-Indian relationships is the source of the Law, as Chief Wallace suggests. I first examine the character of Johnny Looks Twice, then Walter Crow Horse, because they embody two styles of leadership. Finally, I turn to Levoi, the half-breed, the outsider, because he drives home the point that Indians must know themselves, as well as their law, before they can begin to construct a leadership that will address breaches of federal or international law. This message was reiterated throughout the film. Levoi was continuously being told by Maggie Eagle Bear to 'go to the sources'. This is a metaphor not only for the Land, but also for his inner law – that is, the true voice of authority.

The Trickster

I turn first to Johnny Looks Twice, the ARM leader. He is based on AIM leader Leonard Peltier.[15] In the film, Looks Twice is a 'hothead', being taken to jail and wrongly accused of the murders of two policemen, seemingly 'set up' and 'taken away'. His removal allows the focus of the film to turn to Levoi, enabling him to carry out his predestined role as leader. Before that happens, however, Looks Twice is exposed as the *faux* liberation leader of ARM. ARM is the kind of organization found all over the Indigenous world, purporting to speak on behalf of Indigenous people but all the while buying into the system of the white man. No wonder Looks Twice speaks in the empty rhetoric of rights and rules, repeating the slogan like a mantra: 'You have to listen to the old man.' He is the kind of intellectual sellout of whom Alfred (1999: 140) says: 'Those who enlist the intellectual force of rights-based arguments ... concede nationhood in the truest sense.' So it is not surprising that Looks Twice ends up as the subject, rather than master, of the Law – literally caught by its web and imprisoned, which is a metaphor for the prison of rights in which he is symbolically incarcerated. What Looks Twice not only ignores, but finds totally incomprehensible, is the Indigenous path to self-determination because he is so interpellated by the white man's 'rights'.

The Boundary Rider

The figure of Walter Crow Horse is a metaphor for law's boundaries – that is, Crow Horse patrols law's boundaries like a rider overseeing the land. Australian Indigenous Law Man Yami Lester (1993) coins the term 'boundary rider' to explain the role of someone who must guard the boundaries between the two cultures and laws. Walter epitomizes that role and is vigilant in reminding Coutelle and his agents when they are breaching his jurisdiction as a reservation policeman. But he is also vigilant in letting Levoi know when he is breaching Oglala protocol and that his conduct must follow Indian protocol if he wants to find answers to the murders. So Crow Horse is a figure of legal process, of juridical protocol, reminding Levoi of the Indigenous approach to law and life. Throughout the narrative, Crow Horse points out the need for due consideration and deferential behaviour on Levoi's part to Grandpa Reaches, particularly respectful of Grandpa's knowledge of the murder case and also Levoi's own family. So Crow Horse performs a significant, if secondary, role here. He may not be vouchsafed by visions like Levoi, but he knows how to behave – that is, he knows the Law. This is a knowledge that he imparts to Levoi for him to embody in his actions.

The Hero

This injunction to begin at the beginning, or the source, is frustrating for Levoi because he wants immediate answers to the murder case, with no delays. But Grandpa Reaches insists that Levoi's appearance on the scene is more than just forensic (i.e. to solve the case) because he knew he was coming – thereby instructing by revelation. Levoi must explore this connection. This becomes a source of resentment for Walter Crow Horse because, as their relationship strengthens, he realizes Levoi is having visions that instantiate his Holy Man status. That status is affirmed by the content of his visions, in which he sees himself running with the 'ol people'[16] while being massacred by the US Cavalry. Crow Horse, in his annoyance, blurts out that 'a man can wait a whole lifetime for a vision', yet Levoi is gifted with one as soon as he arrives. These gifts are seen as significant metaphors for the Law.

Levoi, however, does not appreciate the revelatory implications of his visions, seeing them instead as hallucinations. However, Grandpa is determined that Levoi will follow the Red Road and insists on situating him in his cosmological ancestry. Slowly, through revelatory experiences, Grandpa guides Levoi into the realization that he is a Minniconjou[17] Sioux and that his ancestor was Thunderheart, a Holy Man of the Great Sioux Nation, who guided the people during the time of the 1890 Massacre of Wounded Knee. By situating Levoi in his historical context, Grandpa is giving him a foundation, a pathway, a road map of his ancestral lands – what the Australian Aborigines would refer to as a Dreaming Track. Grandpa Reaches takes him back, like a Native American equivalent of a psychotherapist, to his childhood, through a ceremony and other experiences in which Levoi sees himself with his Indian father. He learns how this suppressed past is connected to the present situation, particularly his role as a *Minniconjou* who has become an FBI agent. In other words, opposites in Levoi's makeup are being balanced here – that is, the Indigenous and the white, the sacred and the secular. As Grandpa Reaches tells him of his connection to Thunderheart and that 'the same blood of Thunderheart runs through your heart like a buffalo', Levoi realizes what his role is: he must connect with the community, now in a state of crisis, in order to bring balance. By trusting the Red Road and 'feeling' the ancestral holy man Thunderheart, Levoi is able to find the strength to instinctively do what is right. This right way will also allow the community to show its support for him as the chosen leader. However, he is a leader along the lines that Deloria (1972) suggests – that is, he is not a messianic character in the Western model, but rather a messianic figure of change. At the end of the film, Levoi leaves to find himself. But before he leaves, he sets the community on the Red Road – not the Rights Road – which takes place through a declaration: in the final scene, Levoi declares: 'This land is not for sale.'

Rights and Responsibilities

[I]t's about the perpetuation of the American Dream.
(Coutelle speaking to Levoi in *Thunderheart*)

Coming full circle, this last part of the camp returns to the sacred feminine – White Buffalo Calf Woman and her human representatives: women. This section deals with the repression of the sacred feminine and its human counterpart. For it is by studying the role of women and their forms of political participation that the imbalance in the Law of Relationships is illuminated. *Thunderheart*, unfortunately, blatantly perpetuates this imbalance by negating the powerful role of women as the necessary 'other' for the balance of any law. By examining the feminine role – women's rights and responsibilities – I offer a new process of legal engagement: *a walking in a sacred manner*,[18] in which the feminine also *feels the blood of her ancestors running through her heart*. Taking my cue from Maggie Eagle Bear and returning to the 'source', I find both the Plains Indians and the Iroquois historical accounts have sidelined the feminine, casting it into a supportive role. In the case of the Plains Indians, it is the silencing of the tradition of the *Wiyan Wakon* or Holy Woman (St Pierre and Long Soldier (1995: 11).

Referencing another example, in the Iroquois, the same thing occurs with the elimination of the feminine in the 'messianic trinity' of the coming of the *Haudenosaunee* – the Great Law. Both have transformed the feminine and, in its place, given rise to a priestly caste. This is a transformation reminiscent of the Judeo-Christian influences on Roman law, in which the law is symbolically castrated, its sexual union of male and female becoming that neutered, priestly role with no need for the feminine. This, in turn, leads to the masculinization of voice of authority – Levoi, the avatar of *Thunderheart* – while the feminine is either killed off or marginalized. Think about how Maggie Eagle Bear is portrayed as merely collateral damage to the main action, while Grandma is just a harmless old woman. Maggie's character, as mentioned earlier, is based on the real-life character of Anna Mae Pictou Aquash, whose mutilated body was left to rot on the ranch of a Lakota Indian. The cutting off of her hands has deep psychological significance for this reading of *Thunderheart* and for women in the political arena of modernity. I, therefore, examine her death, and its representation in the film, in some detail.

Anna Mae's death is explored in relation to the motif of the *handless maiden*, referencing the work of Jungian analyst Clarissa Pinkola Estes (1995) on the Grimm Brothers' (1857) story 'The Girl Without Hands' (Estes 1995: 35). This is followed by an account of the Plains Indians' circumstances and the call by Tilda Long Soldier in her book *Walking in a Sacred Manner* to honour the *Wiyan Wakon* Holy Women and 'reach out' for what is cosmologically deemed their rightful place and power (St Pierre and Long Soldier 1995). The section concludes with a return to the *H'e Sapa* – the Black Hills – and the ongoing battle for the Land's rightful place in the Law.

To understand this sorry story, and the manner in which women need to 'reach out' to their repressed legal history, it is important to contextualize the film *Thunderheart* – a dramatized version of the Robert Redford documentary entitled *Incident at Oglala*. This documentary records the events that led to the imprisonment of Leonard Peltier, AIM's security chief. As presented in both the film and the documentary, the leadership of ARM/AIM provides a strong and healthy way in which a community may gain its confidence in its traditional ways. Both films insist that women were part of the leadership, becoming martyrs to the cause. Even a 'lost' child like Levoi was able to find his way home. The stated political aim in the film was to aid the threatened communities to recover from colonialism and to build a healthy confidence in the traditional values and ways (*Thunderheart*). At least, this is what one may perceive on a first reading of these records. A second reading, however, yields a very different story – one that turns on what is left out as much as what is included, on what is silenced rather than said. The murder of Maggie – itself based on the horrendous death and mutilation of Anna Mae Pictou Aquash – is a crucial element.

Anna Mae Pictou Aquash was a Canadian Mikmaq woman from Indian Brook, Nova Scotia, who had become part of the AIM leadership (Newhouse, Voyager and Beavon 2005: 215). During the summer of 1975 Aquash travelled with Leonard Peltier to organize security for the Oglala Lakota traditionalists. Both Anna Mae and Leonard were well known to the FBI. They had been called on by the traditionalists to help end the violence that had been unleashed and exercised by government-backed tribal leader Dick Wilson. Around the time of her killing, Wilson was in Washington negotiating the sale of one-eighth of the Lakota People's reservation for uranium mining. In the winter of 1976 Aquash's body was found on the ranch of a Lakota named Amoitte.

The body was taken to the Pine Ridge Public Health Service for an autopsy. For some unknown reason, Anna Mae was not identified by the local people or claimed by the AIM. Her hands were cut off and sent to Washington, DC, for fingerprint identification – an unnecessary (to say the least) and barbaric act. Her cause of death was deemed to be exposure; however, once the family members were notified, they called on the AIM to secure a second autopsy, in which it was revealed she had been shot in the head. The family was also dissatisfied with the fact that it had to prompt the AIM to take action. This lack of inactivity on the AIM's part was strange considering that Aquash had held such a prominent position. Anna Mae's family went to court to prove that the AIM leadership had, in fact, sanctioned her murder, under the pretext that she was a FBI inform-ant (Newhouse et al. 2005: 215). It took 27 years to indict the murderers, but not the leaders. The case has now become a focal point for Native American women within the political movement (2005: 215).

Anna Mae and her film version, Maggie, were not merely killed: they were murdered, execution style, assassinated with a shot in the back of the head. Moreover, Anna Mae had the added humiliation of having her hands cut off by the investigating coroner. What does the cutting off of hands mean? What does this mutilating signify to a legal reading of the text? If we begin with a psychological account of the motif of the cutting off of the hands based on the analysis of the work of Clarissa Pinkola Estes (1995: 406–8) and the Grimm Brothers' (1857) story, 'The Girl Without Hands', the following can be deduced.

'The Girl Without Hands', according to Estes (1995: 36), is a narrative that warns women about making poor bargains, finding themselves sacri-ficed by the father figure or the patrilineal society. When a woman excels, does well, shines her light in whatever manner – in her creativity, beauty, goodness or intellect – she attracts a predator – one that stems from the patriarchal society. He comes in search of what the woman has and will take her through a poor bargain. In the case of Maggie – or the real Anna Mae – she has aligned herself with the patrilineal authority of the AIM – or, if the accusations are correct, with the FBI. Whichever group she was aligned to, neither came to honour her discarded body. The suggestion is that the AIM ordered her execution and the FBI subsequently mutilated her as though to warn other women.

What can we salvage from such an atrocity? According to Estes, one lesson that can be learned is that such a mutilation and decline are about 'a heartfelt return to workable ancient values, more deeply held ideas' (Estes 1995: 406). Estes points out that:

> This motif of cutting as initiation is central to our story. If, in our modern societies, the hands of the ego must be sundered in order to regain our wild office, our feminine senses, then go they must in order to take us away from all seductions of meaningless things within our reach, whatever it is that we can hold on to in order not to grow. If it is so that the hands must go for a while, then so be it.

Let them go. The father wields the silver cutting tool, and though he has a sense of terrible regret, he holds more dear his own life and that of the psyche all around. If we understand the father as an organizing principle, of ruler of the external or worldly psyche, then we can see that a woman's overt self, her mundane, ruling ego-self, does not want to die . . . In aboriginal rites worldwide, the idea is definitely to confuse the ordinary so the mystical can be easily introduced to the initiate.

(1995: 406–7)

Anna Mae epitomized this 'overt self' running with the pack as she was chased across the various counties by the authorities. She was part of the struggle, but it was a struggle for a politically motivated rights discourse, itself based on the dominant culture's indicators of leadership. Women such as Anna Mae fit the dominant culture's criterion as a role model for leadership – that is, as independent, competitive and in emotional control (Estes 1995: 37). These criteria are never seen as wilful or individualistic, but always as 'strong', by Western cultural standards.

In her era, women like Anna Mae were said to be 'processed' by the leadership. Their acceptance was based on their youth and ability to challenge the racist ways of the dominant culture by being media savvy, like Anna. However, as Taiaiake Alfred (1999) contends, such individualistic tendencies move a person away from the community rather than it embracing them. Anna Mae's family accuses the leadership of AIM of using these women and then 'throwing them away' – or, even worse, causing them to end up with a bullet in the back of their heads. In death, Anna Mae is reincorporated into her tribe and has been refashioned as a focal point for re-examining their political organizations and their male domination.

Taiaiake Alfred (1999: 42) reiterates *a Rotinohshonni* teaching about leadership, which is reminiscent of the deeds of White Buffalo Calf Woman: '[A]t the time of grieving a nation is made whole by a leader who reconnects its members with the past and the ancient way of peace, power, and righteousness.'

What, therefore, can be done – and what is being done? Since the 1980s, Lakota Elder Professor Beatrice Medicine[19] has been advocating that women reshape public policy:

Beatrice Medicine is an honoured Native American anthropologist whose research has contested the masculinist Eurocentric research findings that shape public policy in a wide spectrum of fields from education through social services through to governance. In this piece, she sets out the need for Native women to 'begin formulating constructs and tentative hypotheses based upon our own unique experiences' and to locate these within 'the superordinate society's parameters and influences [in order to] focus upon the reactions of females of all tribes to the common experiences of oppression in US society.' Her goal is to have gendered cultural-specific accounts of life experience that can inform public policy and cultural interpretations.

(Medicine 1988: 86–92)

Following in Beatrice Medicine's footsteps, Barbara Mann, a Seneca,[20] challenges the Iroquoian historians in her book *Iroquoian Women: The Gantowisas* (2000) and her paper 'The Beloved Daughters of Jingosaseh' (cited in Johansen 1995). In these works, she sets out to 'resurrect' Jingosaseh from her historical 'murder' by historians and 'breathe life' back into her historical role within Iroquois feminine history. She posits that male historians have deliberately eliminated Jingosaseh, whose participation was essential if the Great Law of Peace was to be accepted by the people. There is no doubt that a female must have been a powerful player for, under *Haudenosaunee* (The Great Law), 'clan mothers choose candidates (who are male) as chiefs. The women also maintain ownership of the land and homes and exercise a veto power over any council action that may result in war' (McGary, n.d.).

Clan mothers in the Iroquois Confederacy still hold power, but one must question why intellectuals do not reference them as powerful sources of knowledge. The answer, Mann argues, is that:

While a high degree of gender equity existed in Iroquois law, sex roles often were (and remain) very carefully defined, right down to the version of history passed down by people of either sex. Men, the vast majority of anthropological informants, tended to play up the role of Deganawidah and Hiawatha, which was written into history. Women, who would have described the role of Jingosaseh, were usually not consulted.

(Johansen 1995: n.p.)

According to Mann: '[I]t is only after the Peacemaker agrees to her terms that she throws her considerable political weight behind him ... She was, in short, invaluable as an ally, invincible as a foe. To succeed, the Peacemaker needed her' (Johansen 1995: 62–63). 'Jingosaseh is recalled by the Keepers as a co-founder of the League, alongside Deganawidah and

Hiawatha,' writes Mann. 'Her name has been obliterated from the white record because her story was a woman's story and nineteenth-century male ethnographers simply failed to ask women whose story hers was, about the history of the League' (Johansen 1995: 62–63).

It is evident from today's political scene, and that played out in *Thunderheart*, that Indigenous males also believe such power is either historically dead or has moved into the realm of the rhetorically empty. It is not that I am arguing that women should have their faces plastered all over the media, but rather that the men should be referencing the women in their speeches and the community decision-making process. By allowing oppressive governments to impose their institutional suppression of the voice of authority of women in the structure of governance bodies, they are, in fact, becoming compradors.

However, let me now return to the Oglala and what perhaps can be seen as a conscious 'reaching out' to the legal status of women. Tilda Long Soldier, an Oglala Lakota, takes up Professor Beatrice Medicine's challenge to make women the authoritative voices about their history. They set out to rectify the gross ignorance and appropriation by the New Age movement of the role of the Plains Indian Holy Woman. Long Soldier collected the oral history of the Medicine Women of the Plains Indians – that is, the healers, dreamers and pipe carriers – and gave them a voice in the book *Walking in the Sacred Manner* (St Pierre and Long Soldier 1995). This is a voice, Long Soldier argues, that has been appropriated by the Medicine Men – whom Fools Crow laments have politicized their holy role. By collecting the oral histories, Long Soldier saw her role as reminding women that in 'their hearts . . . and in the subconscious landscape of their dreams, the spirits still live and communicate with the people' (1995: 11). By re-sacralizing the role of the *Wiyan Wakon* Holy Woman, Long Soldier is calling for Indian women to 'reach out' to their ancestors and honour the roles they have put in place for them in their legal system (1995: 11). Such roles, however, require a type of endurance rather than the 'flash' fame of the political dualistic account with the oppressor.

In *Thunderheart*, Maggie Eagle Bear begs Levoi to come to that same understanding. Media savvy and educated, she has learnt that the white law is impotent when it comes to protecting the sacred Land and the traditions of Native Americans. She implores Levoi to go to the source – which on one level is Red Deer Table, the source of the polluted river and ultimately the civil disruption and murders on the reservation. More importantly, on another level, it is the source of Levoi's visions of his ancestors, which brings him in touch with his own inner voice of authority and law.

Maggie, therefore, becomes the signpost to the source and keeps pointing to the polluting of the river and maintaining that something must be done. Even the old Grandma references the importance of finding the source of the poisoning of the river rather than finding the murderer. However, Levoi cannot let go of his white law and debates with Maggie the naivety of not believing in the ability of the white man's law to bring justice for the Native Americans.

Maggie then 'makes a poor bargain', due to Levoi's pleading with her to help him with the evidence – in other words, to join the white man's law. The result of joining that law is a bullet in the back of the head. Levoi, however, gains from her sacrifice and comes to realize she was right after discovering her discarded body. The price of following the white law is not only the death of Maggie, but also that of the murderer, who had been beaten into submission to comply with Coutelle's breach of his own law. In the end, Coutelle is protected by his law and a 'whitewash' (as Crow Horse puts it) has occurred. Levoi learns that Maggie was right and then turns to her media informants to try to get the truth of the story out to the public. In other words, even in death Maggie still helps him.

The weakness in *Thunderheart* lies in the fact that Levoi never admits that he led Maggie into a poor bargain and caused her death. It was a price she was willing to pay for the protection of the source, but not for the white man's legal process. Maggie, just like the other traditionalists, was trying to show him a different approach to a legal case. In other words, he was being asked to look at the bigger picture, the historical picture of the cyclical Wounded Knee encounters with the US Cavalry. Furthermore, he was being asked to take what I call an Indigenous legal approach to the murder case. It is important to look beyond the victim and perpetrator to the Land and the context – present, past and future, seen and unseen – to provide information about why a murder has occurred. Instead, Levoi hangs on for dear life to the Western law and in the process Maggie is sacrificed. It is Maggie who tells him that she is going to the source and he must follow. In other words, she has to lead him at the price of her own life. A poor bargain has once again been struck and her sacrifice goes unnoticed, other than as 'sorrowful' collateral damage.

This section, therefore, is about the real trauma of the law in *Thunderheart*. The trauma is embodied in the silencing of the voice of the feminine as the signpost to the source – being the Land, the *H'e Sapa*, better known as the gold-rich Black Hills of South Dakota. This area has been the 'warring fields' of white/Indian treaty negotiation and subsequent breaches. These resources have also been exploited by Indians themselves, in the form of Wilson and his GOONs. His arguments are depicted in Coutelle's attitude to the Oglala, a people who have to be dragged into the twenty-first century. It has been argued emphatically throughout the Indigenous political landscape that economic development is our only hope (Pearson 2003). Indigenous people such as Wilson would have seen themselves as helping their 'ignorant' brothers who needed to be taken in hand with such heavy-handed tactics as those used by the GOONs. By placing economic development before the protection of the Land, they are looking at what is best for them. They are looking to their rights rather than to their responsibilities to future generations. Furthermore, they are blocking off the voice of their ancestors, who might be trying to help them see a way of living rather than surviving.

The all-pervasive white law makes it hard for a young woman to make a 'good bargain', as she is constantly being told her economic status and that of her people are the indicators of her success. There is no looking back to see that her ancestors have survived 700 years of invasion in the Americas and are still standing strong in their Law – a Law that is not about 'How much can I gain?' but about 'How much can I give?'

The Living Dead

At this juncture, I will return to Anna Mae's tribal ancestor, nineteenth-century Mikmaq Quill worker Christianne Morris. Even though not directly connected by blood, Christianne is still born of the same land and if Ruth Whitehead's assumptions are correct, Christianne was buried not far from where Anna Mae was born in the area of the old Shubenacadie Reserve.[21] Christianne and her female contemporaries who were master craftswomen and quill workers were able to make a living from their traditional skills and also engage in the dominant culture with more ease than other women in their society (Whitehead 1982). What I found so fascinating about this woman's life was that she was able to sustain her family and appeared to move with ease among the various strata of society. The legacy of this craftsmanship and ability to relate to the dominant culture was that her works and her image, as well as references to her in newspapers and documents, have survived. At the beginning of the millennium, however, Christianne's life seemed only to be documented by Ruth Whitehead (1977) as part of a collection of stories about quill workers of the period. Ruth was also instrumental in collecting her work and having it displayed and preserved in the Nova Scotia Museum.

Newhouse et al. (2005: 215) present a curious dichotomy regarding how these women were seen. This book was written as a celebration of the achievements of American Indians. It includes the life of Anna Mae as a justice issue, while under the maritime 'furniture' section (Cook 2005:

126), we have Christianne featured in her full glory, with both her image and the magnificent craftsmanship of her cradle; ironically, however, neither the cradle nor her image bears her name. The book includes an account of her achievements, but it is Whitehead's account – the one that has been replicated through all accounts referencing Christianne. No relative has been located and there is no apparent Mikmaq interest in claiming her or wanting to learn more about her. Why is this accomplished woman only remembered by an archivist? Why is it only the female Mikmaq portrayed as a victim who is remembered?

What is this obsession with victim – even when the authors are trying to reverse this 'hidden' focus? As Newhouse and colleagues assert in their introduction: 'It is our hope this book will add a new dimension to the picture of Aboriginal peoples, one that shows them to be industrious, meritorious and accomplished.' (2005: xi) Yet Christianne remains just an unnamed photo and an archivist's account of her life and accomplishments – although when I have spoken to Mikmaq, they all say, 'Well, of course, she has relatives!' However, no one steps forward with any clear lineage, only allusions to lineage.

Why do we forget women such as Christianne, who have been able to maintain their cultural authenticity? This is perhaps equally the case in Australia and other invaded lands. Or are they written off as Indian princesses, with the white man allowing only one or two princesses to get through? Why do we not value these women – why are their cultural artefacts and even their lives not worth examining for the lessons they provide? I believe Christianne has much to teach her descendants about how to achieve equal standing for her cultural difference and how to maintain what is valuable to an individual and to future generations. Christianne achieved a peaceful coexistence with her times. I am sure she would have preferred it to be otherwise; however, like the other women of her era and culture, she had to do the best she could to survive it.

Why, then, is it only the tragic, the abused and downtrodden who fill our minds? This may appear to contradict the words of such cultural activist as Greg Cajete (1994), who asserts:

> We hope that sooner rather than later Western society will realize that Native people are not simply vestiges of the past and sources of interesting and even beautiful ideas, but rather they are very much alive today, and their economic and political issues must be addressed on their own terms.

Unfortunately, I feel that the only 'beautiful ideas' are male caricatures of the noble savage – there no female noble savages come to mind beyond Pocahontas. Sadly, the death of Anna Mae aligns with that of Sitting Bull. Both died around the same time of the year – mid-December – and in a similar manner – killed by their own people with a bullet to the head. Where are the stories of all those females who died in the 'vestiges of the past'?

This brings me back to the words of Gunn Allen (1992), who maintains that men are about death and women about continuity.

Conclusion

> I see no seat for the eagles. We forget and we consider ourselves superior,
> but we are after all a mere part of the creation.
>
> (Lyons, 1985: 21)

I began by discussing cosmology, using that as a point of entry to the reality of the Lakota in order to make sense of the events in their lives. I located the particular site of Wounded Knee as a portal for some recurring imbalance attributed to a lack of rest by the departed. The return of an ancestor in the form of a messianic figure was a catalyst for reshaping the events of the modernity, demonstrating the abuse by those putative adherents to the Law of the Red Road.

Thunderheart's narrative and the documentary on which the film is based remind viewers that it is the death and abuse of women that disturb the sacred balance of the Red Road. By bringing attention to the events of Wounded Knee, the writer Fusco and the Holy Man Fools Crow, we have also brought attention to the murder of Anna Mae. She is a woman who is nearing martyr status – but not, as turns out, for the cause of treaty rights and self-determination; rather, she is revered for having revealed the AIM's abuses. So she is martyred by her own people. The very acronym AIM is an objective – strategic rather than sacred and certainly not about finding a path to blend the two laws into a relationship. Instead, they would usurp one or another at any price, including a human life as collateral damage – a particularly ugly outcome of a political battle.

This rebalancing is still in the making and we will have to be careful that women do not become the types about which Alfred (1999) warns. The pursuit of justice is once again a Western concept aligned with human rights. It is individualistic and abstracted, failing to examine just why we need justice if there is a just system. This is a Red Road issue, not a Western problem. These women should be pursuing the Red Road for the solution. Leadership, or good governance, is about reconnecting with that which gives a community a sense of hope. Following the Red Road rather than the Rights Road reconnects the people with White Buffalo Calf Woman and the cosmology and so once again sacralizes their reason for being – a being judged not on winning or losing, but rather on balance and hope.

CHAPTER 9

The camp from the sparkling waters of the Pacific: *Whale Rider*

And so we leave the camp of the Great Plains and move to the sway of the island songs of the Māori of the Land of the Long White Cloud. The story of the Māori resonates throughout the Pacific, through the epic ventures of the outriggers that sailed up and down the great Pacific currents as though riding the highways of the American Midwest. There is little comprehension in the West of the 'traffic' that navigated the Pacific long before the arrival on the horizon of the European ships. Children mastered basic navigation skills by the age of five, for it took a lifetime to acquire a knowledge of the lore of the sea – the great Pacific Ocean.

It was only while standing in a paddock on the farm of the Māori Queen's Capital of the Royal *Waka* that I began to comprehend how the sky can become a very readable dome, for there are no buildings to block it out. While listening to an experienced sailor of the high seas describe the various star constellations, the sky changed for me from being a mass of stars into a distinctive map of identifiable points of direction. Suddenly, it all appeared so easy to comprehend. I understood how familiarity with this heaven-inspired navigational map would create a certainty of direction.

But what of the creatures that live below the great ocean? How was the meeting of the king of the ocean, the mighty whale, understood in Māori navigational stories? The following examination of *Whale Rider* brought that relationship into strong relief and led me to the place of the people of Paikea. Once again, this is a lived experience.

The Return of the Female Legend

The critically acclaimed feature film *Whale Rider* made a major impact on the world in 2005. *Whale Rider* is 'Māori business'. Central to that 'business' and the film's narrative is the constitution of authority and the jurisprudence that legitimates that authority. Furthermore, the narrative not only engages jurisprudence; it references Māori cosmology, particularly that of the Ngati Konohi. To come into the Māori world, according to Witi Ihimaera (1987), the author of the original narrative *Whale Rider*, one must first enter the Māori cosmology, otherwise, knowledge of these people is purely superficial. This is because, for the Māori, an *iwi*'s[1] (tribe's) cosmological Creation stories and events define the principles, ideals, values and philosophies that inform the legal regime (Ministry of Justice 2001). Controlling the whole Māori legal regime is therefore a value-based system – a set of evolving norms rather than rigid rules, a fluid and dynamic law born out of the intimate knowledge of the land. In Ihimaera's story of a young girl's unprecedented assumption of constitutional tribal authority, *Whale Rider* instantiates those norms, this law and its process of existence (Ministry of Justice 2001).

Thus the legal beauty of this piece of legal fiction is that it complements 'drier' legal forms of knowledge – *matauranga*. An example of this drier form of knowing is *He Hinatore ki te Ao Māori: A Glimpse into the Māori World* (Ministry of Justice 2001). Developed by the New Zealand Justice Department to explain the cosmology and legal system of the Māori, this text will be used as a reference point for the legal concepts articulated in this jurisprudential reading of *Whale Rider*. As I have stated in other camps, this is only one person's reading. A lived experience of the Māori cosmology is the only way of truly knowing and understanding it.

I use the concepts developed in *He Hinatore ki te Ao Māori* to address three fundamental elements and characters of *Whale Rider* in this camp. First, I examine in depth the cosmology and its connection to genealogy. Genealogy is vital to Māori cosmology because it grants not only land title – a legal issue – but tells people why and how they are connected to each other through their ancestral line, which relates back to one of the original *kawai tipuna*.[2] *Whale Rider* references this cosmology directly and genealogy is, of course, one of its central concerns.

Second, I address the legal system of the Māori: 'The *mana* and *tapu* of the *kawai tipuna* affect and pervade all activities associated with everyday life' (Ministry of Justice 2001). That system is shaped into a double helix of relationships between the energy called *mana*, which flows through all of creation, and its regulatory 'other', known as *tapu*. *Tapu* is a version of law, which takes as its pivot the determination of what is sacred and thereby is susceptible to management as a sacred resource, be it physical, intellectual or spiritual. The problem with *tapu* is that it can become a means solely of prohibition rather than facilitation. *Whale Rider* directly addresses the problematic nature of *tapu* because it is, of course, *tapu* for a woman to speak on the *marae*, let alone exercise constitutional authority. So the story of the young girl, Pai, is a story of the breach of *tapu*, as much as one of the need for the dynamism of change within a culture over time. The third argument examined here concerns the cosmological place of the individual in relation to his or her rights and responsibilities. Who is to lead? Who is to follow? These are the questions of authority posed by *Whale Rider* in its dramatization of a society undergoing a constitutional crisis. Before I turn to my reading of the film, I will contextualize it in terms of Māori cosmology and the laws that regulate it, as I understand them.

Māori Cosmology

The fundamental jurisprudence elements I envisage in the Māori cosmology are best imagined through the concentric circle. The outer circle is the all-encompassing circle of the cosmology, which permeates through all the circles, holding them together, binding them into a genealogical network. The second circle is the system of law based on the *mana–tapu* relationship, regulating resources through the forces and spirit. In the centre are individuals, with the associated rights and responsibilities over their personal and their *iwi*'s intellectual property.

To enter the *te Ao Māori*, I begin with the outer circle, which follows through to the individual. The original cosmology is long and complex and only those vested with the knowledge of nuances can convey the essential meaning. However, I would recommend either reading or listening to the account, as this is a complex and beautiful experience. I spent many hours in the Hamilton Library poring over this long and engaging cosmological narrative.

Briefly, the Māori world came into being through the original union of the Ranginui (Sky Father) and Papatuanuku (Earth Mother), figures who are more popularly known as Rangi and Papa (Buck 1950: 15). Rangi represents energy while Papa represents matter. This binding did not allow for Creation to come into being, but it did give rise to children, the *kawai tipuna* (Creator Beings). So the children of Rangi and Papa set about separating them so that Creation, including humans – *te Ao Māori* – could come into being. It was Tane Mahuta who succeeded in carrying out this process and so brought the earth and sky into relationship and Creation into being. I will now turn to the concepts and principles that become evident as one spends time with this cosmological story, which gives guidance to the Māori culture through time and distance. The *He Hinatore ki te Ao Māori* gives a concise description of the concepts and principles, more like Western legal norms.

For the Māori, relationships are first and foremost genealogical – that is, the identification of their *whakapapa* (genealogy) is the 'glue that binds Māori'. As *He Hinatore ki te Ao Māori* puts it:

> [A]ncestral ties bind the people and the (environment). Just as land entitlements, personal identity, and executive function arose from ancestral devolution, so also it is by ancestry that Māori relate to the natural world.[3]

This relationship situates both the individual and the group – specifically, how they find themselves in the cosmos, but also how they respect that which is around them through regard for the *tapu* or sacredness of 'others':

> Animate and inanimate objects have a direct genealogical link with the *kawai tipuna*. The *tapu* of humans, animate and inanimate objects is about the relationship between the physical and spiritual realm. Individuals and groups have responsibilities and obligations to abide by the norms of behaviour and practices established by the *tipuna*. *Tapu* acted as a protective mechanism for both people and natural resources. Making something or someone *tapu* could either protect the environment against interference from people or protect people from possible dangers.[4]

This situating of people within the cosmology brings forth a relationship with the rest of the cosmos in a regulatory manner – what I call the law of the regulatory-intellectual property regime, or the system of law of *mana/tapu*. According to the text, *tapu* is considered a 'supernatural condition' of protection for either the human or the environment. I like this 'equal standing' before the law of both 'land' and human. It is a concept that the governments of both Australia and New Zealand would do well to incorporate into their environmental laws.

The energy that flows through all things is *mana*. Its regulation depends on its status as *tapu* and that set of *tapu* may be analogized to modern intellectual property law. This is because intellectual property regulates and constrains the use and abuse of ideas, images, creations and so on, through patents and copyright. It functions as a set of *tapu*, controlling and ordering the *mana* of the intellect. This is precisely what the Māori have been doing for thousands of years. Indeed, one could go so far as to say that the Māori were the first intellectual property lawyers.

Finally, it is a system of law that I call Rights and Responsibilities. This law regulates the Māori personality in the spatial temporal world. As *He Hinatore ki te Ao Māori* says:

> It was the major cohesive force in Māori life because every person was regarded as *tapu* or sacred. Each life was a sacred gift, which linked a person to the ancestors, and hence the wider tribal network. The individual therefore has a sense of personal security and self-esteem, a sense of belonging. The behavioral guidelines of the ancestors were monitored by the living relatives, and the wishes of an individual were constantly balanced against the greater *mana* and concerns of the groups.
>
> (Ministry of Justice 2001: 187)[5]

Trauma of Law

I now turn to a trauma – the trauma of Māori law and, behind it, Māori cosmology. Those traumas manifest themselves in an imbalance in the cosmic and legal relationship between male and female. Traditional Māori cosmology and jurisprudence would see these two 'energies' – the masculine and the feminine – as being in harmony. It is this harmony that has been disturbed, although the disturbance differs according to gender. I suggest that, under modernity, the Māori female retains her place, while the male has lost his. This is because, in my opinion, Māori masculinity, even more so than Māori femininity, has suffered a brutal and far-reaching blow from invasion and the subsequent colonization process, leading not so much to emasculation as a dysfunctional misogynist's world-view.

So Māori men have been colonized internally as well as externally – with disastrous consequences. The film *Once Were Warriors* depicts how, due to high levels of unemployment and illness and a sense of powerlessness, some Māori males become dysfunctional and psychically abusive towards women. In turn, this provides the illusion of control in a world that basically has no wish to understand their law or validate its worth. This leads the man to be more economically and socially dependent on the woman he abuses, which aggravates the cycle of resentment and abuse. All this, of course, happens in order to prove his empty authority. The Māori male, under modernity, is therefore doubly deprived: he cannot assert either his own law or his right to his own epistemological reality. This double deprivation has a long history and can be traced back to the early days of world colonization.

If I turn back to the previous camp and the mention of the Iroquois, over 250 years ago the Iroquois clearly saw how their missionary-trained youth, educated in the Western sciences, proved to be not only useless in their own environment, but incapable of offering good counsel. This experience drove home the point that, in order to make 'real men' of their youth – that is, men with a positive sense of Native American identity – they needed to train them within their own jurisprudential domain.

> But you, who are wise, must know that different
> Nations have different Conceptions of things and
> You will therefore not take it amiss, if our Ideas of
> This kind of Education happen not to be the same as
> Yours. We have had some Experience of it.
> Several of our young People were formerly brought
> Up at the Colleges of the Northern Provinces:
> They were instructed in all your Sciences; but, when
> They came back to us, they were bad Runners,
> Ignorant of every means of living in the woods . . .
> Neither fit for Hunters, Warriors, nor Counsellors,
> They were totally good for nothing.
> We are, however, not the less oblig'd by your kind
> Offer, tho' we decline accepting it; and, to show
> Our grateful Sense of it, if the Gentlemen of
> Virginia will send us a Dozen of their Sons, we will
> Take Care of their Education instruct them in all
> We know, and make Men of them.[6]

I cite the experience of the Iroquois because it is pertinent to that of the Māori. Both cultures link gender, identity and a sense of self, as well as the communal whole, to the juridical issue of jurisdiction. In short, as I have argued elsewhere (Morris 1997), Indigenous people need a legal space of their own, a space that can only be secured by Indigenous law. This is precisely the problem addressed by *Whale Rider*: the necessity for an Indigenous space secured by Indigenous jurisprudence. In so doing, *Whale Rider* takes seriously the questions posed by Kanien'kehaka (Mohawk) philosopher and activist Taiaiake Alfred (1999: xiv): 'Why do we indigen-ous people so often look away from our own wisdom and let other people answer the basic questions for us?' What Taiaiake Alfred asks about here, and *Whale Rider* affirms, is the need to turn to past wisdom of Indigenous jurisprudence instead of entering debates – standard in (especially) American critical race theory – relating to the failings of the Western justice system. The answer lies in understanding Indigenous jurisprudence – not just because it informs Indigenous legal decision making, but because it underpins and constitutes Indigenous society's reality, values and principles.

To contextualize this return to Indigenous wisdom and jurisprudence, I turn to the theory and praxis of Māori intellectual and activist Aroha Yates-Smith.[7] Yates-Smith is different from most theorists in that she actually has *walked the talk* (and, conversely, talks the walk) – that is, she theorizes activism, leading the way for the repatriation of the effigies of the *atua wahine* (female ancestral beings) of her culture (Yates-Smith 2003). She has begun the task of repatriating to New Zealand from overseas museums many effigies and supervised their replacement on the land from which they were originally stolen. One of the powerful effects of this act of 'return to country',[8] as Australian Aborigines would say, is the way in which these effigies impact on land title. They are pointers – indeed, compass guides – to custodianship of land and the realm of ancestral beings. Also, they are images of the female, reminding both men and women that their female ancestors were and are portals of power, the keepers of cosmological balance – *whare tangata*.[9]

Yates-Smith argues that any decolonizing gesture – be it post-colonial theorizing or political renegotiation of treaties – must be carried out in tandem with these sorts of activity, which reclaim a jurisdictional and jurisprudential 'home'. The focus for the activist-theorist should be on their own historical and tribal background[10] – or, as the Māori put it in relation to Western education: 'People who have been taught on their own *marae* among their own people will stand much more comfortably among their own people than someone who has borrowed from outside and then tried to relate it back to their home situation' (Ministry of Justice 2001). The call here is not to reject a Western education, but to be conscious of the fact that what you learn must be acceptable to the intellectual tradition of your own culture.

The film *Whale Rider* is part of this process of return to the source, looking back to Māori cosmology as a way of steering the youth into the future. It argues for a gentle realignment of the male and female as 'joint', rather than a radical restructuring of the female, usurping the male role as chief. The narrative calls at all times for evolution rather than revolution, for incremental changes, moving forward surely but cautiously and always in accord with the ancestral beings as they reveal themselves. The Māori have a word for this notion of gradual change: *humarie* – kindness and humility.[11] The concept of *humarie* is one of the hallmarks of a leader in Māori jurisprudence. Matiu Dickson,[12] who is of Ngaiterangi descent, expands the concept in terms of attributes for a chief:

> The food of the chief – i.e. talking (debate);
> The sign of chieftain – i.e. humility and caring;
> The work of the chief is to weave people together (and give them
> strength).

I explore this concept, along with the notion of leadership, as represented in the three protagonists of *Whale Rider*: Koro, Porourangi and Pai.

Koro – out of the Past: Cosmology as a Sacred Contract

As *Rangatira* (leader), Koro is positioned as the voice of authority. That voice has its rights through *whakapapa* (genealogy). The *Rangatira*, or leader, gains his *mana* of leadership through his genealogy. However, this inherited leadership is not always a given, because a leader must continue to demonstrate that he is favoured by the *kawai tipuna* through his leadership skills – that is, keeping the peace and conducting rituals commemorating the *kawai tipuna* and its founding story (Ministry of Justice 2001).

To appreciate the cosmological link between the *Rangatira* and the *kawai tipuna*, I will elaborate on the meaning of this link and how it is played out in the film. That link is made explicit in the film's prologue, recounting the mythological migration story of Koro's ancestors. This prologue tells the story of Witi Ihimaera's (1987) own clan and of the revered Ancestor, Paikea the Whale Rider, and his coming with his *whanau* (clan), the Ngati Konohi, to Aotearoa from the ancestral lands of *Hawaiki*.[13] Paikea was saved by the bull whale when his *waka* (canoe) was overturned. By saving Paikea and bringing him to shore, the whale takes on the function, and acts as an agent, of the Law, the *Kaitiaki*.[14] That Law, through its agent the whale, will deem when and where the Ngati Konohi, a sub-clan of the tribe Ngati Porou, is to live in Aotearoa.

Moreover, the whale represents a new law that can and must be established for the new environment. This is a common theme in global Indigenous jurisprudence, as mentioned in the previous camp in relation to the Hopi and the Masaw.[15] The new land, or renewed environment, is not just settled on, but its spirit is addressed as 'titleholder' of the new land. It is a place with a full Law – a mature Law. In other words, you just can't arrive and plant your flag and start drawing up maps as the white invaders did.

Instead, on arrival at the 'given' land, the Māori would set up a *waananga* (house of learning),[16] or a type of research station, to consider the lay of the land and the laws that may be perceived through the patterns found in the landscape of the place before the arriving *iwi* moved inland.[17] Prior to settlement, a sacred contract would thus be negotiated between the Māori, through reading the signs, and the Law in the landscape. The land was received, not taken, and based on a sacred contract rather than 'a discovery' on behalf of a sovereign. The use of land is conditional on keeping the sacred bond, not based on the might of the gun. This bond involves constant communication with Nature, as mentioned previously. In other words, land is cultivated for the preservation of the contract rather than just for material gain.[18] The punishment for a breach of contract with Nature may be 'a long time coming', but eventually Nature will reclaim what is hers through natural disasters, thereby instigating a call for a new cosmology and a new contract to be drawn up.

Therefore, land and settlement are not a human-imposed choice of discovery, accomplished by raising a flag to celebrate sovereignty. Rather, settlement is an intervention that actualizes the Law of the Land – and, in *Whale Rider*, the saving by and depositing of Paikea and the Ngati Konohi at Whangara. The sacred contract of land use requires them to continue the tradition and associated ritual to remind the people to follow the Law of the Land as a way of living. Once again, this is Māori wisdom working with the environment, rather than trying to box it into serving human-kind's idea of the greater good. After all, you can't control an earthquake or a volcano – or, indeed, the workings of Mother Nature and her Laws.

The *Rangatira*[19]

In the film, it soon becomes evident that the ritual and tradition have become like a 'beached whale', unable to swim in the sea of modernity. A crisis of leadership foregrounds this unspoken trauma. The present *Rangatira*, Koro, can no longer ride tradition, as he – like tradition – has become beached, an old whale no longer able to swim, let alone lead his people. He is desperate for his son to take on the role, as the heir to his leadership. But Porourangi prefers to sail the seas of commercialism and has gone out into the world to sell his tradition as a successful sculptor in Europe. This flight of the son has been precipitated by the father's relentless force and his rigid focus on tradition. Rather than combining the human with tradition and the times in which they live, the chief has enforced a blind obedience to tradition, strictly adhering to the letter of its law. In short, he lacks *humarie*, the spirit of accommodation. No wonder, then, that the representative of that spirit – his son – leaves: he is forbidden by his father, as Aboriginal Senior Law Man Bill Neidjie (1989) might say, to 'feel' the Law.

Thus tradition has become static, anthropologized into impotency, all under the guise of a patrilineal genealogy. But this guise is just that: a mask or false appearance, giving the illusion of phallic power, disguising how disorientated the leadership has become. On the one hand, it is large and looming like a beached whale, while, on the other, it is impotent of authority. Thus *Whale Rider* presents us with a critique of patriarchy, which in some respects is the opposite of Western feminism: instead of too *much* testosterone, there is too little. It is this lack of masculine authority that is disturbing the cosmos and plunging the Māori into crisis.

Koro, however, is not completely impervious to his sense of dislocation. While he does not actually learn from it, he does lament his empty leadership, which has become imbalanced and so allowed breaches of the custodial ethic by his own people:

> 'Listen how empty our sea has become.' Koro Apirana's voice dropped and, when he resumed his *korero*, his words were steeped with sadness and regret. 'But we have not always kept our pact with *tangaroa*, and in these days of commercialism it is not always easy to resist temptation. So it was when I was your age. So it is now. There are too many people with snorkelling gear, and too many commercial fishermen with licences. We have to place *rahui* on our fishing beds, boys, otherwise it will be just like the whales.'
> (*Whale Rider*)

He knows he has become a kind of impotent Fisher King, turning his world into a wasteland of *upoko maro* (stubbornness). But instead of embracing change, he clings to the tradition he knows. His arrogance continues even after Pai demonstrates that she is the rightful leader. It is Pai, after all, who finds the *tapu* whale's tooth, the symbol of leadership, after it is thrown into the sea in the hope that a new male heir will emerge from another family by bringing it back. Scenes like this make the point that it is Koro's maleness, and not the overall culture, that is being threatened. This personal crisis is reiterated and reinforced throughout the film by the seemingly idle threats from his wife to leave him. 'Just give me the word and we can get a divorce,' is what Nanny Flowers says and the look on Koro's face tells it all: his reality will fall to pieces if she leaves. This scene represents the power of the feminine in Māori culture and the emptiness that pervades the home and the leadership if the feminine is not present. In other words, the *Ranginui* and *Papatuanuku* relationship becomes null and void. This is precisely the kind of relationship that Aroha Yates-Smith (2003) and other Māori women of authority seek to restore and rescue from colonial domination. By supporting Pai, Nanny Flowers shows Koro that he cannot ignore the rightful place of the feminine in their cosmology, be it the overarching cosmology of the Māori generally or spatial temporal of the *Ngati Kanohi* specifically. Koro acts as an individual, making all the decisions without consultation. So he ignores the group, particularly the Elders, whom it is customary to consult in Māori decision making. There is no sense that a group of males, let alone older women, is being consulted to 'consider' the situation. In other words, Koro has forgotten that he is a 'figurehead' of the group leadership, its public representative. Instead, he has taken on the colonized construct of the 'Native Leader'. In the film, Koro only appears to dictate to, rather than dialogue with, the community.

Moreover, Koro appears to have forgotten that the inner voice must be heard – an inner voice that speaks of the law through *tapu*. In the film, it is the song of the whale that validates the lawful leader and it is only Pai who can hear the whale. As Neidjie (1989) says, the Law is a *feeling*, a sense of 'the sensibility' of the world around us, a sense that points to the urgency in maintaining a sacred site. So Koro's leadership lacks both inner and outer voice. He heeds neither the voice of the community – the elders and his wife – nor his inner voice and the strictures of *tapu*.

The effect of this metaphoric deafness is striking and the result is a people, on the one hand, who are trying hard to preserve a way of life, and invest it with meaning, while, on the other, whose young people are caught up in a meaningless world that has no place for them. In other words, neither group can cope with change. So the film recycles *Once Were Warriors* types, especially in the 'pot-smoking' second son of Koro, who spends most of his time lounging around being doted on by his girlfriend. The converse of this figure of sloth is that of illegal hyperactivity, as exemplified in the father of the boy whom Koro thinks may be a leader. These characters augur badly for the next generation of leadership – and indeed call into question Koro's leadership, suggesting his voice of authority as *Rangatira* has been compromised and the genealogical link with the Ancestral Being has been severed.

Porourangi: Portrait of the Artist as a Young Māori

Porourangi, the sacred heir to the leadership of the *iwi*, is an heir in exile, dislodged not only by the personal trauma of losing his wife in childbirth as well as the son who was Pai's twin, but also by the domineering approach his father has taken towards tradition. His name is of import-ance, according to Matiu Dickson.[20] Porourangi is the progenitor of Ngati Pouro, and therefore the name signifies a role that Porourangi is neither capable of filling nor wishes to fill. Instead, Porourangi flees not just to Germany, but to the world of the arts, becoming a talented sculptor with an international reputation. His father cannot understand Porourangi's desire for recognition and fame. Porourangi's artistic endeavours mystify his family generally. This is because two different cosmologies are at play here – one based on the sacred in all things, the other on the rights of humans to trade all things.

Porourangi returns home and mounts a slideshow of his art. The family members sit in front of the images being shown and try to make sense of Porourangi's understanding of and modern adaptation to his 'identity' as a Māori. They are confused by his art because, for them, identity is lived as a daily reality. For Porourangi, however, identity is something viewed from a distance – not just as a cosmopolite in Germany, but from an aesthetic distance, which can *represent* identity because it is no longer a lived reality. So the film suggests that the representation of identity is predicated on its loss. Porourangi's art and life symbolize that loss of identity. In other words, his *mana* is failing and this propels him on a search for a new identity based on the foreign concepts such as identity politics. Porourangi and his art implicitly replace his *mana* with a new identity, that of the *faux* Māori predicated on a Western concept – *the right to differ.*

This right must be distinguished and is in bold contrast to the rights and responsibilities laid down by the tradition – rights and responsibilities that Porourangi has breached. His contract with his *kawai tipuna* is forgot-ten in favour of a new form of contract, one with the law of marketed identity, exchanged and sold as an aesthetic commodity under the condi-tions of global capital. This law of rights, of identity, turns out to be based on the property rights of the individual to receive something in return for the creative process. So the scenes involving Porourangi rehearse all the debates relating to intellectual property and copyright and the way in which the West differs from the Indigenous in this matter. For the Western intellectual property lawyer, cultural property is perceived, first and fore-most, as a saleable object on the international market. For the Māori, it is a sacred object and art releases and realizes its sacrality. In this competition between the market and the sacred, it is clear what will win: the market devours the sacred, consuming it as another commodity, all the while ignoring the inspirational source – Indigenous culture. This is why Indigenous intellectual property activists such as Henrietta Marrie (Fourmile) have argued that, while objects may become respected and valued, there is no change in the racist behaviour towards the Indigenous peoples of Australia (Fourmile 1994). Native Americans such as Charlotte Black Elk, granddaughter of the famous Lakota Sioux Medicine Man, make a similar complaint:

> One of the dividing lines has been when I tell the New Age practitioners, 'Go prepare for seven years.' Most of them want a hodgepodge of things without embracing the total culture. Those people treat Native American ceremonies like they would a diving vacation to the Bahamas.
>
> (quoted in Burton 2002: 276)

Whale Rider enacts Elk's censure by contrasting Porourangi's European success with that of his dysfunctional brother, Rawiri, and the other males in the film – all of whom are presented as *Once Were Warriors* figures who have become beached human whales living a life of sloth among their own people.

The brothers, however, are not as different as they seem. Both exhibit negative aspects of *kaipaoe*.[21] Rawiri seems to be incapable of hard, sustained concentrated work (at least until Pai asks him to teach and remember his tradition), while Porourangi uses his art as an avenue for *kaipaoe*, appropriating his neighbours' identities, and therefore their *tapu*, for his own use. This is a bold contrast to the Māori craftsman. The Māori artist perceives his art as a vehicle for the sacred to reveal itself. He is the human agent revealing the *mana* of the spirit in the inanimate object. In the intellectual property world, however, the artist is producing a reflection of himself for public display and economic gain. Thus individual rights and responsibilities are no longer born out of his *whakapapa* relationship to the cosmology, neither are they regulated by the principles and values of the *mana/tapu* system of law. The *mana/tapu* relationship becomes redundant in such a world. This is because that world is bent on controlling objects for material gain and an ethos focused on money. This leads to a world devoid of meaning and controlled by rules rather than relationships, by profit rather than *tapu*. Porourangi's return threatens the incursion of this world into the world of *Whale Rider* – the emptiness of Western capital replacing the emptiness of Koro's tradition. Pai, however, stands opposed to both forms of emptiness. I now turn to her as the symbol of feminine plenitude that will redeem this world by responding to the voice of authority.

The future: The Re-creator – Pai as Redeemer of Tradition

> A young girl dared to confront the past,
> change the present and determine the future.[22]

The future is symbolized by the goodness of the young Pai, the daughter of Porourangi, who has been named by her father as the next *Rangatira*. However, she has been rejected by Koro because, in his eyes, a female *Rangatira* is a break with tradition. Koro's concept of tradition, as I have argued previously, is static rather than dynamic – it is a rule-bound world of precedent, with the principles and values of the original cosmology. He lacks *humarie*. This blind obedience to tradition, however, threatens that very tradition with a sexism that comes from elsewhere. That sexism is colonial inspired and raises all the modern-day debates in Māoridom over the rights of females to speak on the *marae*. For years, Māori women have had to remind men that there have been many famous female warriors and leaders in Māori history. These women have been either neglected or trivialized as figureheads, a Māori mimicry of the sexism systemic in the dominant *Pakeha* culture. Unless a woman is a Boadicea leading the charge, she is seen as unable to lead, let alone establish an alternative 'feminine' authority. This sexist approach to history – that is, silencing the Māori feminine – is another way in which Māori men are actually controlled by colonialism, not knowing there are other ways of being, alternative modes of leadership, a politics of difference of which their own culture supplies many examples.

Throughout the film, Pai demonstrates maturity and dignity, which her grandfather cannot but help admire. The characteristics are those precisely of *humarie* and are therefore those of a natural leader. Pai's behaviour evinces *humarie* at all points: she conducts herself in a genteel manner and is peace loving and consensus driven when confronted by her grandfather's stubbornness. It is only when she is goaded that her peaceful disposition is forsaken.[23] This occurs when Koro deliberately ignores her after she has made the decision to stay with the clan rather than leave for a prosperous life with her father in Germany. She makes this decision after *feeling* the pull of the Law as exemplified in the bull whale, which is surging offshore as she leaves with her father. In other words, she *feels* the call of the Law and abides by it, while her grandfather dishonours this choice because it conflicts with his own human-made laws.

None of the young males or older men displays these characteristics. Rather, they exhibit a pathologized warrior culture, one subsumed by, and rendered symptomatic under the dominance of, colonial patriarchy. Yet

Koro stubbornly resists Pai's inevitable leadership claims and thereby draws into question his own *humarie*.

Pai encounters a series of trials, which are meant to test her and her sensibility as the next heir. In other words, she is actually forced to confront the *mana wahine* inside of her so that she can be sure of an indisputable place and position of authority. She must feel – and indeed comes to feel – the law within herself internally, rather than merely observing it externally from codes and precedents. As Neidjie points out, you must feel the law moving through your body. Here, Pai and her alter ego blend in a totemic relationship. By riding the bull whale, Pai recreates the cosmology of the original *kawai tipuna* – Paikea – and draws the other whales out. Pai, then, actualizes the law for her grandfather. She metaphorically rides the law and is therefore a true *mana wahina*, a female *Rangatira* whose *mana* is made manifest for him and for all the community to see from which they can draw strength. This changes the natural world as much as the world of 'humankind'. No longer is the sea empty; rather, it is filled with plenitude – namely the whales as they swim out into the future.

By actualizing the law, Pai points to a new jurisprudence of balance, one in which the creative energy of the female and the male achieve equilibrium. In so doing, *Ranginui* once again becomes the complement of the female *Papatuanuku*. Pai, as a female, is just as worthy as her deceased brother of the clan leadership. After all, she has demonstrated her capacity to adhere to the *manu/tapu* system by finding the whale's tooth and saving the whales. Furthermore, she evinces the rights and responsibilities of leadership, learning how to sing, dance, even fight, in the traditional manner. In so doing, she becomes cosmology's favourite: the embodiment in human time of the departed Ancestral Being, connecting the natural and the supernatural, the political and the spiritual. As Yates-Smith (2003) argues, the recognition of the interconnectedness between the spiritual plane and the political plane could foster Māori female participation in all levels of decision making in their society. She sees the more gender-balanced view of the cosmology as not only aiding women but also fostering a custodial ethic.

Furthermore, she understands the balancing role of *Papatuanuku* to *Ranginui* as a psychological aid for women who are still being abused through the dominant paternalistic system. This balance also allows males to see the relationship between the sexes anew, as a source of strength rather than weakness. It restores a new sense of the Law in all of its senses – relational, rights based and resourced – which will raise the economically depressed *iwi* such as Ngati Kanohi and restore them as a people with an identity, a space and jurisprudence.

Conclusion

Whale Rider is a legal fiction that elucidates and throws into bold relief principles and values that underpin my reading of Māori jurisprudence. They are the cosmology's voice of authority and the genealogical, relational law between the *whakapapa* and the *kawai tipuna*. The characters of both Koro and Pai attempt to actualize this Law of Relationship – although with widely varying success. The character of Koro cannot *feel* the 'Law', and so becomes like a beached whale adhering rigidly to the rules, rather than *feeling* the principles of the Law of Relationship. Pai, however, manifests the converse and *feels* the 'Law'; she 'rides into the future' on the back of the whale – itself a representation of the Law of Relationship. So, as the whale rider, Pai 'recreates' the dynamic relational link between the *whakapapa* and the *kawai tipuna*.

Second, there is the regulatory intellectual property regime or the system of law realized in the double-helix relationship of *mana/tapu*. This relationship is explored through the art and activities of Porourangi and indeed those of the other young men in the film. Left leaderless by Koro's inability to *feel* the Law, they are abandoned to swim in the sea of modernity. Many come close to drowning in this sea, like Porourangi's brother, until Pai calls on him to aid her in her cultural education, which, in turn, draws him to a leadership role of mobilizing the community to help the whales. Others, like Porourangi, survive and swim, but to a Western stroke, which abuses – indeed breaches – the *mana/tapu* relationship with their *iwi*.

The third notion is that of individual rights and responsibilities. This law derives from a respect for the sacredness or *tapu* of others and the world around them. This law takes the form of *humarie*, which is conspicuous by its absence in the traditional form of masculine authority. The females in the film encapsulate this notion. Pai is shaped – indeed crafted – into a *mana wahina*, conscious of the principles and values of *humarie* by another woman, Nanny Flowers. So it is the feminine tradition that challenges and remakes phallic authority, a feminine tradition that exemplifies the principles of *humarie*, principles of gradual but persistent change.

Furthermore, *Whale Rider* shows how the past, present and future can harmonize and complement one another when society's central focus is the cosmological relationship as set down by the *kawai tipuna*. This restored balance is necessary to offset the prevalent and off-balance image of the Māori as a dysfunctional culture, as revealed in *Once Were Warriors*. *Whale Rider* calls for, and summons, a new balance between *Papatuanuku* and *Ranginui* within an overarching cosmological jurisprudence.

As Alfred (1999) says, that balance comes from the turn to *ancient wisdom* and the remembrance of a sense of place in the overarching and spatial temporal cosmologies that manage jurisdictions of their *iwi*. Through this mapping of law – geographic, spiritual and so on – Indigenous will then find their own means for self-determination, particularly the place of the male as 'equal' to his female counterpart in law. This restoration of tradition as a living, organic entity, where women as well as men can lead, is a way of riding into the future on the back of the Law.

There is an interesting twist to the story behind the making of *Whale Rider*, an anecdote with which I conclude. The director, Niki Caro (2003), revealed that a whale beached itself not far from her home just before production began. She described how traumatic that experience was, especially when she got close to the beached whale. As she said: 'Nothing in my experience could have prepared me for being that close to a whale and nothing was more powerful in getting me connected to the story of *Whale Rider* and the film that it would become.'[24] It was as if the Law of Relationship actualized itself in material form and 'directed' the Pakeha director on how to make the film. Or, to put it in slightly different terms, she experienced the trauma of the Law of Relationship and was incorporated into the cosmology through her profound feelings for what she saw and touched.

The beauty of Caro's sentiments is that she talked of what the film was to *become* rather than what she would make of it. It was as if she had learned the system of law that underpins the Law of Relationship, the complex interplay between the *mana* in the whale story and the *tapu* way that the film represents. In short, she – as an individual and a *Pakeha* individual at that – also had a 'responsibility' rather than a 'right' to present the ancient cosmology of the *Ngati Kahoni*. By taking on that responsibility, she no longer thought in terms of her own individual Pakeha expression.

Caro explained that 'the privilege of being close to a whale is impossible to explain'. In such circumstances, this statement seems inexplicable until one thinks of how she was 'privileged'. What was the privilege the whale conferred, what were its gifts to her? Surely it was the privilege of making this film, a representation of the Māori and their jurisprudence, their cosmology. Surely it was Caro's privilege, her gift, to bring forth in *Whale Rider* nothing less than the *mana* or spirit of the Law itself?

PART FOUR
Completing the Circle

To tell this final story of law, I am being influenced by the notion of *yorro yorro* – the title of SLM Mowaljarlai's book. *Yorro yorro* is a legal concept that asks us all to 'stand up for everything in Creation'. This standing up is not an opportunity for the oppressed to have a voice as the saviours of the planet; rather, it requires a following of the Law of the Land and acknowledging that the source of the Law is the Land and that it may be found in the patterns that have been laid down. For the *yorro yorro*, as I understand its meaning, is about following the pattern so that Creation can be regenerated and the idea that humans have a duty to help this rejuvenation. Central to any law, therefore – rather than the economic imperatives of humans and the reaping for the benefits of the garden of nature – is a remembering that we are patterned into a galactic *physis* that requires us to be mindful that our actions have intergalactic implications as well as neighbourly implications. That Law is not for humans to make over with a set of rules for the orderly acquisition of their own imagined necessities; instead, it is intended that humans work with and abide by that into which humanity is patterned. By taking on that responsibility through witnessing the laws of the 'other' – whether that is the planet or a hopping mouse – each in its own way witnesses the human into reality.

Dr Martin Luther King's passionate 'I have a dream' speech is perhaps one of the most famous utterances of the twentieth century. Just before that dream became reality, the dream of the Indigenous peoples of the world also bore fruit in the form of the UN Declaration on the Rights of Indigenous Peoples. On the anniversary of that famous speech by Martin Luther King, the first Indigenous UN Rapporteur for the Freedoms and Rights of Indigenous Peoples, Professor James Anaya – an Apache – visited Australia to gather statements relating to the abuse of Indigenous rights in our country. While here, he presented a paper at a conference I attended. The day before this final presentation marked the birth of my third granddaughter and the death of the last of the Kennedy brothers – brothers said by some to have been gunned down for their support of civil rights.

As I listened to the Rapporteur give an overview of the Declaration, and his call for Aborigines to formulate their solutions in light of the Declaration, it struck me that many of the people in the room – who were mainly Western-educated bureaucrats and young people sprouting their well-rehearsed questions – would have little time for the traditional tales Professor Anaya was using to illustrate his points.

It occurred to me that no contemporary law course would allow students to study traditional stories of any country as valid legal narratives of precedent, to be treated with the same care and respect given to Western legal narratives of precedent. Perhaps they could be studied in tandem with a legitimate legal system, but to give them their own space and recognition would be like implementing the Declaration on the Rights of Indigenous Peoples!

CHAPTER **10**

The end of the journey: A camp of contemporary concerns

And so the *logos* has been revealed: *the Land is the Law*. This dialogical encounter with Indigenous jurisprudence has opened an ancient, but repressed and continuously ignored, paradigm in legal theory – a *logos* posited in Land. I will now revise that jurisprudence and its theoretical shape and pattern, as developed through my *talngai-gawarima* jurisprudential structure. This structure has shaped the book into a journey through a circle of camps, in which a *gawarima* was told and the *talngai* was shone on the *gawarima* through a series of concentric circles. The engagement with these circles took the reader into three rings of meaning: the outermost ring, reflecting the cosmology within which the knowledge of the *gawarima* is situated; the middle ring, showing the system of law in which the knowledge is managed; and the innermost ring, in which individuals ascertain their rights and responsibilities. The knowledge outcome of this jurisprudence, and these journeys, was the realization that the Land is the Law and that Law is sacred in its content, healing in its application and, most importantly, leads the individual into lawful behaviour, in which they carry out their responsibilities and in turn gain natural rights.

This encounter with an Indigenous jurisprudence is not intended to decry a missed opportunity to engage with a fossilized law built on payback and customary lore; rather, it is an opportunity to experience a timely legal paradigm that posits itself in the 'remembrance of the past' and its 'present applicability'. It is, therefore, a timely theory that can help to shape and pattern laws relating to the most pressing issue at the time of writing this book: the imbalance of the *Djang* – or, as it is articulated in the West, *climate change*.

It is this recognition of the imbalance that allows me to integrate one last layer of meaning into my book – one that gives purpose to its writing other than to articulate a theory of an oppositional political fight between Indigenous and non-Indigenous. This layer posits the *talngai-gawarima* jurisprudence as a useful binary jurisprudence to that which presently theorizes the Rule of Law, which regulates the laws that have fostered the imbalance of the *Djang* and so caused the current unpredictable climatic conditions. Climatic conditions in the past have been reasonably predict-able and so validated the regulatory system of law and its economic imperative; however, there is a new story of Land being told – one in which the present economic imperative is no longer in balance with the Land. This imbalance calls for a reassessment of the legal system that regulates such imbalances, a reassessment through another law that can 'witness' its regulatory behaviour. That 'witnessing law' I am advocating should comprise the Indigenous Law systems of each country. This advocacy, however, does not mean a digging up of the anthropological past or the present Western-constructed discourse of the 'politically correct', but rather a refocusing of the jurisprudence towards the 'rights' of the Land and the 'responsibilities' of the human towards the Land. Therefore, this book ends with what basically amounts to a diagnosis of the cause of climate change. It provides a prescription for global health – a prescription that offers an alternative legal consideration when it comes to approaching the climatic crisis.

In making this assertion, I am validating the rationale of the Senior Law Men who have turned to writing, to literary inscription, to get their 'urgent' message out – that is, that humans must pay attention to the *Djang*. That *Djang*, I would argue, is climate change at its most fundamental – climate change is an imbalance of the *Djang* and the result of a legal regime that has seen fit to move its central ethos from that of Land to that of the human. Law that is posited in the 'rights' of the Land has been moved to law that is posited in the 'rights' of humans. No longer is Law sought out through observation of the patterns of Land (such as in cultivation societies), but rather is articulated through a human or community engagement with the resources of the Land. In such a shift, Land is no longer the *source* of the Law, but rather has become a *resource*. That is, it has become privatized and therefore disconnected from its 'commons' nature. Its primordial energy, as Wolcher (2004) asserts, is moved from being a *physis* of the cosmos to that of the phantasmic Mother Nature. This shift, as I argued in my exploration of SLM Mowaljarlai's Ngarinyin cosmology, is a result of the two choices humans would seem to have:

> [T]hen the Snake uncoiled and stretched out. She became Midjelna, 'the one that unwinds her rings and stretches out looking'. Her body was sprouting with a kingdom of living nature. From here she would take over from the Creator. She would persuade man to reproduce by sexual intercourse only, without the spirit portion that put him under the Law of the Universe as Wandjina man. Midjelna offered independence, joint management and knowledge of her own realm and powers – she offered the earth.
>
> Wallanganda came thundering down on her, 'Wandjat! You go out of my sight!' and he said, 'From now on you do your own thing, and don't come back into my territory! Don't think you can make creatures just with sex, without dreaming spirit-part into them!'
>
> (Mowaljarlai and Malnic 1993: 142–43)

This ancient narrative is not about a spiritual quest or the Garden of Eden intellectual dilemma, but rather a quest of law. The narrative points directly to choice – an ongoing choice, not an either/or one. The choice, however, prefigures the age of the phallus – destined to suffer the Oedipus complex and with it the phantasmic motif of Nature as Mother (or seductress). In this trajectory, *Midjelna* (Wandjat) becomes the archetype of later incarnations: Kali, Eve or Spider Woman. The alternative to this human-centred creation is the original ordering of Creation, an order in which Land is Law and the pattern of Law is posited in the Land. In other words, it is a giver of place, life, health and Law.

The connection between Law and health is vital and necessary, as this book has argued. Not that the present legal regime in Australia is much concerned with health – indeed, it is quite the opposite. For Australia is one of the highest *legally* regulated polluters on the planet,[1] its economy turning on the extraction of raw materials *for* pollution as much *as* pollution. Solutions to date have centred on economic concerns such as the Stern Review (Stern 2007). This book offers an ancient and alternative way of looking at this problem – a *lex* that offers alternative approaches to the problems, as discussed in Camp 4:

> The pattern is not a hierarchy. The pattern is a system of relationship. And this is what Mowaljarlai is trying to teach us, about *wurnan*.

It is a system of relationship, the way we related to each other, to species, to land. And when we are in relationship there are no bosses, there are no rulers. Everybody gives and receives in a structured relationship which comes from the land. The power and the authority of that come from the land, not from elected people and not from any decision-making structures within the community.

(Mowaljarlai 1995)

Furthermore, it calls for complementary legal regimes to manage the situation – the dyadic approach, as found in the Law of Relationship. It is important that such law be seen as complementary, as this book has shown it is the Law of Relationship that brings about constructive management of land. Therefore, Indigenous law must be given equal standing with Australian common law on the issue. This approach might not only address the problem of pollution, but will go to the core of the racial divide in Australia, enlisting but also hailing the Indigenous people from their epistemology rather than the 'attempts' at consultation that have amounted to the assimilation of Indigenous knowledge, in turn disempowering that knowledge and the people who are charged with holding and guarding it.

This concluding camp is written with an emphasis on the 'applied' – which also calls for another paradigm shift in relation to women and their law. This call has been misread by feminism, as Paula Gunn Allen (1992) suggests, as meaning equal rights in a man's world, a gender-neutral legal status within a patrilineal regime. This book, however, has argued for a fully gendered legal system – that is, Women's Law and Men's Law. As Allen (1992: 262) asserts in relation to male axis orientations:

Strange things begin to happen when the focus in American Indian literary studies is shifted from a male to a female axis. One of the major results of the shift is that the materials become centred on continuance rather than on extinction. This is true for both traditional tribal literatures and contemporary poetry ... The shift from pessimism to optimism, from despair to hope is so dramatic that one wonders if the focus on male traditions and history that has characterized the whole field of American Indian literature and lore was not part of the plot to exterminate Native American.

I do not fully agree with Allen's conspiracy theory, but it does offer food for thought to the historical role of the male domain – men's business as hunters and warriors, in which near-death experiences are part of their initiation trauma, must surely lead to an obsession with death and decline. This obsession is not exclusive to male Indigenous, but is also endemic to Western males, whose founding narratives are historically centred on invasion or battle. Therefore, it is simply a matter of commonsense that a jurisprudence offering 'continuity' or 'creative' *logos* should be brought to the fore. This is especially the case given the present context of climate change – itself about the impending death of the planet. Therefore, its opposite is needed – that is, 'women's business', the domain of the creative, nurturing and productive healing that is an essential part of the balance of Law and the healing of the Land.

This also explains why the later camps all end with a focus on women's business and Law. This is meant as a call to Indigenous women to honour and implement the feminine domain of their Law. For an imbalance in nature is the central issue for Indigenous people – and, indeed, all people. That objective – the restoration of balance to the Land – should be their focus, rather than critiquing or fighting with what MacNeil (2007: 14) describes as an 'ancient patrilineal regime'. This regime has subjugated Indigenous leaders into relegating Indigenous women into the same categories as those used in the West and, unfortunately, using the same rhetoric, which has been referenced throughout the book by the work of Taiaiake Alfred (1999) and his advocacy for change among Indigenous male leaders. This 'reflective' place of woman in the Western legal regime dispossesses women of their Law and their original 'balancing' role as equal partners within an overarching Law of Relationship.

This final camp contextualizes my theory by setting it within an Indigenous modernity and focusing on the necessary recognition of women's Law. For without that legal balancing, there can be no restoration of imbalance of the *Djang* in Law. As Hinsha Waste Agli Win asserts, unless women articulate their experiences and observations in policy and theory, and so influence educational institutions, and unless women develop theories based on their observations and experience into policy, there will be no change. Her assertion is not that of a feminist, but rather embodies a concern for balancing women's Law into the overall governance patterns that emerge from the Land as the Law. In this last camp, I therefore explore how it is possible to take a narrative and find the jurisprudence that identifies the need for balance, which includes women's Law.

In light of the work of SLM Neidjie, as well as that of *Plains of Promise*, I have concluded that it is the Land that *has feelings and misses its people*. By extension, I argue that the Land misses women and their 'women's business' and Law. It is women's Law that has been written out of history, as Paula Gunn Allen (1992) and other Indigenous women have argued (see Camara Fatou 2004). More importantly, however, it is women's Law that has been denied even by Aboriginal administrators, who see little need for funding women's ceremonial activities (De Ishtar 2005: 100). However, if we take the Senior Law Men's jurisprudence to its logical end, it is they who should be advocating for the propagation of women's Law.

The sidelining of the feminine is not peculiar to Australian Indigenous jurisprudence. For example, when we turn back to the writings of Tilda Long Soldier and the macho behaviour of Lakota society in America (St Pierre and Long Soldier 1995: 169), we see that women and their ritual healing capacities are denied recognition even by their Holy Men, as articulated in the camp that discusses *Thunderheart*. I argue – and it is an argument supported by the works of Alfred (1999) in relation to Indian male leadership and its present lack of resistance to 'black magic' (1999: xiii), such as money, bribes and power – that men only give recognition if the dominant male culture tells them that this is appropriate behaviour. For example, if an economic model of law dictates that Indigenous males give money to 'women's business', then that business will be recognized as such – but as crass, commercial 'business'. What is lost here is a sense of patterned law, of dyadic relationship and balance.

This book has revealed the dyadic nature of law – a dyadic pattern that permeates down from the double moiety system into the overall nature of being on this planet. Therefore, the dyadic is the 'replicating' pattern that needs attention in order for the true voices of authority and balance in gender representation and law to emerge and to guide discussion about solutions to climate change.

During my journey to SLM Marika's country, I recall feeling the deep sense of loss that resonated through the mining town in which the rich bauxite was extracted from the area. My sense of hopelessness was not only personal – Richard Trudgen, a long-time project officer, and the Yolngu people themselves were also in a state of despair. These people had been given money, housing and other Western goods supposedly representative of the good life. But all these things brought – as they do the suburbs of Sydney or Melbourne – was a subtle despair about the sameness of material things, a sameness deadened by prescription drugs and mind-numbing sports/entertainment. They did not bring a depth of cultural biodiversity, let alone equality before the white man's law – a law devoid of ceremony and ritual, a law frightened of its own superstitious past in which ceremony and ritual have been equated with oppression and wars under the banner of a monotheistic moral ordering. In such a context, the mention of legal pluralism is an unthinkable thought – if not an act of terrorism – for it terrorizes the judiciary to think that their law may be wanting, that it is beyond what they determine as its weaknesses. There is no room for a witnessing of its weaknesses, only a self-satisfied knowing that it is not perfect. The judiciary of this law thinks itself gracious in its willingness to consider customary law, generously allowing the natives to have their customs and practices as long as these fit within its idea of the law.

I will now return to the theoretical framework of the book to explore further its applicability to this Land-centred dilemma in which humans find themselves at this point in the geological history of the planet. It is a dilemma, I would argue, that legitimates the need to reveal other laws and other realities. The theoretical framework for establishing this legal premise was provided through an analysis of the works of the three Senior Law Men – SLM Neidjie (Buntji), SLM David Mowaljarlai (Ngarinyin) and SLM Wandjuk Marika (Rirratjingu). The works produced by these Senior Law Men inform not only this book, but also the general population, about the Law of their people. Through the unprecedented capturing of their oratories in writing, these Senior Law Men have alerted us to an urgent problem – the imbalance of the earth. It is this urgency that has made them break with tradition and record their knowledge. That act does seem contrary to the oral tradition and the manner in which lawful knowledge is passed on; however, to hold to such a way is to fossilize the peoples and their law – an act that assumes they are somehow unable to cope with modernity. But there is a warning here: this 'captured' knowledge, as found in their texts and in my book, is not definitive, but rather a snapshot in time. The contextualized authoritative outspeaks my work and any written works, for it remains connected to the Land.

The manner in which I apply this knowledge is through a jurisprudential reading of the actions of one of the most prominent individuals in the West, a man whose work is dedicated to revealing the true level of imbalance our planet is suffering. I refer to US Senator and former Vice-President Al Gore. I have chosen this man not for his missionary zeal based on 'green' ethics, but for his lived experience. What is essential for a *talngai-gawarima* jurisprudential reading is a 'lived' experience, not an abstracted 'desire' or even 'ethic'. This 'truth of the level of imbalance' is reflected in my choice of advocate. The very fact that it has taken the political clout of a former Vice-President of the United States, backed by the autobiographical documentary *An Inconvenient Truth*, to draw attention to this issue heralds the gravity of this problem. His message is aimed at his own people, among the world's worst polluters, who must take responsibility for their actions – or, like Rome of yesteryear, they are destined to fall into oblivion. So Gore functions here as a voice of authority and a Law Man on the issue, much like an Indigenous Law Man, because his status is one not of 'politics' but knowledge, not of power but of the truth.

To reiterate, Gore's advocacy to address climate change amounts to 'an appropriate display of knowledge' of a Law Man. What is that display of knowledge? And how is this exemplary lawful behaviour analyzed through a *talngai-gawarima* jurisprudential reading? I will once again reference SLM Marika's camp and Trudgen's (2000) tests for valid legal authority:

- The credibility of the educator to know and teach this strange new knowledge.
- Whether it was delivered in the culturally correct way.
- Whether it was built on culturally accepted knowledge and truths.
- Whether it survived the intellectual debate.

(2000: 209)

These tests, I would argue, are just as relevant to the modern Westerner facing the facts of climate change as they are to the Indigenous people living in the most remote part of Australia. People need culturally appropriate knowledge and an understanding of its relevance to their situation. Gore's experience, as I will show, was not an easy path: the disclosure of hard data does not change a people, let alone a government. More is needed – an experience, a lived reality. In this, climate change has actually revealed more similarities than differences between Indigenous and non-Indigenous peoples. Both advocate the rebalancing of the *Djang* – even if their idioms differ.

So I once again turn to the concentric circle of analysis, first examining Gore's cosmology in relation to Land. He tells us that he grew up surrounded by nature's beauty and abundance on a large farm beside a river, in which he states he could 'lay down in the grass' and he 'didn't know the difference between work and play' (*An Inconvenient Truth*). This ideal life was interrupted by long periods in Washington and by schooling. By way of contrast, these periods gave Gore a better appreciation of the beauty and abundance that the land offered. During his periods of education, he learnt the 'hard data' from a science professor – a mentor whom he held in high regard. As Gore grew older, he could see that these hard data were confirmed by a rise in the levels of pollution and meteorological disturbances. So his cosmology on the issue came out of a lived experience as well as abstracted knowledge from a voice of authority.

The next level on which we explore Gore's experience relates to the system of law. As Al Gore himself found, generating change is not just a matter of presenting the scientific findings to government and letting the facts speak for themselves. As he states:

> There are good people in politics who hold this [knowledge at] arm's length, because if they recognize it, the moral imperative to make big changes is inescapable. It is deeply unethical to allow such effects to occur.
>
> *(An Inconvenient Truth)*

Gore also learnt that the economic imperative drives decision making and that it is often regarded as better to 'not' understand than to understand – especially for those of lower socio-economic status. Perhaps the most daunting reflection of the economic model comes from the voice of the lesser developed countries, which are adamant in their views when they participate in international fora such as the Kyoto Protocol.[2] These nations do not see why they should halt their 'rights to prosperity' when the West has already prospered. It is a Catch-22 situation, in that the West has benefited from pollution and exploitation of the Third World; in this ghastly scenario, it would seem that the chickens have come home to roost. For example, at the time of writing, China is building a nuclear energy plant every nineteen days (*An Inconvenient Truth*) – the energy may be cleaner, but the mindset of 'use' is no different; neither is the law that regulates this 'use' (*An Inconvenient Truth*). As Gore repeats, this is deeply unethical.

So Gore has found that the system of law and its power to legislate are not sufficient; there are other more pervasive influences at play. As he demonstrates in his documentary, people actually think they have a choice between more profit and a liveable planet. This human-centric view, as mentioned earlier, extends into a childish response in which governments both in the developing world and even in First World countries will not change their behaviour unless other countries follow suit. In other words, there is no sense of individual 'lawful' behaviour or responsibility; rather, the whole process has degenerated into a mob mentality of consumer consciousness and individual rights. I now move to that individual lawful behaviour and examine Gore's road to this lawful conduct by contextualizing it within the theory illuminated in SLM Marika's camp, referenced using the story of Law from SLM Neidjie's camp.

Al Gore's understanding of the seriousness of the state of climate change came through two avenues relating to the transfer of knowledge in Indigenous societies – having feelings and observation. To bring him to the state of having feelings for the planet, Gore experienced a personal tragedy relating to the near-death of his young son. As he states in the film, he felt he had gained an ability *to feel* after the tragedy: it changed his way of being in the world. He said he really 'dug in' to learn more deeply about climate change and so began to travel to places such as Antarctica and the Amazon so he could understand and observe the effects of climate change up close:

> [Through] the possibility of losing what is most precious to me I gained an ability that I didn't have before . . . but when I felt it . . . I felt . . . we could really lose it . . . that what we take for granted might not be here for our children.

Gore has, in fact, chosen to learn through one of the fundamental prerequisites of the Indigenous intellectual landscape as articulated by SLM Neidjie: *having feelings* (not emotions) as a legitimate way of knowing. This has given Gore the stimulus to be more dedicated to spreading the message and in so doing he has used his privilege of place and voice of authority on behalf of the Land.

This voice, however, has been received in tandem with individual citizens also having feelings. Once Gore started pointing out that their 'feeling hot' was legitimate due to the rise in temperature, people were able to make their individual decisions – decisions elected governments were unable to enact due to the economic imperative and the voting reality. It would seem the US government was not even moved to action in 2003 when, over a one-week period, 400 tornadoes[3] hit the United States. Japan also suffered ten devastating typhoons, yet its government barely reacted (*An Inconvenient Truth*).

However, once Gore's 'voice of authority' on the issue became public through the film, change began to occur. Gore put his message into a format that was *culturally correct* for the average American. He built it on *culturally accepted knowledge and truth* by using the history of the cigarette industry – that is, the abuse of the tobacco plant and his own family's profit as tobacco farmers – and the devastating personal loss of his sister to lung cancer from smoking. As he states: 'It takes a long time to make the connection' (*An Inconvenient Truth*). This admission about the length of time it took to make the connection between profit and the end-product in terms of personal loss and Americans' 'lived' history of the devastating effects of cigarettes brought Gore closer to his audience – for, once again, *feelings* (the time it takes to make the connection) and lived experience gave him authority, quite apart from his political status and the scientific evidence he was citing.

This is exactly the knowledge trajectory to which Indigenous epistemology leads – a knowledge trajectory that caused Gore to realize that the loss of the 2000 US presidential election was actually an opportunity to move back to what I would argue is a more democratic process – one reflective of SLM Marika's Yolngu people's call for respect for people's right to receive new knowledge through voices of authority with the appropriate experience and in a format conducive to their learning styles. Gore developed a 'slideshow', as he calls it, which presented knowledge about the imbalance of the *Djang* (environment) in images and language the American people would understand. He informs us in the film that he was prepared to go anywhere people would listen. In other words, he was following the Indigenous democratic process in which the individual decides to participate – that is, attend a 'slideshow' – rather than being told what is important.

Therefore, as Gore works in tandem with the Land by highlighting its state of health through the monitory of its temperature – the hottest year on record being 2005 – he endorses SLM Neidjie's adage that *having feelings* is essential for true knowledge in relation to the Land. This is an individual experience and it requires an individual response of lawful behaviour in relation to Land. As Gore states: 'What changed in the US with Hurricane Katrina was a feeling we have entered A PERIOD OF CONSEQUENCES.' In other words, the moral imperative and the understanding of consequences of actions are now being felt through climate change – *our ability to live on this planet is what is at stake.* I would suggest that Gore's experience is an excellent example of how the jurisprudence of the Senior Law Men has applicability in the present and is not fossilized for its ancient 'extractable' knowledge for the select few – such as archaeologists, anthropologists and scientists. As this *talngai-gawarima* jurisprudential reading of Gore's actions and the Land's sickness has shown, the Senior Law Men's call for a recognition of the *gift* is about consequences and responsibilities, not rights and economic development.

I now move to summarize the *talngai-gawarima* encounter with the gift that is Indigenous jurisprudence. As SLM Mowaljarlai states: 'We have a gift.' That gift is another legal regime, one that comes out of millennia of experience and observation of the processes of the *Corpus Australis* as set down by the Senior Law Men – who have chosen to take this action with a sense of urgency. This same sense of urgency has stimulated me to take the unprecedented step of considering the shape and pattern of an Indigenous jurisprudence based on works by Senior Law People. These actions, as I have argued, are opening up a new educational paradigm that asks Indigenous scholars to revisit their traditions, to find theoretical shapes and models based on ancient thoughts.

I have taken the reader on a series of journeys that patterned my thinking into the cosmology of the native peoples, shaping my choice of contemporary narratives that I later read jurisprudentially. It was from these journeys that I began to shape this book into a school of thought based on a paradigm shift to a unique discourse informed by traditional thought and Law. This discourse is different from that of Indigenous studies – a discipline within an overarching Western discourse that shapes and patterns 'allowable' knowledge into the educational institutions. This shift to a new school of thought, in which personal experience and observations of actualizing the Law and knowledge of the Land play a central role, is occurring in response to the call of the Senior Law Men and Senior Law Women, such as Hinsha Waste Agli Win. It is from those experiences that a theory is formed. As mentioned in *Thunderheart*, Hinsha Waste Agli Win calls women to articulate their experiences and observations in policy and theory and so influence educational institutions – not just as stories of disempowerment, but as empowering narratives framed in an Indigenous theory.

Having revised my theoretical cosmology, I will now revise that jurisprudence, and its theoretical shape and pattern, as they have been developed through my *talnga-gawarima* jurisprudential structure. The structure shaped the book into a journey of a circle of camps in which a *gawarima* was told and the *talngai* was shone on it. The knowledge outcome of this jurisprudence and these journeys was the realization that the Land is the Law and that Law is sacred in its content and healing in its application. Most importantly, it leads the individual into lawful behaviour, through which she carries out her responsibilities and, in turn, gains natural rights.

The first camp entailed reading the prose of SLM Neidjie of the Buntji peoples. By taking selections of his prose, recording them and then translating them into the 'whitefella' vernacular, I was able to elucidate the jurisprudential content of SLM Neidjie's *Story About Feeling* – a book most aptly named for the understanding of his cosmology, which revealed the nature of the *Djang*. This is a primordial energy that permeates the skin of the earth, an energy of which a lawful person is fully conscious. There is a need to maintain that balance of this force known as the *Djang* and the act of maintaining the balance is carried out through an awareness of the *affect* of *having feelings* for the land and the knowledge that the land returns those feelings. This book has demonstrated that, by having such feelings, that the Aboriginal person becomes a 'watcher'. The act of watching then reveals the helplessness of the human to redirect this great energy. It also reveals the importance of the preventative – a preventative built on a relationship between what may be called dimensions of reality. As prefaced earlier in the book, Ramose's triadic community – which takes in the *living dead*, the *living* and the *yet to be born* – works together in this preventive behaviour. The triadic relationship comes into force in the works of SLM Neidjie to support the human relationship to the *Djang*. The gateway to this communication, or registering of the state of the *Djang*, is *having feelings*. As we saw earlier, it was not until Gore *had acquired feelings* that he intuited the level of destruction happening to the Land; however, his experience is an 'after-the-fact' one.

But these feelings are also the gateway to the living dead. The living dead are seen not as intangible ghostly apparitions, but rather sources of knowledge and warning about living on the Land and knowing the Law. Perhaps more importantly, they too are 'watchers' – watchers over the 'living' and their responsibilities to the 'yet to be born'. Communication with this dimension of Indigenous reality is through having feelings. However, this camp also introduced a fourth relationship: that of the totemic, in particular the manner in which the spirit of the totemic animals also assists the human. The intention is not to build up a fantasy of operatic encounters, but rather to make the human more sensitive to their thoughts and actions and so, in turn, to the energy of the *Djang*. In other words, the human becomes a kind of barometer, testing the temperature of society's inner and outer landscape – something that was played out in the figure of Ivy. In that narrative, it became evident that the health of the land was projected into the mental stability of the chosen human.

Hence this cosmological reading opened up not only the subjective nature of having feelings, but also its prerequisite to the intellectual landscape of Indigenous peoples. This camp was entered so that the reader could understand aspects of the cosmology one might find in an Indigenous community. It was meant to be a guide to protocols for observing and engaging with an alternative reality and people's ways of perceiving Land and Law.

The next camp led to an understanding of the system of law which one might find in Indigenous communities. The travel diary of SLM Mowaljarlai and his journey to touch up the great Wandjina cave paintings of the Kimberley brought me into an understanding of the narratives of the ventures of the Wandjina and their laying down of the *Wunnun* sharing system as a Law of Relationship. That law shapes and patterns the human into the archetypal legal system that traverses *Bandaiyan* – not unlike the rule of law that traverses the West and allows for cultural and regional differences in the expression of law and, most importantly (as Gore realized), *consequences* of actions.

It was in this camp that I demonstrated the importance of the dyadic that represents the 'di' of the noun 'Indigenous'. This dyadic structure has been found to be generic among many Indigenous nations across the world. Moreover, its shape permeates nearly all relationships – from that of the dyadic moiety systems of law to that of the men's and women's Law. It was argued that it is this replicating pattern of engagement, rather than some territorial categorization of dualistic laws and gender or even species, that offers individual creativity and democratic participation.

Finally, SLM Marika addresses the role of the individual and the development of their voice of authority as a lawful person following the Land as the Law – a law that looks to the individual as a lawful person and builds character through expecting the individual to develop their voice of authority about why they should be lawful; a law in which the Land would seem to have an effect on the behaviour and choices an individual makes.

In summary, the theoretical elements here point to a cosmological understanding and appreciation of the founding Creation narrative. Such understanding and appreciation are essential for any knowledge of people's intellectual landscape, which consists of their decision making and what they value in their society – that is, a system of Law that looks to the management of relationships on all levels of being, which in turn is connected through networks of moiety kinship systems across the continent that influence many decisions. Finally, it is a law of rights and responsibilities, which deem the individual lawful until proven otherwise. Their very living on their homeland gives them responsibility, which ensures their right to wellness. Therefore, when entering an Indigenous community, the first act of protocol is to learn the founding narrative, learn the system of the Law and respect the people's rights and responsibility to good health that comes from the Land.

Let us turn now to the final group of camps, in which these jurisprudential theoretical rings resonated the theory through a series of 'readings' of the contemporary narratives. As I argued in the first camp, the analysis of the narrative is not an assimilation of the Western discourse of critical legal analysis of law and literature, but rather a return to the storytelling tradition in which the Indigenous jurisprudence is found. The narrative has always been the home of jurisprudence – a home made popular through access by the people. As MacNeil (2007) has argued, *lex* belongs to the *populus* and you must find it in that *populus*, which, in turn, is found in the narrative media of films, novels or the internet (e.g. YouTube or Twitter).

These narratives were chosen on the basis of journeys taken in my formative years of understanding Indigenous laws and culture. As described, these journeys shaped and patterned my understanding of other Indigenous world-views. I therefore chose two films and one novel to reflect that lived experience. So my choice of the films, *Whale Rider* and *Thunderheart*, and the novel, *Plains of Promise*, was based not just on their jurisprudential richness, but also my lived experience and observations of the peoples and the Land. An important addition to each of these chapters, as mentioned earlier, was the shift from the jurisprudential reading of the theory found in masculine text to that of the lived experience of women and what these narratives had to say to women about their Law. Hence the Law of Relationship, with its necessary balance of women's and men's Law, was found within each chapter.

The first narrative examined, the novel *Plains of Promise*, is situated in my home territory: Australia. Based somewhere on the Queensland/Northern Territory border, this narrative dramatically poses many questions that shift the legal paradigm from the courtroom or the constraints of the missionary reserves to that of 'actualizing' the Law from the Land. This narrative, more than any I have read, 'actualizes' the law for a reader. However, had I not had my own personal experiences in this place, I do not think I could have done such a *talngai-gawarima* jurisprudential reading. For it is in the experience of Land as the source of Law, and the feelings it imbues, that one comes to know the Law.

This drama offers a sweeping vista of the history of the invasion of Australia and its ongoing 'disease', which infects the people to this day. However, this is a healing story and tells a journey of healing. It is a journey in which the Land calls back its chosen or loved ones – its little ones, who it rejoices in seeing. This act of rejoicing is manifested as a replenishment of a water supply – a break in the drought.

When I met with Alexis Wright at the Brisbane Writers' Festival in 2006, she told me that she had drawn inspiration for her story from her grandmother's life experience. Wright brings us into a very busy world of legal interaction between neighbouring tribes. Both tribes are steeped in their legal knowledge of their country, but both are also deeply concerned about the obvious 'imbalance' in their land – the drying up of the great lake. Wright skilfully uses a Creation story to cosmologize the situation. In other words, she brings us into the cosmology of the people, where we can gain knowledge of their classic history and thought. We learn where the imbalance has occurred, but it is up to the people to bring back that balance. It is a balance that is inhibited by the dualism of laws: the imposed invader's law and that of the Land. The story then becomes a balance of the two laws – a balance that does not look for solutions, but rather for processes to bring about change. It thus becomes an inter-generational 'sorting out'. Like any true healing, this takes time. In this case, the mental illness is in the land and is projected on to the character of Ivy. The healing will occur when the people become lawful. The character of the young Law Man Elliot epitomizes that lawfulness. It takes Elliot a lifetime to become lawful, a lifetime of pain and hurt brought about mainly through his own unlawful arrogance, which hits up against another law that controls and seduces him into a position of power over his own people.

The healing occurs over many decades, for it takes time for the right people to do the right thing and the right people to return. It is only then that the Land can truly be healed and the people themselves made well. This story, more than the others, demonstrates that the Land is the Law and that being a lawful person comes from a voice of authority of a lifetime of experience living *in* the Land rather than *on* the Land.

Thunderheart offers a close look at the Law of Relationship and the legal paths one can take, which easily mislead one into thinking that Western law will bring about freedom and respect for people's rights. A path can lead down the Red Road based on the traditional legal narratives or one can go down the politically conservative legal path of Western discourse and its construction of an 'indigeneity' through fictions like customary lore, native title and other 'acts' that are said to offer Indigenous peoples individual legal rights – rights and their immediate solution that eventually pull the Indigenous away from the focus of law being on their responsibilities to Land and future generations. It is the conflict between the immediacy of rights overriding longer term planning for responsibilities to future generations that is played out in *Thunderheart*. These rights include political as well as economic rights. The political clashes with the economic here, with both declaring that their methods are for the benefit of the people. This is a common catchcry in Indigenous rights regimes; however, as the narrative reveals, these 'benefits' lead the people away from the Red Road – a road that validates who and where the people came from and where they are going, a road that does not lead to political and economic gains, but rather to a strong sense of well-being. This is some-thing that is only just beginning to be understood, as Trudgen (2000) argues, as being fundamental both to people's health and welfare and to their desire for economic prosperity.

Questions of Law in relation to women are played out dramatically in this narrative with the murder of the female protagonist. The story is based on the real-life drama of the after-effects of Siege at Wounded Knee in the early 1970s. This camp is heavily weighted, cautioning women that following the politically conservative can end as badly as the path of the 'comprador'. This story, therefore, is a warning from the battlegrounds of the Great Sioux nations, which have fought long and hard with the most powerful nation in the world – the United States. The Sioux are a people who have learnt to move the battle from one of the sword and the arrow to one of the pen, TV screen and internet. The representation of the image of Native peoples is being fought hard and in a multiverse of media domains and is a battle that it is hoped will lead back to the Red Road and the rebalancing of women as leaders and holy people, as well as followers.

The final narrative chosen was *Whale Rider*, coming from our nearest neighbour – Aotearoa – and its Māori cosmology. This narrative, as I pointed out, was written after the appearance of a whale in the Hudson River of New York, where writer Witi Ihimaera (1987) was contemplating writing a new novel for his young daughter. It was the whale that gave him inspiration, as it is the Creator Being from which his *iwi*'s *whakapapa* claim their descent. Furthermore, when the novel was adapted to film, the director Caro also had an encounter with a whale – the beaching of the whale just before shooting began. As Caro explained in her interview (2003), the feeling engendered by seeing the whale beached brought a new depth to her role as director. So it was the encounter with an aspiration of the ancestor that imbued both writer and director with a feeling for the telling of this tale of constitutional challenge.

It was this constitutional level – in particular, the constitutional authority level of the Māori *iwi* – that was the central concern of the jurisprudential reading of *Whale Rider*. This camp focused on the importance of knowing the cosmological narrative of peoples so as to be able to unpack the imposition of the Westphalian model of sovereignty (Morris 2000) and its values and notions about the source of an authoritative voice – a source that pointed to a lineage that, in fact, as was pointed out, was the very same source as that for the Māori: the *whakapapa*. The Māori *whakapapa* was explained and its powerful influence on the gender bias of the voice of authority revealed.

I argued that it is the influence of the *ancient patrilineal regime* that spins what is seemingly a kind of 'black magic' over the leaders and their gender bias when it comes to the voice of authority. The narrative, however, depicts the future generation in the characters of a young girl, backed by ancestral force and knowledge of the *whakapapa*, who is herself a revelation of the true cosmology. This is a rebalancing of women into the *Ranginui* (Buck 1950) and *Papatuanuku* dyadic relationship of the cosmological narrative of the Māori. For it is important at this cosmological level that women be balanced back into the overall equation if the Māori are to have balanced constitutional governance. To sublimate women is to cause an imbalance in the overall cosmological ordering – one that follows through with an imbalance of constitutional authority by sublimation of half the population. If there is such enormous inequity, then there can be no real constitutional authority and what comes about is an autocracy – a one-eyed version of a people's future as a community.

This camp has much to offer for the leaders whom Taiaiake Alfred (1999) critiques, especially those who claim grassroots or 'real black' status as authoritative figures. It is therefore, the cosmology, not the politically correct, that defines a people's principles and values.

The intention of this book was to introduce the reader to a dialogical encounter with a *talngai-gawarima* jurisprudence, which argues that the Land is the Law and that adherence to this Law is through the following of *feeling* – having feelings for the Land and enjoying the feelings from the Land that heal and balance the human personality, but at the same time instil in humans the need for balance and their responsibility to maintain that balance.

Balance comes through the Law of Relationship – a relationship with all that is around us. Any relationship demands the witnessing of another – that other being another way of seeing the world. A Law of Relationship is one between laws – laws that hold at the most fundamental level that the Land is the Law. There must be a natural understanding of polarization rather than consensus – that is, acknowledging the need to polarize before consensus can be reached, a double-helix pattern of political and social relationships. The Law of Relationship teaches and gives protocols for dealing with difference and honouring diversity – giving the human a special responsibility to care for their totemic other. It is a Law that calls for settlement of disputes to be through protocols and ritual – for example, the *Markatreeta*[4] in Arnhem Land.

And finally, it is a Law that calls the individual to be a lawful person – a lawful person coming out of their experience and observations as their voice of authority. Such a voice honours the experiences of others, which vary from their own. It also honours their responsibility as caretakers of another species. Finally, it honours their responsibility to *care for country*!

Notes

1 My camp

1 My mother's mother's people are the Kombumerri and her father's people are the Munaljahlai. These two clans are neighbours and, therefore, share a language.
2 A South-East Queensland Aboriginal language group, including the Kombumerri, my grandmother's people, and Munaljahlai, my grandfather's people.

2 The camp of the *talngai-gawarima*

1 PIE, or Proto-Indo-European, is the hypothetical reconstructed ancestral language of the Indo-European family. The timescale is much debated, but the most recent date proposed for it is about 5500 years ago.
2 'The reconstructed Proto-Indo-European root of this looks like *yewes- and among its relations are Irish huisse "just". Though the root later meant "law", probably it originally was a term of religious cult, perhaps meaning "sacred formula" (cf. Latin *iurare*, "to pronounce a ritual formula", Vedic *yos*, "health", Avestan *yaoz-da-*, "make ritually pure"). In language, if not in life, law and religion are blood brothers.' Available at http://www.etymonline.com/index.php?search=Indigenous&searchmode=none (accessed 17 November 2006).
3 '1340, "wisdom to see what is virtuous, or what is suitable or profitable", from O.Fr. *prudence* (13c.), from L. *prudentia* "foresight, sagacity", contraction of *providentia* "foresight" (see *providence*). Secondary sense of "wisdom"

(c. 1375) now only in *jurisprudence* (q.v.).' Available at http://www.etymonline.com/index.php?search=prudence&searchmode=none (accessed 17 November 2006).

4 '1646, from L.L. *indigenus* "born in a country, native", from L. *indigena* "a native", lit. "in-born person", from Old L. *indu* "in, within" (earlier *endo*) + *gen-*, root of *gignere* (perf. *genui*) "beget", from PIE **gen-* "produce".' Available at http://www.etymonline.com/index.php?search=Indigenous&searchmode=none (accessed 17 November 2006).

5 South-East Queensland Aboriginal language group including the Kombumerri, my grandmother's people, and Munaljahlai, my grandfather's people.

6 Taiaiake Alfred (1999: 12) refers to the Mohawk philosophy as being a similar question: 'human purpose consists in the perpetual quest for balance and harmony'.

7 Taiaiake Alfred (1999: 12) also points out that the Mohawk philosophy that 'peace is achieved by extending the respect, rights and responsibilities of family relations to other peoples'. This interpretation is slightly different from the one above.

8 Ms Graham has held many significant positions in relation to Aboriginal community politics and child welfare. She and Lilla Watson developed ground-breaking courses in Indigenous tertiary education in Queensland in the 1980s.

9 Ms Watson is a descendant of the Kangaulu and Birrigubi clans of South-East Queensland, Australia. An Indigenous scholar who has made a significant contribution to Indigenous tertiary education, she is also an artist of international repute and many of her works hang in places of significance in Australia.

3 Feeling the *Djang:* The camp of Senior Law Man Neidjie

1 Senior Law Man (or Woman) is an honorific title to indicate the level of education that is required for an Indigenous person to reach the status; it is equivalent to what in Western law would be a High Court Judge.

2 SLM Neidjie's clan is the Buntji clan of Northern Australia's Kakadu National Park.

3 Dr Gregory Cajete, Santa Clara Pueblo, New Mexico. He was the founding Director of the Institute of American Indian Arts in Santa Fe and is currently an Associate Professor in the College of Education at the University of New Mexico.

4 The spider or the web? The camp of Senior Law Man Mowaljarlai

1 Some of the oldest surface rock – 4.4 billion years old – can be found in the Jack Hills of Narryer Gneiss Terrane of Western Australia.

2 Interview with Mowaljarlai about the concept of the university. Available at http://www.abc.net.au/rn/talks/8.30/lawrpt/lstories/lr100996.htm (accessed 17 November 2006).

3 I thank Louis Wolcher, University of Washington for bringing this to my attention during the Critical Legal Conference in South Africa in 2003.

4   I refer to orality as being limited only in relation to its access by a wider audience than that for which it was originally intended. It has nothing to do with either its substance or its posterity. For only the land-based clans can keep the accurate account alive for posterity.

5   The Ice Age occurred during the Pennsylvanian and Permian periods (between about 350 and 250 million years ago).

6   Gavin Pretor-Pinney, in *The Cloudspotters' Guide* (Sceptre, 2006), points out that landscape is static. Only the atmosphere makes it dynamic. Morning Glory cloud is the world's biggest and most frequently stratocumulus roll cloud, at times 1000 kilometres long.

7   Kallawa Anggna Kude is the name of a celestial occurrence, a 'star with trails' (Wunambal language group) (Mowaljarlai and Malnic 1993: 209).

8   'Walkabout' is a term that can be used in a derogatory way. It refers to an Aborigine who must travel a distance to attend either a ceremony or other Aboriginal business.

5 Health and land: The camp of Senior Law Man Wandjuk Marika

1   Yalanbara is also known as Port Bradshaw of north-east Arnhem Land in Australia's Northern Territory.

2   Isaacs has worked on many pictorial publications with Indigenous people. She has had a long-time friendship with Marika and his clan.

3   A series of land councils was set up in each state as semi-representative bodies to deal with government.

4   'This version of the story is not the *manikay* – the song, the religion. He does not impart the detailed religious knowledge that was his great power. Today, songs and ceremonial knowledge of Djangukawu are considered profound Yolngu knowledge and property. This book simply places the Djangukawu in context so that all could understand his life, and his purpose' (Marika 2000: 32).

5   '*Madayin* is the name for the complete system of law of Yolngu (Aboriginal people of North-East Arnhem Land). It embodies the rights of the owners of the law or citizens (*rom watangu walal*), who have the rights and responsibilities for this embodiment of law.' Available at http://www.ards.com.au/info7.html (accessed 17 November 2009).

6   Both brothers have been named Australian of the Year, Galarrwuy in 1978 and Mandawuy in 1998.

7   A form of Indigenous knowledge from east Arnhem Land; see Hughes (2000).

8   The Garma Festival is an annual festival held in a bush setting in remote Northern Australia.

6 The journeys: From camps of old men to camps of young women

1   These were the people who lived in the Arizona area before the Navaho. The cliffs are now in what is termed Navaho country.

2   *The North American Indian* by Edward S. Curtis is one of the most significant and controversial representations of traditional American Indian culture ever

produced. Issued in a limited edition from 1907–30, the publication continues to exert a major influence on the image of Indians in popular culture. Curtis said he wanted to document 'the old-time Indian, his dress, his ceremonies, his [sic] life and manners'. In over 2000 photogravure plates and narrative, Curtis portrayed the traditional customs and lifeways of 80 Indian tribes. The 20 volumes, each with an accompanying portfolio, are organized by tribes and culture areas encompassing the Great Plains, Great Basin, Plateau Region, south-west, California, Pacific north-west and Alaska.

3   Available at http://www.lanl.gov (accessed 10 June 2006).
4   Available as http://www.lanl.gov/news/index.php?fuseaction=home. story& story_id=7396 (accessed 10 June 2006).
5   Popular TV Westerns in the 1950s and 1960s.
6   Shaka established the Zulu Nation, an area covering the province of KwaZulu-Natal. However, the battle tactics of Shaka and his warriors were portrayed as aggressive rather than skilful.
7   Religious dance of Plains and Plateau Indians.
8   SFIC, Regina Saskatchewan, Canada is seen as one of the most significant First Nations tertiary institutions.
9   The legal myth on which Australia was able to be occupied by the British.
10 Available at http://aotearoa.wellington.net.nz/imp/mata.htm (accessed 12 December 2006).
11 Available at http://www.maori.org.nz/tikanga/?d=page&pid=sp30&parent=26 (accessed 12 December 2006).
12 Māori sacred knowledge. *Tikanga* can be described as general behaviour guide-lines for daily life and interaction in Māori culture. Available at http:// www.korero.maori.nz/forlearners/protocols (accessed 12 December 2006).
13 Available at http://aotearoa.wellington.net.nz/imp/mata.htm (accessed 12 December 2006).
14 The Waikato River is a major river system running through the west side of the North Island of New Zealand, through the fertile plains of the Waikato district.
15 The replication of the tattered Treaty is on display in the Te Papa Museum in Wellington.
16 The New Zealand Wars were fought in New Zealand between 1845 and 1872.
17 Māori tribe.
18 War canoe.
19 According to Māori tradition, Paikea is an ancestor of Ngāti Porou, a Māori tribe of the east coast of New Zealand's North Island. Available at http:// en.wikipedia.org/wiki/Paikea (accessed 17 November 2009).

7 The camp of 'caring for country': The world of *Plains of Promise*

1   The Dreaming in the Australian Aboriginal world-view is the primordial energy from which all things emerge and into which they disappear.
2   In 1896, Archibald Meston was asked to report to the government on conditions at the mission stations and reserves. In his report, Meston spoke of the frequent

kidnapping of Indigenous children by settlers. He urged that Indigenous people be isolated on reserves to the 'total exclusion of whites' in order to prevent further kidnappings. Meston's suggestion was taken up by the government and would form the foundation of its policies until 1965. Indigenous people, including children, were to be isolated on missions and government settlements, well away from non-Indigenous society. The government acted on Meston's advice soon after by passing the Aboriginal Protection and Restriction of the Sale of Opium Act 1897. This allowed government officials under the Chief Protector's control to remove Indigenous people to reserves and to separate children from their families. All that was needed was administrative approval from the minister. There was no court hearing. The Act also allowed 'orphaned' and 'deserted' mixed-descent children to be removed to an orphanage.

3   As mentioned previously, I shall reference these Senior Law Men through the acronym SLM as an honorific to acknowledge their long and arduous education and training in the jurisprudence of their law. This honorific was prompted by SLM Mowaljarlai's complaint that Senior Law Men are given little recognition of their status by the media. He felt quite indignant that he should be simply called 'David' when interviewed: 'After all, no one calls a High Court Judge Tom, Dick or Harry,' but rather their honorific is used – for example, Chief Justice or, in speech, Your Honour. I have therefore decided to use the acronym SLM to honour SLM Mowaljarlai's wishes.

4   The novel was shortlisted in the Commonwealth Writers' Prize, *The Age* Book of the Year and the New South Wales State Premier's Award – all prestigious literary awards in Australia for a new writer.

5   The National Inquiry into the Separation of Aboriginal and Torres Strait Islander Children from their Families was established in May 1995 in response to efforts made by key Indigenous agencies and communities. They were concerned that the general public's ignorance of the history of forcible removal was hindering the recognition of the needs of its victims and their families and the provision of services. Available at http://www.hreoc.gov.au/social_justice/stolen_children (accessed 17 November 2009).

6   I denote affluent when referring to tribes that received royalties from their land resources.

7   African spider motif.

8   De Ishtar (2005: 137) points out that the ritual was a combination of Christian and European secular elements with traditional mythology and ritual and that it was introduced to Balgo through Fitzroy Crossing after having travelled from the west coast. It contained many song sections and elements and took several years for the Balgo people to learn.

9   The unacknowledged invader.

8 The camp from Turtle Island: *Thunderheart*

1   Chief Stephen Augustine, Elsipogtog Heredity, New Brunswick and Curator at the Canadian Museum of Civilization, Ottawa, Canada.

2　The Lakota, sometimes known as the Teton Sioux, moved to a region west of the Missouri River. The Lakota became the largest of these groups, developing what is known as the Plains Indian Culture after receiving the horse in the seventeenth century. They are divided into seven bands: the Oglala, now on the Pine Ridge Reservation in South Dakota; Sicangu or Brulé, who are now on the Rosebud and the Lower Brulé Reservation in South Dakota; Hunkpapa, who are now at the Standing Rock Reservation in South Dakota and North Dakota; Miniconjous, now at the Cheyenne River Reservation, South Dakota; Sihasapa or Blackfoot, now at Standing Rock or Cheyenne River; Itazipacola or Sans Arc, now at Cheyenne River; and Oohenupa or Two Kettle, also at Cheyenne River (later declared to be tribes by the US government). Available at http://www.hanksville.org/daniel/lakota/Lakota.html (accessed 17 November 2009).

3　The names the people we call Sioux have for themselves are the Lakota, Nakota or Dakota, meaning 'friends . . . allies . . . to be friendly'. At an earlier time, the Sioux evolved into three main groups, speaking different dialects of the same language. The Dakota were the largest group and are considered to be the mother group. The Nakota were next in size, followed by the Lakota. Winter count records indicate that there was strife within the Sioux tribal family, which may have been associated with a rise in power of the Lakota. Available at http://www.hanksville.org/daniel/lakota/Lakota.html (accessed 17 November 2009).

4　The Mikmaq people are from Nova Scotia and New Brunswick, Canada.

5　Available at http://www.dickshovel.com/annalay.html.

6　The American Indian Movement, more commonly known as AIM, was active in Indian politics in the Civil Rights era of America.

7　The Red Road is also known as the Pipe Religion or, in Lakota language, Canku Luta (St Pierre and Long Soldier 1995: 66). It should also be noted that the Lakota have issued a Declaration of War against people who exploit their spirituality. It was declared and documented at the Lakota Summit V, June 1993. Available at http://www.elexion.com/lakota/rites/index2.html (accessed 17 November 2009).

8　Attorney Chief Harry Wallace reminds Indigenous peoples that the Federal Indian Law is a recent apparition in his multimedia presentation for the University of New Mexico Law School's Tribal Law Journal. Available at http://tlj.unm.edu/multimedia/interview_with_chief_harry_wallace.php (accessed 13 December 2006).

9　Lester is a Pitjantjatjara Senior Law Man.

10　*Thunderheart* – Grandpa Reaches speaking to Levoi.

11　The Creation story began long, long ago when Waziya, the Old Man, lived beneath the earth with his wife, Wakanka. Their daughter, Ite, grew to be the most beautiful of women, thereby captivating the attention of one of the associate Gods, Tate the Wind. Although not a Goddess, Ite became the wife of Tate, who lived at the entrance to the Spirit Trail. She bore Tate four sons, quadruplets – the North, West, East and South Winds. The first son became cruel and hard to get along with, so Tate took his position as first son and gave it to his boisterous second son, West Wind. Thus the order of the Winds became West, North, East and South. Because of the association with the influential good and helpful Gods through the marriage of Ite to Tate, Waziya became dissatisfied and yearned to have the power of the true Gods. Iktomi, the Trickster, always anxious to further discontentment and promote ridicule, bargained with Waziya and Wakanka and Ite, promising them great power and further beauty for Ite if they would assist him in making others ridiculous. He even promised Ite that her enhanced beauty would rival that of the Goddess Hanwi, the Moon, who was the pledged wife of the great Sun God, Wi. So Waziya, Wakanka and Ite agreed to Iktomi's bargain (St Pierre and Long Soldier 1995: 44).

12 Available at http://www.manataka.org/page163.html (accessed 10 November 2009).

13 Lakota word for Holy Man.

14 Lakota intellectual Vine Deloria Jr, in discussing leadership, points out that: 'So there is a group of Indians frantically trying to buy into the system, and they clog up the analysis of our problems because they seem to be co-opted, but they are really just selling out. One way to avoid that is to have a council governing the tribe and have it choose a particular person as spokesman for different occasions. Many tribes practised that successfully with similar institutions. The Sioux used to appoint people to make different speeches, without vesting the power to negotiate in any of them' (quoted in Alfred 1999: 91).

15 Available at http://www.freepeltier.org (accessed 10 November 2009).

16 The 'ol people' are the ancestors, who are seen in a ghostly form.

17 Band of the Great Sioux Nation.

18 A concept taken from the title of St Pierre and Long Soldier (1995).

19 Dr Medicine is Professor Emeritus of Anthropology at California State University.

20 Seneca – one of the tribes of the Iroquois confederacy; see Mann (2000).

21 Christianne was referenced under many names over the years, such as Mary Christianne Morris Paul, Christy Anne and Christina Morris, as was the custom of the time due to the Mikmaq's different way of naming.

9 The camp from the sparkling waters of the Pacific: *Whale Rider*

1 *Iwi* is the largest independent politico-economic unit in Māori society.

2 The *kawai tipuna* are the superior beings and controllers (Ministry of Justice 2001: 14).

3 The full quote is: 'Ancestral ties bind the people and the [environment]. Just as land entitlements, personal identity, and executive functions arose from ancestral devolution, so also it is by ancestry that Māori relate to the natural world. Based on their conception of the creation, all things in the universe, animate or inanimate, have their own genealogy; genealogies that were

popularly remembered in details. These each go back to *paptuanuku*, the mother earth, through her offspring gods. Accordingly, for Māori the works of nature; the animals, plants, rivers, mountains, and lakes are either kind, ancestors, or primeval parents according to the case, with each requiring the same respect as one would accord a fellow human being.' Available at http://www.justice.govt.nz/pubs/reports/2001/maori_perspectives/part_1_ mana.html# 175 (accessed 17 November 2006).

4 '*Tapu* is a supernatural condition. Animate and inanimate objects have a direct genealogical link with the *kawai tipuna*, particularly Tane, whose attempts to produce the human element resulted in all these things. The *tapu* of humans, as well as animate and inanimate objects, is about the relationship between the physical and spiritual realm. Examples of these relationships are found in *waiata* and *karakaia*, each of which has its own *tapu* nature. Everything was regarded as *tapu*. Individuals and groups have responsibilities and obligations to abide by the norms of behaviour and practices established by the *tipuna*. *Tapu* acted as a protective mechanism for both people and natural resources. Making something or someone *tapu* could either protect the environment against interference from people or protect people from possible dangers they may encounter.' Available at http://www.justice.govt.nz/ pubs/reports/2001/maori_perspectives/part_1_mana.html#175 (accessed 17 November 2006).

5 'It was the major cohesive force in Māori life because every person was regarded as *tapu* or sacred. Each life was a sacred gift, which linked a person to the ancestors, and hence the wider tribal network. This link fostered the personal security and self-esteem of an individual because it established the belief that any harm to him [sic] was also disrespect to that network which would ultimately be remedied. It also imposed on an individual the obligation to abide by the norms of behaviour established by the ancestors. In this respect, *tapu* firmly placed a person in an interdependent relation with his *whanau, hapu* and *iwi*. The behavioural guidelines of the ancestors were monitored by the living relatives, and the wishes of an individual were constantly balanced against the greater mana and concerns of the group' (Ministry of Justice 2001: 187).

6 Canasatego, Iroquois, on turning down the offer of the commissioners of Maryland and Virginia to educate Iroquois young men at William and Mary in 1744, the James Madison University. Available at http://www.jmu.edu/ madison/center/main_pages/madison_archives/era/native/franklin.htm (accessed 15 December 2004).

7 Dean, School of Maori and Pacific Development, Waikato University.

8 The phrases 'return to country' or 'sitting down country' refer to a kind of 'grounding' or going back to one's roots and remembering where one came from.

9 These cosmological beginnings are mirrored in the processes of conception and birth. From the *kākano* (seed) develops the *koi ora hou* (a new life),

which – while within the *whare tangata* (womb) – possesses *mauri, whakapapa, wairua, hau* and *pūmanawa* (natural talents). It is then born into the world of light. Available at http://www.bioethics.org.nz/index.html (accessed 15 December 2004).

10 In my own case, in the early 1980s I participated in my clan's activities on the Gold Coast to repatriate the human remains and assist in the reburial of our ancestors remains, which dated back over 1200 years. This grounding in my Kombumerri history has become an important intellectual strength.

11 '*Humarie* is the human nature, which is accommodating to all sorts of people and all sorts of situations. Accommodating in the sense that rather than react in a very violent and active way, one will tend to, not necessarily take it on the chin, but will act in a way which is becoming of the gentleperson. This is not to be read as a weakness but rather that the person has control of his or her feelings and emotions and by that very nature will often assist in settling disputes and bringing about resolutions much more quickly than someone with a more volatile nature. This is a person of a rather peaceful disposition but there will be situations outside of the general context in that if *humarie* people are goaded enough they will forsake their peaceful disposition. Generally, though, the expectation of *humarie* people is that they have such a way or manner that enables others to work with them.' Matiu Dickson, personal correspondence with author.

12 Personal correspondence with author. Matiu Dickson's *hapu* is Ngai Tukairangi. He is a Senior Lecturer at the University of Waikato.

13 The land from which they come, Hawaiki, is said to be a mythical land, which has been destroyed – in other words, a place that is not of the present cosmology or part of the history of the present civilisation. Available at http://www.spiritsouthseas.com/hawaiiki.htm (accessed 17 November 2009).

14 *Kaitiaki*: guardian, steward. The meaning of *Kaitiaki* in practical application may vary between different *hapu* and *iwi*.

15 However, when compared with the oldest cosmology in the Americas – that of the Hopi – and the concept of former worlds – which are subsequently destroyed once the inhabitants forget their sacred contract with their Creator – this is a common theme. Even in the Australian case, it is not dissimilar: former worlds and their law exist in the Kimberley area. SLM Mowaljarlai refers to the need for the Law to be brought once again to cope with life after the Ice Age. The present people and their law have been laid down by the Wandjina – Creator Beings.

16 Hirini personal communication, Melbourne, December 2002.

17 In the case of the Hopi, the following of a cloud to the new homeland reminds us of the similarity of the meaning of Aotearoa – the land of the Long White Cloud. It is as if a cloud has also been followed.

18 Hopi land claim, Connecticut presentation.

19 'Additional *mana* could be acquired through the way *rangatira* conducted their actions during their reign as leader. The *mana* of the *rangatira* is enhanced

when the people recognise and acknowledge the ability of the *rangatira* to succeed in defeating other tribes or forming new alliances with other tribes. The *mana* of a *rangatira* was integrated with the strength of the tribe, which was the result of these achievements' (Ihimaera (1987: 175). The success of the *rangatira* may have been because of the advisers or other leaders within the tribe assisting him or her, but outsiders will give sole recognition to the *rangatira* as the figurehead of that tribe; see Buck (1950: 345).

20 Personal communication, Griffith University, 2005.
21 '*Kaipaoe* in a narrow sense refers to someone who is generally incapable of hard, sustained, concentrated work, especially agriculture. The person who is not given to hard work tends to walk among relatives outside the immediate family group and prey on their goodwill to obtain a *kete* of potatoes. It is similar to neighbours who knock at your door and ask whether you have any sugar or other foodstuffs on a regular basis. Thus a *kaipaoe* is someone who poaches food from someone else' Ministry of Justice 2001).
22 Official website http://www.WhaleRiderthemovie.com (accessed 17 March 2005).
23 Matiu Dickson, personal correspondence with author.
24 Available at http://www.movienet.com/Whale Rider.html (accessed 17 April 2005).

10 The end of the journey: A camp of contemporary concerns

1 Others are the United States, China and India.
2 The United Nations Framework on Climate Change meeting resulted in the Kyoto Protocol.
3 A team of experts from National Oceanic and Atmospheric Administration (NOAA) in the United States released a service assessment on the performance of its forecast operations during the severe weather outbreak that struck portions of 19 states in May 2003, resulting in 39 deaths and nearly 400 tornadoes during a six-day period. Available at http://www.noaa.gov (accessed 17 November 2009).
4 An Australian Aboriginal legal agreement in dispute resolutions among north Arnhem Land tribes.

Bibliography

Alfred, G.R. (1995) *Heeding the Voices of Our Ancestors: Kahnawake Mohawk politics and the rise of native nationalism*, Toronto: Oxford University Press.

Alfred, T. (1999) *Peace, Power and Righteousness: An Indigenous manifesto*, Toronto: Oxford University Press.

Allen, P.G. (1992) *The Sacred Hoop: Recovering the feminine in American Indian traditions*, Boston: Beacon Press.

Anker, K. (2005) 'The truth in painting: cultural evidence as proof in Native Title', paper presented to the McGill International Roundtable for the Semiotics of Law, Montreal, April.

Australian Medical Association (2006) 'Report confirms death rates a continuing disgrace', 6 August. Available at http://www.ama.com.au/web.nsf/doc/WEEN-6SC63B (accessed 21 November 2006).

Belich, J. (1988) *The New Zealand Wars and the Victorian Interpretation of Racial Conflict*, Auckland: Penguin.

Bell, H. (1998) *Men's Business, Women's Business: The spiritual role of gender in the world's oldest culture*, Toronto: Inner Traditions International.

Borrows, J. (2007) *Recovering Canada: The resurgence of Indigenous Law*, Toronto: University of Toronto Press.

Buck, P.H. (1950) *The Coming of the Māori*, Wellington: Māori Purposes Fund Board and Whitcombe & Tombs.

Burton, L. (2002) *Worship and Wilderness: Culture, religion, and law in public lands management*, Madison, WI: University of Wisconsin Press.

Cajete, G. (1994) *Look to the Mountain*, Asheville, NC: Kivaki Press.

Camara Fatou, K. (2004) *Power and Justice in Black People's Tradition*, Paris: L'Harmattan.

Caro, N. (2003) Director of *Whale Rider*, interview with author.

Central Land Council Protocols – Going Bush (1998) Personal communication with author. [This is a confidential document.]

Commission on Human Rights Sub-Commission of Prevention of Discrimination and Protection of Minorities Working Group on Indigenous Populations (1993) *The Mataatua Declaration on Cultural and Intellectual Property Rights of Indigenous Peoples*, Whakatane, New Zealand. Available at http://aotearoa. wellington.net.nz/imp/mata.htm (accessed 17 November 2009).

Cook, J. (2005) 'Native and newcomers in the new world: maritime furniture and the interactions of cultures', in E. Newhouse, C. Voyager and D. Beavon (eds), *Hidden in Plain Sight: contributions of Aboriginal peoples to Canadian identity and culture*, Toronto: University of Toronto Press.

Curtis, E.S. (1907–30) *The North American Indian: Photographic images*, 20 vols, Northwestern University Library, Evanston, IL. Available at http://memory. loc. gov/ammem/award98/ienhtml/ curthome.html (accessed 12 December 2006).

Day, R. (2000) Chairman of Murray Island, Torres Strait Islands, interview with author, 10 July 2001.

De Ishtar, Z. (2005) *Holding Yawulyu White Culture and Black Women's Law*, Melbourne: Spinifex Press.

Deloria, V., Jr (1972) *Custer Died for Your Sins: An Indian manifesto*, New York: Avon.

—— (1979) *The Metaphysics of Modern Existence*, New York: Harper & Row.

—— (1995) *Red Earth, White Lies: Native Americans and the myth of scientific fact*, New York: Scribner.

Doi, T. (1981) *The Anatomy of Dependence*, Tokyo: Kodansha International.

Dorsett, S. and McVeigh, S. (2002) 'Just so: the law which governs Australia is Australian law', *Law & Critique*, 13: 289–309.

Duthu, N.B. (2000) 'Incorporative discourse in federal Indian law: negotiating tribal sovereignty through the lens of Native American literature', *Harvard Human Rights Journal*, 13: 141–90.

Estes, C.P. (1995) *Women Who Run with the Wolves: Myths and stories of the wild woman archetype*, New York: Ballantyne.

Fanon, F. (1965) *The Wretched of the Earth*, New York: Grove Press.

—— (1967) *Black Skin, White Masks*, New York: Grove Press.

Fourmile, H. (1994) 'Aboriginal arts in relation to multiculturalism', in S. Gunew and F. Rizvi (eds), *Culture, Difference and the Arts*, Sydney: Allen & Unwin.

Freire, P. (2000) *Pedagogy of the Oppressed*, New York: Continuum.

Graham, M. (1985–2007) Personal communications with author.

—— (1992) Interview with Carolyn Jones, *The Search for Meaning*, ABC Radio National, 15 November.

—— (1999) 'Concepts of time', in *Worldviews: Environment, culture, religion 3*, Cambridge: White Horse Press.

Grimm Brothers (1857) 'The Girl Without Hands', in C.P. Estes (1995), *Women Who Run with the Wolves: Myths and stories of the wild woman archetype*, New York: Ballantyne.

Hughes, I. (2000) 'Ganma: Indigenous knowledge for reconciliation and community action', Action Research e-Reports. Available at http://www2.fhs.usyd.edu.au/arow/arer/014.htm (accessed 17 November 2009).

Human Rights and Equal Opportunity Commission (HREOC) (2005) *Bringing Them Home: Report of the National Inquiry into the Separation of Aboriginal and Torres Strait Islander Children from Their Families*, Canberra: Australian Government Publishing Service.

Ihimaera, W. (1987) *The Whale Rider*, Auckland: Heinemann.

Isaacs, J. (1980) *Australian Dreaming: 40000 years of Aboriginal history*, Sydney: Lansdowne.

Jackson, M. (1988) *Māori and the Criminal Justice System: he whaipaanga hou – a new perspective*, Wellington: Department of Justice.

—— (1990) 'Criminality and the exclusion of Māori', in N. Cameron and S. Francis (eds), *Essays on Criminal Law in New Zealand: 'Towards reform?'*, Wellington: *Victoria University Law Review*, Monograph 3.

—— (1995) 'Justice and political power: reasserting Māori legal process', in M. Hazlehurst (ed.), *Legal Pluralism and the Colonial Legacy*, Aldershot: Avebury.

Jennings, F., Fenton, W., Druke, M. and Miller, D. (1995) *The History and Culture of Iroquois Diplomacy: An interdisciplinary guide to the treaties of the six nations and their league*, New York: Syracuse University Press.

Johansen, B.E. (1995) 'Dating the Iroquois Confederacy', *Akwesasne Notes New Series*, 1(3&4): 62–63.

Jones, R. (1990) 'The world's water', *Time*, 11 November.

King, T. (1994) *Grassy Green Running River*, New York: Bantam.

Law Commission (New Zealand) (2001) *Māori Custom and Values in New Zealand Law*, Study Paper 9, Wellington: Law Commission.

Lester, Y. (1993) *Yami: The autobiography of Yami Lester*, Alice Springs: IAD Press.

Levinas, E. (1990) *Nine Talmudic Readings*, Bloomington, IN: Indiana University Press.

Lyons, O. (1985) 'Traditional native philosophies relating to Aboriginal rights', in M. Boldt, J. Long and L. Little Bear (eds), *The Quest for Justice*, Toronto: University of Toronto Press.

MacNeil, W. (2007) *Lex Populi: The jurisprudence of popular culture*, Stanford, CA: Stanford University Press.

Mann, B. (2000) *Iroquoian Women: The Gantowisas of the Haudenosaunee League*, New York: Peter Lang.

Manning, E. (n.d.) Report in *High Country News*. Available at http://www.hcn.org/servlets/hcn.Article? (accessed 27 November 2006).

Marett, A. (2005) *Songs, Dreamings, and Ghosts*, Middletown, CT: Wesleyan University Press.

Marika, W. (1995) *Wandjuk Marika: Life story*, Brisbane: University of Queensland Press.

Marmon Silko, L. (2006) *Ceremony*, New York: Penguin.

Matthiessen, P. (1992) *In the Spirit of Crazy Horse*, New York: Penguin.

McGary, D. (n.d.) *The Emergence of the Chief: A donation of an outdoor sculpture for the Loyola campus*, exhibition brochure, Concordia University. Available at http://web2.concordia.ca/publicart/documents/McGaryChiefbrochure.pdf (accessed 16 October 2009).

McVeigh, S. (ed.) (2006) *Jurisprudence of Jurisdiction*, London: Routledge-Cavendish.

Mead, H.M. (2003) *Tikanga Māori: Living by Māori values*, Wellington: Huia.

Meadows, M. (2001) *Voices in the Wilderness: Images of Aboriginal people in the Australian media*, Westport, CN: Greenwood Press.

Medicine, B. (1988) 'Native American (Indian) women: a call for research', *Anthropology & Education Quarterly*, 19: 86–92.

—— (2001) *Learning to be an Anthropologist and Remaining 'Native'*, Urbana, IL: University of Illinois Press.

Ministry of Justice (New Zealand) (2001) *He Hinatore ki te Ao Māori: A glimpse into the Māori world*. Available at http://www.justice.govt.nz/pubs/reports/2001/Māori_perspectives/175 (accessed 17 November 2009).

Moore, M. (2003) 'A conversation with Vine Deloria, Jr about evolution, creationism, and other modern myths: a critical inquiry: MariJo Moore asks Sioux author Deloria to shed new light on ancient truths', *New Life Journal*, October–November. Available at http://www.findarticles.com/p/articles/mi_m0KWZ/is_2_5/ai_110265052 (accessed 17 November 2009).

Morris, C. (1991) 'Oral tradition under threat: an Australian Aboriginal experience', *National Ethnic Association Journal*, 14(2): 33–40.

—— (1994) Guest Editor for Literature in *The Encyclopaedia of Aboriginal Australia: Aboriginal and Torres Strait Islander history, society and culture*, Canberra: Aboriginal Studies Press.

—— (1997) 'Indigenous intellectual property rights: the responsibilities of maintaining the oldest continuous culture in the world', *Indigenous Law Bulletin*, 4(2): 9–10.

—— (1999) 'A full law', in D. Posey (ed.), *Cultural and Spiritual Values of Biodiversity: A complimentary contribution to the Global Biodiversity Assessment*, Geneva: United Nations Environment Programme and Intermediate Technology. Available at http://www.un.org/Pubs/textbook/e00035.html (accessed 16 June 2005).

—— (2000a) 'A full law', *Griffith Law Review*, 9(2): 209–11.

—— (2000b) 'Constitutional dreaming', in C. Sampford and T. Round (eds), *Beyond the Republic: Meeting the global challenges to constitutionalism*, Sydney: Federation Press.

—— (2001) 'Digital songs and multimedia dreaming', *New Internationalist*, March.

—— (2002) 'Indigenising the effects of global media', *Media International Australia*, 105: 19–29.

—— (2003) 'Intellectual property and traditional law', *Media Development Journal*, WACC, London. Available at http://www.wacc.org.uk/ publications/md/ archive.html (accessed 16 June 2005).

—— (2004a) 'Foreword', in P. Steven (ed.), *No-nonsense Guide to World Media*, Oxford: New Internationalist Publications.

—— (2004b) 'Shape-shifting through reality: the interactivity of parallel universes in the daily life of the ancients', in M. Punt (ed.), *From the Extraordinary to the Uncanny: The unusual and inexplicable in art, science and technology*, special issue of the *Leonardo Electronic Almanac*, 12(11).

—— (n.d.) 'A touch of cloud', unpublished manuscript of the life and times of Christianne Morris.

Morris, C. and Meadows, M. (2003) 'Framing the future: Indigenous communication in Australia', in N. Couldry and J. Curran (eds), *Contesting Media Power*, Boulder, CO: Rowman & Littlefield.

—— (2004) 'Digital dreaming: Indigenous intellectual property and new communication technologies', in G. Goggin (ed.), *Virtual Nation: An Australian internet reader*, Sydney: University of New South Wales Press.

Mowaljarlai, D. (1995). 'Aboriginal law', interview with Susanna Lobez on *The Law Report*, ABC Radio National, 31 October. Available at http://www.abc.net.au/rn/ talks/8.30/lawrpt/lstories/lr311001.htm (accessed 9 November 2006).

Mowaljarlai, D. and Malnic, J. (1993) *Yorro Yorro*, Broome: Magabala Books.

Murphy, L. (2000) 'Self-determination', in 'Who's afraid of the dark: Australia's administration in Aboriginal Affairs', unpublished MPA thesis, Centre for Public Administration, University of Queensland.

Neidjie, B. (1989) *Story About Feeling*, Broome: Magabala Books.

Neihardt, J.G. (1963) *Black Elk Speaks: Being the life story of a Holy Man of the Oglala Sioux*, Lincoln, NE: University of Nebraska Press.

Newhouse, E., Voyager, C. and Beavon, D. (eds) (2005) *Hidden in Plain Sight: Contributions of Aboriginal peoples to Canadian identity and culture*, Vol. 1, Toronto: University of Toronto Press.

Pearson, N. (2003) 'On leadership', 2003 Leadership Lecture. Available at http:// www.leadershipvictoria.org/speeches/speech_pearson2003.htm (accessed 14 November 2005).

Peats, D. (1995) *Blackfoot Physics*, London: Fourth Estate.

Ramose, M. (2002) *African Philosophy Through Ubuntu*, Harare: Mond.

—— (2005) 'The philosophy of the Anglo-Boer War', in *A Century is a Short Time: New perspectives on the Anglo-Boer War*, Pretoria: Nexus Editorial Collective.

—— (2006a) 'The king as memory and symbol', in M. Hinz (ed.), *The Shade of the Leaves*, Windhoek, Namibia: University of Namibia.

—— (2006b) Interview with Christine Morris, *Symposium of the South* DVD, July.

Romero, E. (1994) 'Identifying giftedness among Keresan Pueblo Indians: the Keres study', *Journal of American Indian Education*, 34: 35–38.

Ryans, P.M. (1994) *Dictionary of Modern Māori*, Auckland: Heinemann.

Siko, L.M. (2006), *Ceremony*, Harmondsworth: Penguin.

Simpson, L. (2003) 'Traditional ecological knowledge: marginalization, appropriation and continued disillusion'. Available at www.snowchange.org/snowchange/content/view/28/2 (accessed 16 June 2005).

Smith, Huston and Cousineau, P. (2006) 'A seat at the table: Huston Smith in conversation with Native Americans on religious freedom', Berkeley, CA: University of California Press.

Stern, Sir N. (2007) *The Economics of Climate Change: The Stern Review*, London: UK Treasury. Available at http://news.bbc.co.uk/2/shared/bsp/hi/pdfs/30_10_06_exec_sum.pdf (accessed 9 December 2007).

Stokes, E. (2002) *Wiremu Tamihana Rangatira*, Wellington: Huia.

St Pierre, M. and Long Soldier, T. (1995) *Walking in the Sacred Manner: Holy women, healers, and pipe carriers – Medicine Women of the Plains Indians*, New York: Simon & Schuster.

Tolkein, J.R. (1954) *Lord of the Rings*, Sydney: Allen & Unwin.

Trudgen, R. (2000) *Why Warriors Lie Down and Die*, Darwin: Aboriginal Resources and Development Services Inc.

Unaipon, D. (2001) *Legendary Tales of the Australian Aborigines*, Melbourne: Miegunyah Press.

United Nations Intergovernmental Panel on Climate Change (IPCC) (2008) Climate Change 2007, Geneva: IPAC, UN. Available at http://www.ipcc.ch/publications_and_data/publications_and_data_reports.htm#1 (accessed 17 November 2009).

Wallace, Chief H. (2001) Interview, University of New Mexico, School of Law, *Indian Law Journal*. Available at http://tlj.unm.edu/multimedia/interview_with_chief_harry_wallace.php.

Waters, F. (1963) *Book of the Hopi*, New York: Penguin.

Waters, F. and Fredericks, O. (1977) *White Bear: Book of the Hopi*, New York: Penguin.

Watson, Lilla (n.d.) Personal communication with author over two decades.

Whitehead, R.H. (1977) 'Christina Morris: Micmac artist and artist's model', *Material History Bulletin*, 3: 1–14.

—— (1982) *Mikmaq Quill Work: Micmac Indian techniques of porcupine quill decoration, 1600–1950*, Halifax, NS: Nova Scotia Museum.

Wilde S.A., Valley J.W., Peck W.H. and Graham C.M. (2001). 'Evidence from detrital zircons for the existence of continental crust and oceans on the Earth 4.4 Gyr ago', *Nature* 409: 175.

Wilkins, Kerry (2004) *Advancing Aboriginal Claims: Visions, strategies, directions*, Saskatoon, SK: Purich.

Williams, N. (1986) *The Yolngu and Their Land: A system of land tenure and the fight for its recognition*, Canberra: Australian Institute of Aboriginal Studies.

Willis, R. (1990) 'Story about feeling', unpublished honours dissertation, University of Queensland.

Wolcher, L. (2004) 'Nature and freedom', *Independent Review*, IX(2): 263–70.

Wolf, A. (1985) The quantum physics of consciousness: towards a new psychology', *Integrative Psychiatry*, 3(4): 24.

Wright, A. (1997) *Plains of Promise*, Brisbane: University of Queensland Press.

Yates-Smith, A. (2003) 'Reclaiming the ancient feminine in Māori society: Kei wareware i a tātou te Ükaipö!' *He Puna Kōrero: Journal of Māori and Pacific Development*, 4(1): 10–19.

Yazzie, R. (2005) 'Healing as justice: the Navajo response to crime, justice as healing Indigenous ways', in *Writings on Community Peacemaking and Restorative Justice from the Native Law Centre*, Minneapolis, MN: Living Justice Press.

Youngblood Henderson, J.S. (2006) *First Nations Jurisprudence and Aboriginal Rights: Defining the just society*, Saskatoon: Native Law Centre, University of Saskatchewan.

Yunupingu, G. (1997) 'Concepts of land and spirituality', in A. Pattel-Gray (ed.), *Aboriginal Spirituality: Past, present, future*, Melbourne: HarperCollins.

Yunupingu, M. (1993) 'Boyer Lecture 1993: Voices of the land – presented by six Indigenous Australians in IYWIP: Getano Lui, Dr Ian Anderson, Jeannie Bell, Mandawuy Yunupingu, Dot West and Noel Pearson'.

—— (1994) 'Yothu Yindi: finding balance', in Mandawuy Yunupingu et al. (eds), *Voices from the Land*, Sydney: ABC Books.

Zuni Cruz, C. (1997) 'Domestic violence and tribal protection of Indigenous women in the United States', *St John's Law Review*, 69: 69–170.

—— (1999) '[On the] road back in: community lawyering in Indigenous communities', *Clinical Law Review*, 5(2): 557–603.

—— (2003) 'Indigenous Pueblo culture and tradition in the justice system: maintaining Indigenous language, thought and law', in *Judicial Review in Land, Rights, Laws: Issues of Native Title*, Vol. 2, Canberra: AIATSIS.

—— (2005) 'Four questions on critical race praxis: lessons from two young lives in Indian country', *Fordham Law Review*, 73(5): 2133–60.

Films and Documentaries

Benny and the Dreamers (1992), Dir. I. Burum, CAAMA, Alice Springs.

Incident at Oglala (1992), Dir. M. Apted, Miramax Films.

An Inconvenient Truth (2006), Dir. D. Guggenheim, Paramount Classics.

The Motorcycle Diaries (2004), Dir. Walter Salles.

New Zealand Wars (1998), Dir. T. Stephens, Air NZ.

Once Were Warriors (1994), Dir. Lee Tamahori, South Pacific Films.

Thunderheart (1992), Dir. Michael Apted, Columbia TriStar.

Tuaiwa Hautai Kereopa Rickard (1998), Tuaiwa Hautai Kereopa whanau/Moko Productions, Wellington.

Whale Rider (2005), Dir. Nicki Caro, South Pacific Films.

Index